...ed and carryed on by Papists and other Wicked and Traitterous Persons fou...
...on from France to subvert our Religion Laws and Liberty: We whose
...nts and other Members of the Company of Clockmake...
...his present Majesty King William is Rightfull and Lawfull King of
...assist each other to the utmost of our Power in the Support and...
...of James and all his Adherents. And incase his Majesty...
...Freely and Unanimously Oblige our Selves to Unite...
...their Adherents; and in Supporting and Defending the...
...of King William and Queen Mary, Intituled, An Act...
...ling the Succession of the Crown—

John Hicker   Langley Bradley
Elias Burges
Tho: Morgan   Phill: Corderoy
William Neighbour   Thomas Wise
George Stower
William Norton   Wm Watson —
Jno: Finch   Samuell Clowes
George Deane
Samuel Vernon   John Trubshaw
Tho: Lumpkin   Thomas Davis
How: Killminster   Daniel le Count
Michael Knight   Thos: Merryman
Daniel Landwin   John House
Daniel Beckman   Francis Asselinne
George Wilson   James DeHandes
John Howard
Edw: Orton   John Jones
Geo: Childs   Thomas Burwhisell
                                Joseph Biddle
Tho: West   John Wise
Leonard Patterson   Cha: Halsted
Tho: Darlew
Tho: Walkden   James Jackson
John Barnard   John Stower
John Winn   Henry Elliott

Frontispiece: A striking clock by James Gregory in a case veneered with ebony with fine gilt metal mounts and a balustered superstructure surmounted by a gilt metal figure of Cupid upon a dolphin after a sketch by Reubens. (The back of the clock is shown in Plate 255.)

Early English Clocks

A discussion of domestic clocks up to the
beginning of the eighteenth century

Percy G. Dawson,
C. B. Drover & D. W. Parkes

Antique Collectors' Club

© 1982
Percy G. Dawson
C.B. Drover
D.W. Parkes
World copyright reserved
ISBN 0 902028 59 6

British Library CIP data
Dawson, Percy
    Early English clocks.
    1. Clocks and watches, English — History
    I. Title   II. Drover, Charles   III. Parkes, Daniel
    681.1′13′0942   TS543.G7

Published for the Antique Collectors' Club
by the Antique Collectors' Club Ltd.

Printed in England by Baron Publishing, Woodbridge, Suffolk

Acknowledgements

The authors wish to acknowledge the help which they have received from many quarters, without which it would have been impossible to complete this book. In particular, our thanks are due to Robert Foukes, upon whose researches much of Chapter II is based; to Tom Robinson for compiling the index and for giving help with the bibliography; and to Michael Hurst for agreeing to write the foreword.

For the use of illustrations from their collections we are grateful to Her Majesty the Queen; the Directors of the Art Gallery of South Australia; the Ashmolean Museum, Oxford; the British Museum; the Castle Museum, York; La Chaux de Fonds Museum; the Fitzwilliam Museum, Cambridge; the Fogg Art Museum, Harvard; the National Museum of Antiquities of Scotland; several properties of the National Trust; the Salisbury Museum; the Science Museum, London; the Time Museum, Rockford; the University of St. Andrews; the Worshipful Company of Clockmakers; the Museum for the History of Science, Leyden; the Victoria and Albert Museum; the Metropolitan Museum of Art, New York, and the Trustees of the Chatsworth Settlement.

A number of antique dealers have been most helpful in providing us with photographs, particularly Messrs. Ronald Lee (Fine Art) Ltd., but also Messrs. Camerer Cuss, Algernon Asprey, Christie Manson and Woods, Derek Roberts Antiques, Malcolm Gardner, Godden of Worthing, Gerald Marsh, the Pelham Galleries, Sotheby Parke Bernet and Strike One. *Apollo* and *Country Life* magazines have also helped as has the Antiquarian Horological Society.

A large number of private individuals have very generously allowed us to photograph clocks in their collections and, in many instances, to entirely dismantle them for this purpose. It is a matter of regret to us that considerations of security prevent us from mentioning them by name, but we wish to express to them all our most grateful thanks.

Contents

Colour Plates

*Endpapers: extracts from the Association Oath Roll of Members of the Clockmakers'
Company, 1697*   Crown Copyright

Erratum: Frontispiece caption, *for* Reubens *read* Rubens.

Foreword

The authors have invited me to write a foreword to this book and I am much honoured by this invitation. I have long felt that there has been a need for such a book as this, which would incorporate the general early history of clockmaking in England and describe in detail the productions of the second half of the seventeenth century, which culminated in the period when English clockmaking led the world.

The skills and techniques developed subsequently, through clockwork, provided, on a larger scale, much of the mechanical expertise necessary for the Industrial Revolution and were thus one of the reasons for Britain being "the workshop of the world" in the nineteenth century.

The authors are well known in antiquarian horological circles.

Charles Drover, a former Assistant of the Clockmakers' Company and Chairman of the Antiquarian Horological Society, who has made a lifetime study of early clocks and clockmaking, has dealt with the historical section.

Daniel Parkes, a Liveryman of the Clockmakers' Company and a fourth generation practical clockmaker, is an authority on seventeenth century clockwork, having spent much of his working life on its repair, restoration and study; he has contributed the sections on clock movements.

Percy Dawson, who took on the difficult task of bringing the work together, is a second generation clock case maker and his tremendous depth of knowledge of all facets of this subject, based on many years of work and research, has gone into the sections on clock cases.

The book is carefully balanced and apportioned as between history, development, cases and movements, describing many details which will be new to the reader. Thomas Sprat (History of the Royal Society 1666) refers to "a universal desire, and appetite after knowledge" engendered after "late times of Civil War and confusion"; where better could this be illustrated than by the clockmakers of the period whose work is described in these pages?

The historical section sets the scene for the formation of the Clockmakers' Company and gives much contemporary information on the working practices of clockmakers. This leads on to the innovative part played by the Fromanteels in the development and production of clocks of a new design that has not before been described in such detail, clearly showing that it was from their work that the normal eight-day movements of later years evolved.

The detailed descriptions of movements and their mechanisms have not appeared before and will appeal, not only to those who are mechanically minded, but to all who have a feeling for the sheer beauty of the artefacts themselves. The details of various components adopted by individual makers, groups of makers or their suppliers, together with practical information of techniques used in clockmaking will also be new to the reader.

The evolution of clock cases, their styles and construction as used by various clockmakers, or their case makers, is fully explored and there is much information on woodwork, formation of mouldings, etc., with contemporary directions for polishing.

In these pages we find accurate information concerning many fascinating clocks made during the formative years of clockmaking history. This is the first time that the subject has been dealt with in such a wealth of specific detail of actual movements and cases, and is the fruit of many years of painstaking observation and labour.

This record of the ingenuity of our early clockmakers will, I am sure, fascinate and inspire many readers and on their behalf I acknowledge their considerable debt to the authors.

Michael Hurst

Chapter I

The Period up to the
Early Seventeenth Century

The weight-driven mechanical escapement clock appears to have been invented in the second half of the thirteenth century, probably in Western Europe and possibly in England. The earliest clocks appear to have been clocks *inside* cathedrals, abbeys and monasteries and many of them carried elaborate astronomical indications.

It is recorded that in 1283 a clock was placed over the *pulpitum* (i.e. the stone screen dividing choir and nave) in Dunstable Priory Church.[1]

In 1286 Bartholomew the Clockmaker was working on a clock at St. Paul's Cathedral, London, and it is apparent from the will of Robert le Senescal, a minor canon, which was dated 1298, that the clock was inside the cathedral church.[2] The movement was replaced by Walter the Organer in 1344.[3]

In 1290 or before, Norwich Cathedral had a clock and this was replaced by a great new clock inside the cathedral church between 1323 and 1325. It was started by Robert de Turry and after his bankruptcy was completed by Roger and Laurence of Stoke.[5]

In 1291 or before, Ely Cathedral had a clock, probably in the South transept, which was probably destroyed by the fall of the central tower in 1322.[4]

In 1292 a great new clock was constructed in Canterbury Cathedral Church at a cost of £30. That this was inside the church and in the South transept is clear from Leland's description when he saw the clock in his itineraries between 1535 and 1543.[6]

After completing the clock in Norwich Cathedral, Roger and Laurence of Stoke went on to St. Alban's Abbey where Richard of Wallingford was building a most elaborate astronomical clock. Thanks to the researches of Dr. John North of the Museum of the History of Science at Oxford, we have a full description of this clock including its escapement, which is an early form of verge escapement with a foliot

---

1. *Annales Monastici,* Vol. III, ed. H.R. Luard, 1866. See also *Antiquarian Horology,* Vol. 10, No. 2 (Spring 1977), pp. 189-196.
2. *Domesday of St. Paul's,* Camden Society, No. 69, p. 172, and St. Paul's Docs. A Box 66, Doc. No. 10.
3. British Museum Cart., Cotton XXI. 24.
4. *Sacrists' Rolls of Ely,* ed. F.R. Chapman, Cambridge, 1907.
5. Sacrist Rolls of Norwich Cathedral, Nos. 218, 229, 230 and 231.
6. *Leland's Itinerary in England, 1535/43,* ed. Lucy Toulmin Smith, Vol. 4, 1909 edition, pp. 39-40.

controller and from which the crown wheel and verge escapement as we know it today was probably developed.[7]

Turret clocks (i.e. mechanical escapement clocks striking the hours on a bell in a belfry so as to give public notice of the passing of the hours) appear to have been a later development of weight-driven mechanical escapement clocks. The turret clock was probably an Italian invention, and what is believed to be the first one was installed in the Church of San Gottardo in Milan in 1335.[8]

It is thought that the first turret clock in England was that installed by Edward III at Windsor Castle in 1352. The installation was carried out by three Lombard clock-makers, who seem to have come from Italy for the purpose. It seems likely that they made the clock mechanism in Italy and brought it with them, although that is not entirely certain. What is known is that the clock mechanism was transported from London to Windsor at a cost of 1s. 6d. (presumably by water up the Thames) and one supposes that it was imported into London from Italy.[9]

Between 1366 and 1369 turret clocks were installed at Sheen Palace (Richmond, Surrey), the royal manor of King's Langley, Queenborough Castle and Westminster Palace. In 1368 Edward III granted a safe-conduct to three Dutch clockmakers of Delft to practise their art in England for one year. It is tempting, and probably correct, to say that they installed the mechanisms of the four clocks mentioned above, all of which were in royal buildings.[10] Nevertheless, the conclusion should not be drawn that there were no English turret clockmakers at the time. The Sacrists' Rolls of Ely Cathedral record that in 1371/72 Alan Clockmaker was paid £4. 6s. 8d. for new-making the "cloke" (i.e. a turret clock as distinct from an "horloge" which did not strike the hours on a large bell)[11] and the Fabric Rolls of York Minster record that in 1371 a new "clok" was made by John of Clarebergh for £13. 6s. 8d. exclusive of the cost of the weights and the bell.[12] Although fourteenth century records are somewhat scanty, it is a fair assumption that by the end of the century every cathedral, abbey, monastery and parish church of any size had its own turret clock, for the regulation of its own services and for the convenience of the local populace. For example the churchwardens' accounts of St. Michael's Church, Bishop's Stortford (which must have been a small place in those days), records that a new clock made by Bukberd was installed in 1431, replacing an earlier clock.[13] St. Peter's Church, Barnstaple, had a turret clock installed in 1389.[14]

Domestic clocks, on the other hand, were few and far between in England until the end of the sixteenth century. To take one example, in the very detailed inventory of the contents of Ingatestone Hall, Essex, of 1600, not one domestic clock is referred to, though the inventory records that the house had a turret clock.[15] Henry VIII purchased a very large number of clocks and watches and many transactions are

---

7. J.D. North, *Richard of Wallingford*, Oxford, 1976, Vol. 1, pp. 441-526, and Vol. 3, pp. 61-74.

8. G.H. Baillie, *Watches*, London, 1929, p. 32, quoting from *Fiamma's Chronicles*.

9. W.H. St. John Hope, *Windsor Castle — An Architectural History*, London, 1913, 2 vols., pp. 138 *et seq.*

10. R. Allen Brown, "King Edward III's Clocks", *Antiquarian Horology*, Vol. 3, No. 5, Dec. 1960, pp. 124-6.

11. Ely Cathedral Sacrists' Rolls, roll No. 18.

12. *The Fabric Rolls of York Minster*, ed. James Raine, the Surtees Society, Vol. 35, 1859.

13. *The Records of St. Michael's Parish Church, Bishop's Stortford*, ed. J.L. Glasscock Jnr., London, 1882.

14. Chanter and Wainwright, *Reprint of the Barnstaple Records*, Barnstaple, 1900, Vol. II, pp. 38-40.

15. *Ingatestone Hall in 1600. An Inventory*, Essex Record Office Publications, No. 22, 1954.

Plate 1. *Anne Boleyn's clock, dated circa 1533. The dial and movement were replaced in the 17th century.*

Reproduced by gracious permission of Her Majesty the Queen

Plate 2. Detail of the coat of arms on top of Anne Boleyn's clock shown in Plate 1.

Plate 3. The weights from Anne Boleyn's clock, engraved with Henry's and Anne's initials and a true lovers' knot.

recorded in his privy purse expenses from November 1529 to December 1532, but it is noteworthy that the purchases are made mainly from Frenchmen, i.e. Vincent Quesnay and one Drulardy.[16]

Possibly one of these clocks might have been the clock which Henry gave as a present to Anne Boleyn whom he married in 1533. The clock is illustrated in Plates 1-3 and is presently in the royal library at Windsor Castle. Plate 1 is a general view of the clock and shows that the dial was replaced probably in the seventeenth century. The movement has also been replaced, no doubt at the same time. Plate 2 shows the detail of the coat of arms held by the bear at the top of the clock and Plate 3 shows the detail of the weights engraved with Henry's and Anne's initials and a true lovers' knot. The clock is 10ins. high to the top of the finial and 4ins. square at the base.

At the time in question, Nicholas Oursian, a Frenchman, was the royal clockmaker and a second Frenchman, Sebastian Le Sene, joined the staff in 1538. There are various inventories of Henry VIII, Edward VI and Queen Elizabeth I which show

16. N. Harris Nicolas, *The Privy Purse Expences of King Henry the Eighth from Nov. 1529 to Dec. 1532,* London, 1827.

Plate 4. Weight-driven clock by Francis Nawe, London, dated 1588. The dial, bell and super-structure and movement are later replacements.
Christie, Manson and Woods Ltd.

that these were made in England. There is evidence that in 1572 the Dutch community in London imported clocks from Holland[17] and in or about 1594 William Shakespeare wrote the well-known lines in *Love's Labour Lost* (Act III, Scene 1) which are spoken by Biron, one of the lords attending on the King:

> "What! I love! I sue! I seek a wife!
> A woman, that is like a German clock,
> Still a-repairing, ever out of frame,
> And never going aright, ..."

German clocks, i.e. the clocks of Nuremburg and Augsburg, must clearly have been well-known in England and many must have been imported.

---

17. Letter dated Dordrecht, 8th October 1572, from Bartholdus Wilhelmi to the Minister and Elders of the Dutch Community, London. (*Ecclesiae Londonio — Batavae Archivum Epistulae Tractatus,* Vol. 3, No. 209, p. 177).

Plate 5. The original chapter ring of the clock shown in Plate 4. Note the beautiful engraving on the case.
Victoria and Albert Museum

While there is evidence that domestic clocks were imported into England in the sixteenth century, there is very little evidence as to the extent of the domestic clock industry in England up to about 1575. If there was any such industry, it must have been very small. A few iron weight-driven clocks may have been made but, if so, these cannot be identified today because they were probably made by blacksmiths and were unsigned.

The earliest domestic clocks which were made in England, and of which we have record, were those made mainly by Huguenot emigrants from Flanders. The extant examples were all made after 1575 and very few can have been made as the sixteenth century survivors can almost be counted on the fingers of two hands. There are three weight-driven clocks of this period known, one by Francis Nawe dated 1588 (Plates 4-5), one by Nicholas Vallin dated 1598 (Colour Plates 1-2) and one which is anonymous and undated (Plates 6-7). There are eleven spring-driven clocks known

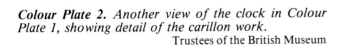

Colour Plate 1. *A general view of a weight-driven carillon clock by Nicholas Vallin, dated 1598.*

Trustees of the British Museum

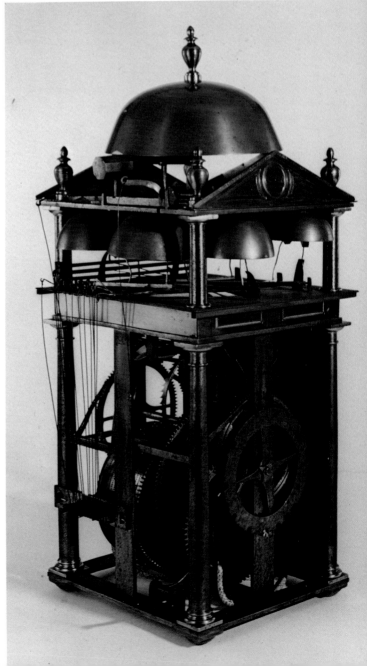

Colour Plate 2. *Another view of the clock in Colour Plate 1, showing detail of the carillon work.*

Trustees of the British Museum

Plate 6. Weight-driven English/Flemish clock, unsigned.

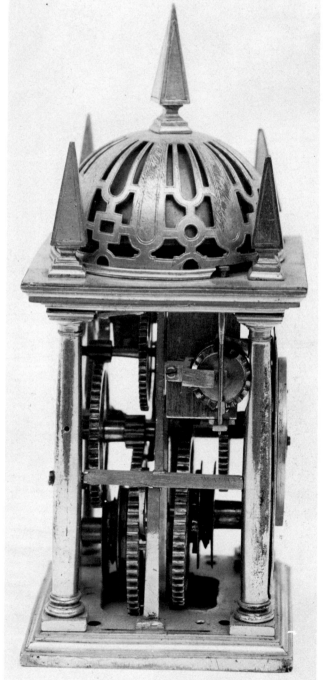

Plate 7. Side view of the clock shown in Plate 6 with plates removed.

Plate 8. *Small drum clock by Nicholas Vallin having astronomical indications (now in the Science Museum, London).*

to be surviving in whole or in part, of which seven were made by Nicholas Vallin (Plates 8-20), and one by Gilles van Ghele (Plate 21), both immigrants from what is now Belgium, two by Bartholomew Newsam (Plates 22-27), an Englishman in the parish of St. Mary-in-the-Strand, London, and one by Edmund Bull. There is one case for a spring-driven clock in the British Museum which is clearly of English/Flemish origin, but it is unsigned (Plates 28-29).

Gilles van Ghele (his name is spelt variously in records as Vangaile, Vangaland, Vangand) is recorded as being in London between 1576 and 1591 and several watches by this maker are extant. The clock referred to above and shown in Plate 21 is, however, the only known clock by him to survive. Francis Nawe (Noway, Nouwe, Nauwe) is recorded as being in London between 1576 and 1593 when he died of the plague together with three of his daughters. He came to London from Antwerp. Michael Nouwen (Nawe, Nauwe) came from s'Hertogenbosch in South Holland and is recorded as being in London between 1571 and 1609. Nicholas Vallin and his father John came to London from Brussels and records show Nicholas was in London between 1590 and 1603 when he died of the plague.

The cases of all the above clocks are of gilded copper or brass (except the case of the drum clock by Bartholomew Newsam (Plates 22-25) which is of silver). Some of the cases are plain but for the most part they are richly engraved with various designs of the period.

The mechanism of these spring-driven clocks invariably follows the French and never the German pattern. The vertical clocks (Plates 11, 19 and 26) are of the

Plate 9. Another small drum clock by Nicholas Vallin with astronomical indications. Compare with Plate 8.
Time Museum, Rockford, Illinois

Plate 10. Top plate of the clock shown in Plate 9, showing the signature and beautifully decorated cock.

Plate 11. *Spring-driven vertical clock by Nicholas Vallin, dated 1600, having a later dial and movement.*

Plate 12. *Base plate of clock shown in Plate 11, showing signature and date.*

Plate 13. *Drum shaped striking clock with alarm by Nicholas Vallin.*

Plate 14. *Movement of drum clock by Nicholas Vallin in the Banff Museum, Scotland.*
Antiquarian Horological Society

Plate 15. *Top plate of clock shown in Plate 14 showing cock and balance wheel.*

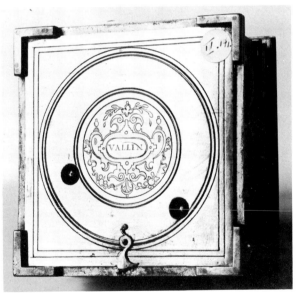

Plate 16. *Horizontal clock signed "Vallin". This may be Nicholas Vallin or his father John. The dial is a later replacement.*

Museum of International Horology,
La Chaux-de-Fonds, Switzerland

Plate 17. *Bottom plate of the case of the clock shown in Plate 16 showing the signature.*

Plate 18. *Top plate of the movement showing cock and balance wheel of the clock shown in Plate 16.*

Plate 20. Compass in the cupola on top of the clock case shown in Plate 19. The similar clock by Bartholomew Newsam also has a compass in the cupola.

Plate 19. Case of a vertical table clock, signed Nicholas Vallin. Compare with the clock by Bartholomew Newsam, Plate 26.

Plate 21. Drum clock by Gilles van Ghele, late 16th century.
Sotheby Parke Bernet

French 'double-decker' design with the striking train in the lower stage and the going train above. They have fusees and the going train is controlled by a balance wheel and not by a foliot. Sometimes an alarm train was included. The wheelwork, fusees and spring barrels are normally of gilded brass, and the pinions and arbors of steel. The drum clocks also follow French designs both in layout and materials. Where the drum clocks are striking clocks, the bell is on top of the movement but below the dial so that the drive to the hand had to come through the bell (Plates 13, 16 and 22). More frequently these drum clocks were purely timepieces and contained neither striking nor alarm work.

The similarity of these spring-driven clocks to French clocks of the period prompt the compelling inference that the Flemings derived their clockmaking techniques from the French and in turn imparted them to the English.

There is one very characteristic feature of these vertical English/Flemish clocks and that is the pierced strapwork designs of the dome-shaped bell covers (see Plates 6, 11, 16, 19, 22, 26 and 28). This feature is frequently found in clocks manufactured by English or Flemish makers but not, apparently in clocks of other manufacture. It also has to be remembered that in the latter part of the sixteenth century and early part of the seventeenth century the clock and watch industry in Flanders had largely disintegrated owing to religious persecution and the wars of religion, and it is a fair inference that clocks of the late sixteenth and early seventeenth century, with this particular type of dome cover, are mainly of English manufacture (though there are of course others, e.g. Hans de Evalo, a Fleming, was making clocks in Madrid).

It is difficult to find any French trend in English/Flemish weight-driven clocks, since no weight-driven clocks of this period are known which can be attributed to French manufacture with any certainty. Also, of the three English/Flemish examples known, one of them lacks the whole of its original movement. The unsigned example (Plates 6-7) has gilded wheelwork and steel pinions and has a weight-driven alarm train.

The weight-driven clock by N. Vallin (Colour Plates 1-2, page 19) has a particularly interesting movement, though, like most of these very early clocks, it has received some restoration over the years. The movement is largely of steel and consists of three trains, going, hour striking and quarter chiming. The chiming mechanism is indeed so elaborate, that the clock might almost be described as a musical clock. The going train is placed so that its wheels are parallel to the dial. The striking and chiming trains are at right angles to the going train, with one train on each side of it.

The clockmaking traditions which had been introduced into England by the Flemings, continued into the seventeenth century. Plates 30-31 show a magnificent spring-driven clock by David Ramsey, the royal clockmaker and first master of the Clockmakers' Company. The case bears strong French characteristics and it is probable that it was imported from France as David Ramsey is known to have imported watch cases from Blois. The scene depicting the pope's nose being ground on a grindstone, which is on the base plate (Plate 31) would not suggest a Roman Catholic country for its provenance, but it is possible that the base plate was originally plain, and was engraved when the case arrived in England.

A rather later example of about 1620 is the clock by Christian de Wellke shown in Plates 32-33. This is a fine striking clock with alarm. A fusee trap door, a distinctly French feature, can be seen in the side of the clock; the purpose of this was to enable anyone to see whether or not the clock required winding.

22

Plates 22-25. Silver drum shaped clock with original leather case by Bartholomew Newsam.
Metropolitan Museum of Art,
Gift of J. Pierpont Morgan

23

24

25

Plate 26. *Vertical striking clock by Bartholomew Newsam now in the British Museum.*

Plate 27. *Movement of the clock shown in Plate 26. The going train is on top and the striking train below.*

Colour Plate 3. Table clock by Ahasuerus Fromanteel and Edward East. (Other views of the clock are shown in Plates 46-51.)

Plates 28 and 29. *Spring-driven clock case (unsigned) but the table of sunrise and sunset engraved inside the side plates (Plate 29) shows that it was made in England.*

28

29

Plate 30. *Fine striking table clock by David Ramsey.*
Victoria and Albert Museum

Plate 31. *Base plate of the clock shown in Plate 30 depicting the pope's nose being ground on a grindstone.*

Plate 32. Striking clock with alarm by Christian de Wellke, dated circa 1620.
Sotheby Parke Bernet

Plate 33. Top plate of the clock shown in Plate 32.

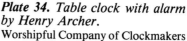

*Plate 35. Movement of the
clock shown in Plate 34
seen from below.*

Another similar clock is that by Henry Archer which is today in the Clockmakers' Company museum at the Guildhall Library. This is another fine horizontal striking drum clock with the dial on top and is illustrated in Plates 34-35. Henry Archer was appointed senior warden (and deputy master) of the Clockmakers' Company in its Charter of 1631 though he never became Master.

To demonstrate how this tradition of clockmaking in England persisted well into the seventeenth century, the case with movement and top plate of a fine spring-driven striking clock by David Bouquet is illustrated in Plates 36-38. David Bouquet was of French origin but spent most of his working life in England. He became a member of the Blacksmiths' Company in 1628, joined the Clockmakers' Company in 1632 and died in 1665. The date of this clock is about 1635.

Plate 36. Spring-driven clock by David Bouquet, dated circa 1635.

Science Museum, London

Plate 37. Movement of the clock shown in Plate 36.

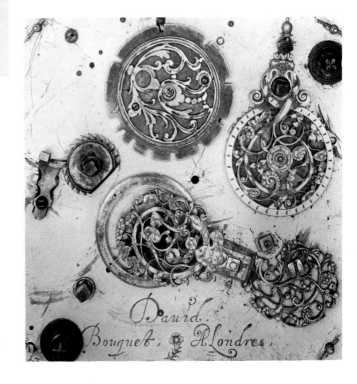

Plate 38. Top plate of the clock shown in Plate 36 showing the finely pierced pinned-on cock.

Plate 39. *Table alarm clock by Robert Grinkin, general view.*
John D. Fleming and Co., Dulverton

Plate 40. *Movement of the clock shown in Plate 39 showing the barrel and fusee of the going train.*

Plate 41. *Top plate of the clock shown in Plate 39.*

Plates 39-41 illustrate a fine table alarm clock by Robert Grinkin which dates from the middle of the seventeenth century. Robert Grinkin was originally a member of the Blacksmiths' Company, being master in 1609. He joined the Clockmakers' Company in 1631, being junior warden in 1640, renter warden in 1641/3 and was master in 1648 and 1649.

Another fine clock of about the same period is a striking table clock by Edward East (Plates 42-44). Edward East had a very long life, being born in 1602 and dying in 1698.[18] He was originally a goldsmith and became the junior member of the Court of Assistants on the formation of the Clockmakers' Company in 1631. He was renter warden in 1639 and 1640, and master in 1645 and again in 1652.

---

18. H. Alan Lloyd, "The One and Only Edward East", *The Horological Journal*, May 1950, pp. 296-298, and June 1950, pp. 370-377.

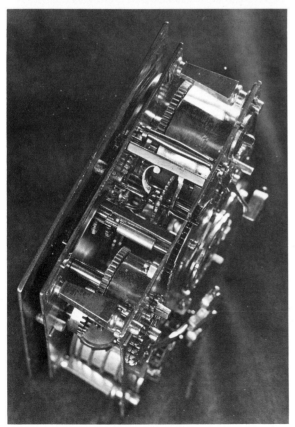

43

44

37

Plate 45. General view of table clock by Fromanteel and East. The clock is also shown in Colour Plate 3, page 30.

This series of clocks reaches its climax in an exceptionally fine clock in a case of fire-gilt brass, its overall dimensions being 5⅛ins. high and 4½ins. square (Plates 45-51). The sides of the case are engraved with the Four Seasons from Wensel Hollar's *Theatrum Mulierum* of 1644. The engraving is undoubtedly by the hand of a master.

The silver dial (Plate 46) at the centre is pierced and engraved with floral subjects and the chapter ring is divided into three parts of 60 minutes each, as the minute hand revolves once in three hours. The corners are engraved with individual *amorini*.

The hands, which are not original, are of pierced brass. They are copied from original examples from an early clock by Edward East which has a velvet covered dial.

This unique clock, which has a duration of 29 hours, incorporates full grande sonnerie striking, and is the earliest recorded example of a clock with this feature.

The movement is contained in four tiers. The one immediately below the dial houses part of the quarter striking mechanism including the bell. The next down contains the going train of four wheels and fusee, the verge and the quarter striking train of four wheels. The very narrow tier between the going and striking trains is occupied by the balance wheel and regulator control. The bottom tier is fully occupied with the hour striking train of four wheels and fusee.

The two fly wheels are solid and the chains are of very early type.

The movement is gilt throughout other than the steel parts, some of which are blued, and the mechanism in the top tier which is hidden from view.

The base plate carries the count wheel (Plate 47). This is engraved with floral subjects and gilt. The silver count ring is engraved with numerals depicting the hours, between which the quarters are represented by dots, e.g. .:: The hammer, in the form of a grotesque animal head, is of polished steel.

Plate 46. Dial of table clock by Fromanteel and East shown in Plate 45.

Plate 47. Top plate and bell of the clock shown in Plate 45.

Plates 48-51. *Four views of the movement of table clock shown in Plate 45.*

49

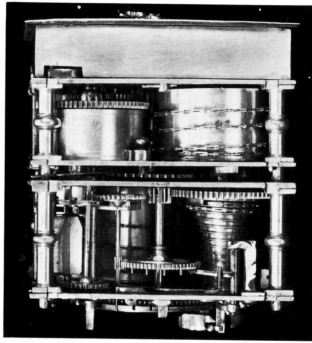

50

51

The count wheel hand, hour striking release, strike/silent lever, and other decorative steel work retains the original blueing, except the regulator pointer which is a replacement. The hour bell is secured in the hinged base cover by engraved cross straps. To operate the quarters' strike/silent lever, the movement has to be partly removed from the case.

The signatures of the joint makers are engraved on the base plate: "A. Fromanteel Fecit" and "Edwardus East Londini". That of East has been engraved before gilding was carried out, and that of Fromanteel afterwards.

It is a matter for conjecture how East and Fromanteel came to be engaged on the same job. There is no other recorded instance of a clock or watch being signed by them both. It would appear that East was largely responsible for the decorative side of the case work as the piercing of the dial follows closely that on watches signed by him. One suggestion put forward is that the two makers started to work jointly but fell out because East wished to claim credit for the whole work, whereas the movement is typical of Fromanteel's work, hence the "fecit".

The clock has to be 'read' to ascertain the time, as in the earliest longcase movement by Fromanteel. In this the minute hand revolves four times in the hour, possibly to indicate split minutes as required by an astronomer.

The Fromanteel/East clock is in a remarkable state of preservation, the quality throughout being of the very highest order. The only restorations are the hands, the regulator pointer and the spring to the securing lever of the hinged base cover.

The clock was made between 1658 and 1660 and is one of the first to have a minute hand following the invention of the pendulum.

Chapter II
The Clockmakers' Company and Associated Matters

The Clockmakers' Company [1]

From the twelfth century onwards, trade in London and the other principal cities of Western Europe was organised in craft guilds. These guilds were corporations, their members were citizens of the cities concerned, and their constitutions enabled them to control the working conditions, the quality of work of their members and the regulation of apprenticeship.

In the early days there were relatively few of these craft guilds, but with the advance of technology and the increasing specialisation of economic life the number of guilds gradually grew.

As will have been apparent from Chapter I of this book, there were few clockmakers in the City of London in the early part of the sixteenth century. Such clockmakers as there were were mainly turret or 'great' clockmakers or clockmakers working mainly in iron, and it would be a natural thing that they should be largely members of the Blacksmiths' Company. Indeed in some early records, clockmakers who attended to the repair of turret clocks are referred to as 'clocksmiths'.

Some clockmakers were, however, members of other companies. For example Randolph Bull (who had a number of apprentices over the years including Nicholas Ridgdall [2]) was a member of the Goldsmiths' Company. On the whole Bull confined himself to producing watches and clocks with finely gilded cases, but it should be remembered that he also undertook work of a larger nature and he did in fact make the clockwork for Thomas Dallam's celebrated organ clock which was presented to Mohammed III 'Sultan of Turkey' in 1599. [3] Incidentally Thomas Dallam, a famous organ maker, was a member of the Blacksmiths' Company.

It has to be emphasised that it was normally by being a member or freeman of a craft guild that anyone could be a freeman or citizen of London and only a citizen had the right to work at a craft in the City. It was also possible to obtain freedom of

---

1. For a fuller account of the history of the Clockmakers' Company see *Some Account of the Worshipful Company of Clockmakers of the City of London* by S.E. Atkins and W.H. Overall, 1881.

2. There is a watch by Nicholas Ridgdall in the Victoria and Albert Museum, South Kensington.

3. *Antiquarian Horology,* Vol. 1, p. 150.

the City by purchase and *The Gentleman's Magazine,* December, 1737, records that the Lord Mayor and Court of Aldermen resolved "that the fine for purchasing the freedom of the City of London, for the future shall be £50. which has been sold lately for £30." This sum, which was undoubtedly large, would seem to have been restrictive by nature in order to control the entry of outsiders wishing to set up in business within the City boundaries.

There were, however, exceptions. There were districts, either on the edge of, or just outside the City, called liberties, where people could work at crafts without being citizens. There were liberties at St. Clements and in Blackfriars and it was in these areas that the Protestant clockmakers and others from Flanders and France tended to congregate on emigrating to London.

Then 'foreigners' (the expression bore a wider meaning in those days than someone from overseas) proved an early bone of contention to those citizens carrying on the then infant trade of domestic clockmaking. While the foreigners undoubtedly brought their skills with them, which no doubt proved of assistance to clockmaker citizens who could copy their work and work methods, they were very potent competitors who had the added advantage of not having to contribute to the dues and quarterages which citizens had to contribute to their craft guilds.

By the early part of the seventeenth century the small band of English domestic clockmakers were beginning to flex their muscles and grow jealous of the dominance of their industry by foreigners.

In 1622, sixteen clockmakers, stated to be all the clockmaker householders in London, petitioned the King asking that no foreign clockmaker should be allowed to work in this country except under a master of English nationality and that the import of foreign work should be prohibited. To support their petition, the English clockmakers avowed that their trade was disgraced by the bad workmanship of the foreigners and that the public was deceived because their work was externally beautiful and attractive but internally of poor workmanship.[4] How untrue this statement was can be readily seen by examining the extant work of, say, Cornelius Mellin of Blackfriars, who was one of the foreigners specifically mentioned by name in the petition.

This petition failed to achieve any result, probably because the allegations it contained were not supported by the evidence and probably also because it was not supported by one of the established City Companies.

In the meanwhile, it seems that the French clockmakers in the Liberties had petitioned the King for a grant of Letters Patent authorising them to carry on their trade in the City. In 1627 the free clockmakers persuaded the Blacksmiths' Company to petition the Court of Aldermen to use their influence to persuade the King against the grant.

It seems that this opposition must have been successful and in 1628, the free clockmakers, as a body, were in communication with the Blacksmiths' Company with a view to being incorporated with them. These negotiations came to nothing, though they did not stop certain individual clockmakers from seeking admission to the Blacksmiths' Company. Among these were Richard Gray in 1628, Josias Cuper in

---

4. The petition is in the Public Record Office, *State Papers, Domestic Series,* 14, Vol. 127, quoted by R.W. Symonds in *Thomas Tompion, His Life and Work* at pp. 301 to 303 and referred to at p. 7.

Plate 52. The original box in which the Clockmakers' Company charter was stored.
Worshipful Company of Clockmakers

1629 and in 1630 Ahasuerus Fromanteel was ordered to bring in his certificate of his seven years service as an apprentice, which he duly did.

However, the sense of community which the negotiations had given to the clockmakers was probably directly responsible for sowing the seeds of the more ambitious project; namely the incorporation of all the free clockmakers into a Clockmakers' Company.

In the year 1630 a number of clockmakers banded together, undertaking between them to find the necessary funds to petition the King, and they appointed Francis Forman and Richard Morgan (a member of the Blacksmiths' Company) to be suitors to His Majesty and Sampson Shelton (also of the Blacksmiths' Company) to be Treasurer of their funds raised for the purpose.

In accordance with the usual custom, the petition was submitted by the King to the Lord Mayor and Court of Aldermen for their recommendations, and a favourable certificate being produced, a charter of incorporation was granted on the 22nd August, 1631.

This is a lengthy document engrossed on two large skins of parchment, richly ornamented and having a full length portrait of Charles I in the right hand corner (see Colour Plate 4, page 47).[5] The original box in which the charter was stored is illustrated in Plate 52.

The charter decreed "that all and singular the Clockmakers and other person and persons whatsoever, as well as freemen of or in our city of London, as also all other our natural freeborn subjects, using the Art or Mystery of Clockmaking within the same city, liberties or suburbs thereof, or within any place within ten miles of the same city, as well within liberties and places exempt, as in other places, be and shall be by virtue of these presents, for ever hereafter, one body corporate and politic, in deed and name to have continuance for ever by the name of The Master, Wardens and Fellowship of the Art or Mystery of Clockmaking, of the city of London . . . . ."

---

5. The charter is quoted in full by Atkins and Overall, *op. cit.,* at pp. 7-19.

The charter then goes on to confer various powers on the company including power to elect a master, wardens and assistants who were to constitute a court with various powers over the members of the company. The charter appointed David Ramsey to be the first master and Henry Archer, John Wellowe (Willow) and Sampson Shelton to be the first wardens. The first assistants were also named. They were James Vautrollier, John Smith, Francis Forman, John Harris, Richard Morgan, Samuel Lynaker, John Charlton, John Midnall, Simon Bartram and Edward East.

The court was given powers in the charter to make laws and ordinances for the government of its own members, to punish deceitful practices, to regulate the manner in which clockmakers throughout England should carry on their trade, and to fine and punish offenders against these laws. The court was also given power to search for and seize and break work if unlawfully made or made of bad materials. All apprentices were to be bound to a free clockmaker only and no alien (who was not naturalised or a denizen) was to work within the limits of the charter except only with a free clockmaker. To prevent frauds and abuses no one was permitted to import any clocks without bringing the same to the court to be viewed and marked.

In 1632 bye-laws for the good government of the craft were (in accordance with a statute of Henry VII) submitted to the Lord Chancellor and the chief justices of the Court of King's Bench and the Court of Common Pleas and duly approved by them.[6]

Among these bye-laws it was ordained that the company should be a "Livery of Company" but generally speaking they legislate for the detailed application of the powers conferred by the charter. It is interesting to note that apprentices who had served their terms and had been admitted freemen of the company, had to serve two years as journeymen, and at the end of that period produce their masterpieces, whereupon they were to be admitted 'workmasters'. No foreigner was to be employed by a freeman without the approval of the court. A journeyman had to give his master three months' notice of his intention to leave and a master had to give a similar period of notice to a journeyman to terminate his employment.

It may seem odd to us in these democratic days that a sovereign could of his "especial grace, certain knowledge and mere motion" impose liabilities on third parties without their consent or without an Act of Parliament, but the powers of the sovereign fell within the royal prerogative which had not by then been largely superseded by parliamentary powers.

However the charter was not as sweeping as it would seem to be on a first reading, as it became clear that the rights and liabilities only attached to those who had applied for and been admitted to the freedom of the Company and had voluntarily agreed to adhere to its rules and regulations.

In 1671 the company acquired the right to bear arms, the arms, crest, supporters and motto being described in the grant as "Sable, a Clock ye 4 Pillars thereof erected on four Lyons, and on each Capital a Globe with a Crosse, and in the Middest an Imperiall Crowne all Or, and for their Crest upon an Helmet Proper Mantled Gules Doubled Argent and Wreath of their Colours a Spheare Or the Armes Supported by the Figures of a Naked Old Man holding a Scithe and an Hour Glass representing

---

6. For the full text of the bye-laws see Atkins and Overall, *op. cit.*, at pp. 22-49.

Plate 53. The arms of the Clockmakers' Company taken from a copy of the charter and bye-laws published in 1825.
                                                          Worshipful Company of Clockmakers

Time, and of an Emporour in Roabes Crowned holding a Scepter; Their Motto *Tempus Rerum Imperator''* (see Plate 53).[7]

Nevertheless, by its charter, the company did not achieve the predominant position in the trade that its sponsors sought nor did the charter convey all the powers that its court needed.

In particular, the court had no powers to compel clockmakers to acquire the freedom of the company and many clockmakers acquired their citizenship of the City of London by becoming freemen of other guilds, notably the Blacksmiths' Company.

In the result, although by the end of the seventeenth century the clockmakers of London were leading the world in their techniques and workmanship, the Clockmakers' Company lacked local prestige and with it membership and the funds which a larger membership would have produced.

From the latter part of the seventeenth century onwards, the Clockmakers' Company made strenuous efforts to improve their position.

In 1696 the court petitioned the Lord Mayor and Aldermen and the Common Council to the effect that persons using the trade of clockmaking and allied trades should cause all their apprentices to become freemen of the Clockmakers' Company

---

7. Atkins and Overall, *op. cit.*, p. 73.

Colour Plate 4. *Detail of the Clockmakers' Company charter showing a portrait of Charles I in the initial letter of the charter.*   Worshipful Company of Clockmakers

at the conclusion of their apprenticeship. This petition was strongly opposed by the Blacksmiths' Company who could see the danger to their own membership, and in the result the clockmakers' petition failed.

The matter then remained in abeyance for a prolonged period, but in 1764 the matter was re-opened — this time with success — and an Act of Common Council was passed with effect from Christmas 1765. After that time no person who was a clockmaker should be admitted a citizen of London except by freedom of the Clockmakers' Company.

The clockmakers also sought to increase their prestige by obtaining a grant of livery. Their bye-laws made in 1632 purported to confer a grant of livery on the company, but this was nugatory since according to the custom of the City of London, a livery could only be granted by the Court of Aldermen and then only upon proper application made. The effect of a grant of livery is that the guild concerned is allowed to have the number of liverymen specified in the grant, and the liverymen have the privilege of voting in the City of London at the election of the City officers including the Chamberlain of London. So the grant of livery would make the Clockmakers' Company an integral part of the government of the City of London.

On the other hand, the Court of Aldermen were only interested in conferring a grant of livery if, to use the words in the petition of 1776, "divers of the Members of the said company were able and willing to bear the expense of a livery and to contribute and assist on all public occasions for the honour and service of this City".

So it was rather a vicious circle. The lack of a livery was a discouragement to the company but a livery would only be granted if the company showed themselves to be worthy of it.

The first petition for a grant was made in 1749 and this was unsuccessful.

In 1768, however, a further petition was lodged on 10th June and this was successful. The company was constituted a Livery Company, the number of liverymen being fixed at sixty. (This number has subsequently been increased.)

From then on the company obtained its present prestige though many of its powers were falling and continued to fall into disuse. It has never been a really wealthy company and has never had its own hall, and the court had to meet in taverns or in the halls of other companies. Today the court and livery meet almost exclusively in the Goldsmiths' Hall. The company however has a fine and very valuable collection of antique clocks and watches and a fine and extensive horological library, all of which are available to the public in the Guildhall Library.

The Apprentice[8]

It was enacted by the Statute of Artificers in 1563 that all craftsmen living in town or country had to acquire the skill of their trade by being apprenticed to a master for seven years. It was generally accepted that following the apprenticeship period, a tradesman worked as a journeyman for hire, prior to setting up in business on his own. Apprenticeships varied somewhat with the master. Although the usual term of binding was seven years, on occasion seven and a half years, eight years or even longer periods have been recorded. An entry in the Court Minute Books of the Clockmakers' Company for 22nd July, 1691, clearly indicates the ages between which it was possible for an apprentice to be bound:

---

8.   C.E. Atkins, *The Company of Clockmakers, Register of Apprentices, 1631-1931.*

"...that as it was illegale and contrary to the Custome of the Cittie of London That any person being under the age of 14 years should be bound Apprentice; Soe was it also, That any person above the age of One and Twenty yeares should be bound Apprentice."

The binding of apprentices to clockmakers seemed to be getting out of hand by the end of the third quarter of the seventeenth century. This was no doubt due to the abusing of the regulations by many clockmakers who saw in the apprentice a means of cheap labour. A court held on 6th November, 1676, brought matters to a head, when it was recorded that, "This Court taking into Consideration the great inconvenience arising to the Company by the multiplicity of the Apprentices taken, have Ordered the Clarke to issue out Ticketts to all and every the Members of the Company to give notice to them, that henceforward noe Apprentice will be allowed to be bound unto or taken by any member of the Company, Otherwise than according to the Ordinances of the Company."

This order evidently did much to restore the balance of apprenticeship within the company for the next fifteen years, for no further major comment is made until a quarter court held on 6th July, 1691, when a long entry was made, referring to the order of November 1676 ... "ffrom which time, it hath hitherto bin practiced, and insisted upon as a Rule; That noe member having One Apprentice, might take a Second, till his former should have served his full ffive yeares of his time." This restraint was modified and clockmakers were henceforward allowed, "That he who hath One Apprentice bound for seven yeares may binde a second when his first hath served Two yeares, — and he who hath one bound for Eight yeares, may binde a second when his ffirst hath served Three yeares; the ffirst Apprentice in either case having ffive yeares to serve."

At a quarter court held on 20th January, 1700, the regulations were further modified, it being "now voted and ordered that till further order any Member haveing but one Apprentice bound to himselfe may take another and bind him to himselfe although the first Apprentice has not been bound full two yeares. Yet nevertheless noe Member to have more than two Apprentices bound to himselfe at One time."

During the third quarter of the seventeenth century it was a not infrequent occurrence for a clockmaker to pay a fine to the company in order to bind an additional apprentice which otherwise he would have been unable to do, having the number laid down in the ordinances. The fines ranged from a few shillings to two pounds and were probably based upon what the company considered the clockmaker could afford to pay. Thus both were satisfied, the company's coffers were enhanced and the clockmaker secured his additional apprentice. It was no doubt this state of affairs that paved the way to the issuing of the court order of 6th November 1676.

The fee paid for apprenticeship seems to have varied with the whim of the master. *The London Tradesman* (first edition 1747)[9] gives the amount payable as £10-£30 and incidentally states the hours of working as a clockmaker from 6 a.m. to 8 p.m.

There was a custom among the London apprentices, during their holidays and particularly at Shrove Tuesday, to seek out ladies of easy virtue in order to have them imprisoned during Lent. Samuel Pepys records in his diary on 24th March 1668/9, "great talk of the tumult at the other end of the town, about Moorefields, among the 'prentices, taking the liberty of these holidays to pull down brothels." As a result of these occurrences a number of pamphlets were published at about this

9. R. Campbell, *The London Tradesman, 1749 and 1757.*

ELIAS ALLEN.

Apud Anglos Cantianus, iuxta **Tunnbridge** natus, Mathematicis Inſtrumentis ære incidendis ſui temporis Artifex ingenioſiſſimus,

Obijt Londini, prope finem Menſis Martij, Anno a Christo nato 1653 ſuæque ætatis

Plate 54. *Portrait of Elias Allen.*

Science Museum, London

50

time with such intriguing titles as "The Wh-s Petition to the London Prentices", "The Citizens' Reply to the Wh-s Petition, and the Prentices' Answer" and "The Poor Wh-s Petition to the Illustrious Lady of Pleasure, the Countess of Castlemayne"!

The Workshop and Living Accommodation

No contemporary illustration of the interior of an English clockmaker's workshop has so far been recorded though engravings of such European workshops exist dating from the late sixteenth century.[10] The nearest source that can be taken is Wenceslas Hollar's etching of Elias Allen dated 1660 which portrays this instrument maker at his bench with a variety of instruments and several tools in a rack on the wall behind him (see Plate 54).

Allen, fourth master of the Clockmakers' Company held that office from 19th January 1636 to 29th July 1638, considerably more than the accepted period of one year.

It is, therefore, only possible to construct a mental picture of the type of workshop that existed by drawing from contemporary documentation. The Clockmakers' Company Court Minute Books and certain rate and tax books give some indication of the workshop within the framework of the building as a whole.

On 17th March 1681, a search was made by four members of the Clockmakers' Company, together with the beadle, of the "Shop & House" of John Martin of White Gate Alley, London, on account of irregularities in the binding of an apprentice. "They then found in the shop his wife and his Apprentice Richard Print. Martin, having been out at the time, was questioned upon his return and required to show his work roome above stairs ... the said Martin with the Wardens, Assistant, Clerk & Beadle went up higher into his Work Roome, where they found that Boy supposed to be the Apprentice soe unduly bound as aforesaid, at a Work Board, with a near unfinished Clock Wheel in his hand, and divers other parts and pieces of Clock Work, and divers usuall Clockmakers' Tooles, before and neare him in the Roome ..."

Clearly John Martin had his living and business premises under one roof and extended through the house.

The rate books of St. Dunstan's in the West give an indication as to the type of establishment kept by Joseph Knibb. An entry in 1678 gives more than usual details. It sheds light not only on the number of occupants of the house next Serjeant's Inn, but indirectly confirms what sort of household Knibb kept. The rent of the house was shown as £30 thus bringing it into line with those kept by Thomas Tompion and Henry Jones. Whereas these last mentioned makers occupied sections only of their respective houses, Joseph Knibb is shown as inhabiting, together with his ménage, the whole house. The extract from the Rate Book is as follows:

Joseph Knibb and his wife	12/ –
1 child and 3 apprentices	4/ –
Peter Knibb Journeyman	11/ –
Anne Ball, maid servant	4/ –

Thus there were eight occupants as compared with fourteen at the house where

---

10. See for example the frequently reproduced engraving by Gallé of Jan van der Straet's (Stradanus) painting of a Clockmaker's Workshop painted in Florence c.1588.

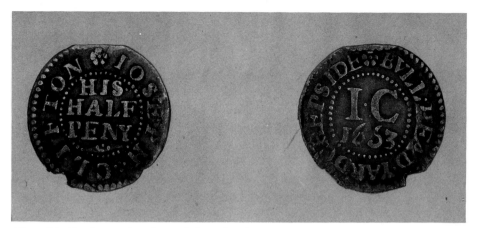

Plate 55. Tradesman's token of Joseph Clifton as found in the case of a clock by Ahasuerus Fromanteel.

Thomas Tompion had his establishment. At this time, it seems to have been much commoner for houses to be shared. No doubt even twelve years afterwards, the Great Fire of 1666 was still having its repercussions. Generally speaking the more successful makers in the trade would have had the more commodious premises.

Division of Labour

Even from its infancy, clockmaking in England had some division of labour. During the earliest period, in addition to the clockmaker, the services of the engraver and gilder were called for as and when required.

Following the restoration of the monarchy, quite apart from those engaged upon the construction of the movements, there came into being the specialist wood case maker. One or two of the London cabinetmakers must have been quick to see the business potential upon the introduction of the pendulum clock into England in 1658 and the provision of cases for these when they must have been regarded as strikingly revolutionary timekeepers. Some twenty to thirty years later, the more prolific makers undoubtedly had their workshops organised somewhat in the manner of a production line, drawing their labour from apprentices, journeymen and outworkers. By the end of the seventeenth century, there could have been as many as ten or a dozen specialist workers involved in the creation of one clock.

Purposely inserted into the carcase of a clock case by Ahasuerus Fromanteel was a tradesman's token inscribed "Joseph Clifton, Bull Head Yard, Chepside. His half-penny 1663"[11] (Plate 55). It may be correctly assumed that this token had remained in the carcase since the construction of the case, but unfortunately, while such a token has been previously recorded, research has so far failed to identify the trade followed by Joseph Clifton. Even so, it may not be unreasonable to surmise that he was among these few early cabinetmakers and associates who were the first to

---

11. On 14th May 1616 a Joseph Clifton petitioned the Painter Stainers' Company and was admitted free, 16th October 1617. This was probably the father. The marriage of a Joseph Clifton to Susan Tanfield was recorded at St. Olaves, Park Street, on 17th October 1657.

specialise in clock case construction.

Those of the seventeenth century that it has been possible to identify are listed below:

GUTCH, JOHN. "John Gutch a Case Maker was Admitted and sworn a Brother of this Company paid for his Admission Twenty shillings and promised his Conformity to the orders of the Company." (Clockmakers' Company, Quarter Court, 7th April, 1673.)

PLAYER, ROBERT. "Robert Player Case and Cabinett Maker (free of the Company of Joyners) was Admitted and Sworne a Brother of this Company paid for his Admission ffifteene shillings and sixpence, and promised his conformity to the Orders of the Company." (Clockmakers' Company, Quarter Court, 8th April, 1678.)

LOW, JOHN. "John Low Case maker being a Branch of the Art of Clockmaking was Admitted and Sworne a Brother of this Company Paid for his admission Twenty shillings and promised his Conformity to the Orders of the Company.
Witnes his hands
(Signed) John Low"
(Clockmakers' Company Quarter Court, 4th July, 1692.)

BARBER, EDWARD. Poll Tax Records. Year 1698. Cripplegate Without Ward. Edward Barber Clock-Case Maker.

A manuscript in the Clockmakers' Company library at Guildhall dated 26th June, 1662, entitled "A List of all the Clockmakers both ffreemen and fforieners alians and outliers" itemises under streets or districts the names of 168 clockmakers and kindred tradesmen. Five engravers are included.

Another engraver, George Deane, a member of the Clockmakers' Company, was in all probability undertaking work for Henry Jones during the middle 1670s. (See the Clockmakers' Company Court Minute Books 24th September 1677, MS 2710/1.)

Unfortunately it is presently impossible to identify a particular case with its case-maker except possibly in the above-mentioned instance of Joseph Clifton.

Contemporary Prices and Values

Few contemporary references to prices and values survive. Now and again it is possible to glean such information from odd manuscript sources and even so there seem to be more references to watches than clocks. R.W. Symonds cites an account dated 23rd June, 1664,[12] which included the following items:

"A pendilum clocke to goe 8 dayes with a lampe to show the houre of the Night £45" and "A pendilum clocke £5".

At a Quarter Court of the Clockmakers' Company held on 19th January 1673 (Court Minute Books MS 2710/1) it was recorded that:

"Mr. Henry Jones Clockmaker acquainted this Court that he having heretofore made for the King a Clock of the value of One Hundred and ffifty pounds whereon was engraven Henricus Jones Londini with which it stood in his Maties Closett about Seaven Yeares but being by his Matie given unto a Lady it came to the hands of Robert Seignior Clockmaker to make some addition to the worke . . ."

---

12. R.W. Symonds, *Masterpieces of English Furniture and Clocks*, p. 144.

Assuming the value placed on the clock to be correct, it was at the outset greatly more expensive than the normal domestic clock of the period.

Sir Richard Legh writing to Lady Legh on 29th April 1675[13] records:

"I went to the famous Pendulum maker Knibb, and have agreed for one, he having none ready, but one dull stager which was at £19; for £5 more, I have agreed for one finer than my Father's, and it is to be better finish'd, with carved capitalls gold, and gold pedestalls with figures of boys and cherubines all Brass gilt. I would have had it Olivewood, (the Case I mean), but gold does not agree with that colour, soe took their advice to have it black Ebony, which suits your Cabinett better than Wallnutt tree wood, of which they are mostly made. Lett me have thy advice herein by the next."

In due course Lady Legh replied to Sir Richard:

"My dearest Soule,.... as for the Pandelome Case I think Blacke suits anything."

R.W. Symonds records the following prices extracted from accounts at the British Museum, Public Record Office and the Lord Chamberlain's Department:

"Augt 16 (1693). A spring clock in a Tortoise Shell case, £40."

"March ye 28 (1693) A large Month Clock a fine wallnut tree case wth ye Diall plate Capitall and Bases Gilt £25."

1695. "Thomas Tompion for a fine clock £600."

From Michaelmas 1697 to Michaelmas 1698.

"For a new spring repeating quarter clock an Ebony case and fine silver Ornaments, £95."

"For a new spring clock with an Ebony case & silver Ornaments, £75."

Both the above mentioned clocks were presents from William III to the Government of Tunis.

R.W. Symonds also records in an account to the Honourable Robert Harley, under the year 1701:

"August 7   For a Spring Clock & Stand. £31.10.0

And for a month clock in an extraordinary case £17.10.0.

August 23 For a 30 houre clock in a black case £6."

---

13.   Raine's Collection, Chetham's Library, Manchester.

Chapter III
The Lantern Clock

Some time in the early part of the seventeenth century, probably around 1620,[1] there appeared in England a simple domestic clock with a case of largely brass construction and having going and hour striking trains. The trains were normally placed 'back and back' with the going train in front and the striking train behind. These clocks almost invariably had an hour hand only, which was ample for the needs of the times, and were sometimes fitted with an alarm mechanism. All were weight driven. Sometimes the clocks were made to stand on a bracket; others hung from a steel stirrup on the back plate which had two spurs at the bottom to keep the clock parallel to the wall.

It is not known precisely when or by whom these clocks were first designed, though one can say with complete certainty that the design is that of a maker working in England and that they attained instant and continued popularity. Until the introduction into England of Huygens' application of the pendulum to the domestic clock in 1658 (and apart from a few table clocks) they were virtually the only English domestic clocks (though other types were no doubt imported from abroad) and despite the introduction of longcase and bracket clocks, they continued to be made and enjoyed great popularity well into the eighteenth century, no doubt because they were relatively cheap and quite adequate for the less elaborate households of the time.

It may be asked why they were almost invariably made of brass especially since, although there was a brass industry in England from about 1570 until the time of the Civil War, its products were not of good commercial quality and manufacturers of brass articles preferred to import their raw material.[2] The reason no doubt is that brass was easier to work than steel, possibly cheaper, rustless and easy to clean and keep clean by lacquering.

These clocks are today almost exclusively referred to as lantern clocks although it

---

1. There are two or three reputedly dated lantern clocks prior to 1620: (i) an iron lantern clock in the Science Museum, South Kensington, signed by John Holloway at Lavington, has the date 1611 scrathed on the underside of the base; (ii) a clock by Wm. Paynes in East Smithfield, formerly in the Webster collection and illustrated in Cescinsky & Webster, *English Domestic Clocks,* 1913, has the date 1618 scratched on the arbor frame behind the dial plate; (iii) Mr. L.F. Miller in an article "The East Anglian Lantern Clock" in the *Horological Journal,* May 1978, at p. 3, states that there is a lantern-type clock in a private collection in the U.S.A. which is signed by John Smith of (King's) Lynn and dated 1610.

2. For further details of early English brass manufacture see Rupert Gentle and Rachael Feild, *English Domestic Brass and the History of its Origins,* London, 1975.

Plate 56. *A transitional clock with the front (not original) removed.*

Plate 57. *Side view of the clock shown in Plate 56.*

is not known when that name first began to be used or whether it is used because the clocks bear some resemblance to lanterns of the period or is a corruption of the word 'latten' meaning brass. Other names for them are 'Cromwellian', 'bird-cage' and 'bed-post' clocks, all being entirely unsuitable names.

Lantern clock design appears to have derived from the weight-driven iron, or so called Gothic clocks, which were made on the Continent. For an example of a transitional clock the reader is referred to that illustrated in Plates 56-57. This clock was formerly in the Ilbert collection and is now in the British Museum. The four corner corner pillars are typical of the Gothic clocks of the period and while the rest of the clock resembles a lantern clock, it is not known how much of that part of the design is original. Certainly the brass front and the hand are not accepted as original by the British Museum authorities. There is no evidence that this clock is by a maker working in England.

Once designed and produced, the lantern clock quickly established itself as the standard English domestic clock. In later years, its manufacture spread to some countries abroad, notably France.[3]

As already indicated it cannot be reliably stated when the first lantern clock was produced. Its popularity spread so rapidly over the country that one is inclined to deduce that it first appeared in London and found instant favour. A number of extant early examples were made by William Bowyer. Baillie quoted this maker as working between 1626-47 and states that there was a lantern clock by him in the Webster collection dated 1626.[4] Extant examples suggest that William Bowyer was a prolific maker of lantern clocks and might well have been their originator though it has to be conceded that there is no definite evidence to support this theory.

Since lantern clocks were first produced around 1620, they were originally made with crown wheel and verge escapements and balance wheel controllers. There is no extant example of a lantern clock with an original foliot controller and it is very doubtful if any were made. With the advent of the pendulum, lantern clocks began to be made first with crown wheel and verge escapements and bob pendulums and later with anchor escapements and long pendulums. Nevertheless lantern clocks continued to be made with balance wheel controllers almost to the end of the seventeenth century and the example by Samuel Stretch, who worked first in Birmingham and later in Bristol, cannot be much earlier than 1685 or 1690 if Stretch was born only in 1657 as is stated in Baillie's *Watchmakers and Clockmakers of the World*. The balance wheel of this clock is undoubtedly original.[5] (See Plates 58-60.)

Balance wheels are almost invariably made of brass and not of steel and they are chamfered underneath so as to adjust them to the correct weight to give more or less accurate timekeeping. Final adjustment was made by making the driving weight as an open bucket filled with shot so that shot could be removed or added to if it was desired to make the clock go slower or faster. It is remarkable how good a time-

3.   W.F.J. Hana, "French Lantern Clocks", *Antiquarian Horology,* Vol. IV, No. 9 (Dec. 1964), pp. 266-269.

4.   Lot 213 at Sotheby's sale of Part II of the Webster collection, 19th October 1954, where the clock is described in the catalogue as "a rare dated brass Lantern Clock by William Bowyer of London". Clearly G.H. Baillie's starting date of 1626 for this maker in *Watchmakers and Clockmakers of the World* must have been taken from the date of this clock and it is likely that he was in business before this date. Incidentally William Bowyer was a subscriber to the fund to pay the expenses of obtaining the Clockmakers' Charter.

5.   This clock was sold by auction about thirty years ago as a lot in a general furniture sale and when the auctioneer offered the clock he stated: "The pendulum of this clock is missing"!

Plate 58. *Lantern clock by Samuel Stretch with original balance wheel dated about 1685.*

Plate 59 *(left). Side view with plate removed of the clock shown in Plate 58.*

Plate 60 *(right). Back view showing original balance wheel of the clock shown in Plate 58.*

61

62

Plate 61. *Lantern clock with original balance wheel by William Bowyer, dated c.1620. (Also shown as Colour Plate 5, page 67.)*
Trustees of the British Museum

Plate 62. *Side view of the clock shown in Plate 61 with plates removed.*

Plate 63. *View of the alarm mechanism of the clock shown in Plate 61.*

Plate 64. *View of the balance wheel, taken from above, of the clock shown in Plate 61.*

63

64

Plate 65. Lantern clock by Nicholas Snowe of Salisbury, dated 1636.
Salisbury Museum

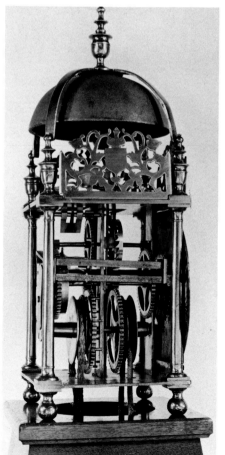

Plate 66 (left). Lantern clock by Thomas Knifton at the Cross Keys, Lothbury, circa 1650.
Science Museum, London

Plate 67 (right). Side view of the clock shown in Plate 66 with plates removed.

Plate 68. Back view of the clock shown in Plate 66.

Plate 69. Silver lantern clock by David Bouquet, c. 1650. The low bell suggests that the clock was originally designed to fit in a case.

Victoria and Albert Museum

keeper a balance wheel clock can be if it is in good condition and regulated properly.

Balance wheel lantern clocks normally went from twelve to fifteen hours at one winding, depending upon the height at which they were hung on the wall. The great wheels of both going and striking trains turned in opposite directions and there was a click spring fitted to each great wheel. The trains were operated by separate ropes with a weight and counterpoise to each. The striking hammer was invariably on the right.

Lantern clocks with original balance wheels are extremely rare and it is doubtful if there are many more than half-a-dozen extant today. A great many balance wheel clocks have been converted to pendulum control over the years but over the last thirty years or so it has become fashionable to re-convert them back to the balance wheel, their original form of controller.

One of the earliest extant clocks with an original balance wheel controller is that by William Bowyer which is illustrated in Plates 61-64. (Plate 61 is also shown as Colour Plate 54, page 67.) This clock was acquired by the late Courtenay Ilbert from the Drummond Robertson collection and then went to the British Museum (where it still is) when the Ilbert collection was acquired.

Its height to the top of the finial is 16⅜ ins., the clock is 5 ¹³/₁₆ ins. square and the diameter of the chapter ring is 5⅞ ins. The clock is fitted with an alarm mechanism which is intact and original. It will be noted that the chapter ring is narrow, only ¹³/₁₆ in. wide compared with about 1 ³/₁₆ ins. wide on later clocks of similar size and the narrow chapter ring is an early feature (see Plate 61).

The next clock in order of date is a clock by Nicholas Snowe of Salisbury. Despite the fact that it has lost its frets, it is illustrated because it is dated 1636 and thus provides us with a milestone. This clock is in the Salisbury Museum (see Plate 65).

The next clock illustrated is a clock in the Science Museum, South Kensington, by Thomas Knifton at the Cross Keys in Lothbury. Thomas Knifton was free of the Clockmakers' Company from 1640 to 1662 and while this clock was undoubtedly a balance wheel clock when first made, its present balance does not appear to be original and it would seem to have been re-converted. Its height to the top of the finial is 15¾ ins., the diameter of the dial is 6¼ ins. and the clock is 5³/₁₆ ins. square. The hand appears to be a replacement (see Plates 66-68).

A nice little alarm clock in the Victoria and Albert Museum, South Kensington, is the clock by David Bouquet shown in Plate 69. The case of this clock is made entirely of silver and is the only lantern clock known which is made of this metal. The clock is signed "David Bouquet a Londres". He was a French immigrant who was admitted to the Blacksmiths' Company in 1628 and joined the Clockmakers' Company as a founder member in 1632. He died in 1665. The present clock was probably made in about 1650. It is 8 ins. high overall, 3 ins. square and the dial has a diameter of 3½ ins. The movement may not be original.

An example of a clock which originally had a balance wheel, but was later converted to an anchor escapement with a long pendulum, is the clock by John Pennock. The clock is signed "John Pennocke at Lond. Within Bishopsgate fecit". It is known that he was in Bishopsgate in 1630 and still there in 1638 but by 1647 he was in the parish of St. Margaret's Lothbury. It would therefore appear that the clock was made after 1629 but before 1647. John Pennock was renter warden of the Clockmakers' Company in 1654 and 1655, master in 1660 and again in 1663. The clock has finials which screw down and fasten the top plate to the pillars. This is the

usual method of construction but sometimes the pillars are each made in one piece, the plates being let into the pillars by grooves. The alarm train has been removed. The overall height of this clock is 16¼ ins. high and it is 5¾ ins. wide (see Plates 70-71).

The next clock is signed "Peter Closon Nere Hoborn Bridge Fecit" (Plates 72-74). It was formerly in the Ilbert collection and is now in the British Museum. Baillie (*op. cit.*) says that Closon was in London in 1630, a subscriber to the incorporation of the Clockmakers' Company and was a member of that Company from 1632-1653. He was senior warden from 1636-39, though he was never master. The alarm mechanism is missing. The overall height of the clock is 15⅜ ins., the width 5¾ ins. and the diameter of the dial 6¼ ins.

When the pendulum was introduced into England, lantern clocks began to be made with crown wheel and verge escapement with bob pendulums. It seems that at much about the same time the Huygens endless rope arrangement was fitted, so that both going and striking trains operated from one weight.

Plate 72. Front view of a clock by Peter Closon.
Trustees of the British Museum

Plate 73. Side view of the clock shown in Plate 72.

Plate 74. Top view of the clock shown in Plate 72 with the bell removed.

Plate 75. Side view of a clock by Edward Webb showing heraldic frets.
Science Museum, London

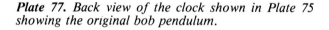

Plate 76. The top plate of the clock shown in Plate 75, with the bell removed showing original crown wheel escapement.

Plate 77. Back view of the clock shown in Plate 75 showing the original bob pendulum.

These clocks can be identified by the fact that although the great wheels of each train revolved in the same direction, there was a ratchet on the great wheel of the striking train only and the striking hammer was on the left hand side as one faced the clock.

An example of this type of clock is one in the Science Museum, South Kensington, by Edward Webb of Chewstoke which is dated 1688.[6] As can be seen from Plate 75 the clock has heraldic frets with lion and unicorn and crown supporters and a shield in the middle to take the owner's initials. The view of the top plate (with the bell removed) shows the original crown wheel and the pallets of the escapement (Plate 76). Plate 77 shows the original bob pendulum. The overall height of the clock is 16⅛ ins., the width is 5¾ ins. and the diameter of the chapter ring is 6 ins.

However there are always exceptions and not all clocks with original bob pendulums and verge escapements had Huygens winding arrangements. An example is a clock by Jacobus Markwick of London which was formerly in the Ilbert collection and is now in the British Museum. This clock has an original verge escape-

---

6. There is also a lantern clock in the Victoria and Albert Museum signed "Edward Webbe in Church Stoke 1676" and one in the Clockmakers' Company Museum signed "Edward Webb of Chewstoke, 1692".

Colour Plate 5. *Lantern clock with original balance wheel by William Bowyer. Circa 1620. (Other views of this clock are shown in Plates 62-64.)*

Plate 78. *Clock by Jacobus Markwick.*   Trustees of the British Museum

Plate 79. *Side view of the clock shown in Plate 78.*

Plate 80. *Back view of the clock shown in Plate 78 showing the original bob pendulum and the half-hour bell.*

ment with bob pendulum but it does not have the Huygens endless rope winding arrangement. Both great wheels revolve in the same direction, there are ratchets on both great wheels but the bell hammer is on the left as one faces the clock. Exceptionally the clock strikes one blow at each half hour on a half-hour bell; this striking arrangement being operated by the star wheel. The alarm dial is probably a replacement though the alarm mechanism is missing with the back plate. Jacobus Markwick was free of the Clockmakers' Company from 1666-98. The clock has an overall height of 15¼ ins., a width of 5¾ ins. and the diameter of the dial is 6⅜ ins. (see Plates 78-80).

A nice little clock is that by Thomas Tompion shown in Plates 81-82 which is in the British Museum. Its overall height is approximately 10 ins., the clock is 3⅜ ins.

Plate 81. *Small lantern alarm timepiece by Thomas Tompion.*

Trustees of the British Museum

Plate 82. *Side view of the clock shown in Plate 81, showing the alarm mechanism and the original bob pendulum.*

square and the dial has a diameter of $4^3/_{16}$ ins. It has its original crown wheel and bob pendulum. It is a timepiece, i.e. it does not strike the hours, but has an alarm with the alarm fitted as usual on the back of the case. Also as usual, the alarm is weight-driven. The clock is engraved with Tompion's name in the centre of the dial. This is where Tompion always signed his lantern clocks; he never signed them on the chapter ring. The clock is number 518 which is stamped at the bottom of the back right hand column.

Towards the end of the seventeenth century, a specialised form of lantern clock appeared, namely, the winged lantern. In these clocks the trains were normally pitched between four bars so that the pendulum with a fluked anchor bob could swing out into wings mounted on the doors. Plate 83 shows an example of the winged lantern. This clock is by Joseph Knibb and has an alarm.

In other respects winged lantern clocks were similar to ordinary lantern clocks with verge escapements and bob pendulums.

Lantern clocks with original wings are extremely rare, probably rarer than lantern clocks with original balance wheels, though a good number have had restored wings

Plate 83. *Winged lantern clock by Joseph Knibb.*

Sotheby Parke Bernet

Plate 84. *Very small lantern clock with date circle and alarm, unsigned.*

Plate 85. *Very large carillon quarter striking clock.*
Christie, Manson and Woods Ltd.

Plate 86.
Lantern clock by George Graham with its original oak travelling case with compartments for the weights.

fitted. It is unlikely that all these clocks have lost their wings over the years and the more likely explanation is that they were never fitted with wings, the pendulum being allowed to swing on either side of the clock through slits cut for the purpose.

Although the standard lantern clock had an overall height of 15 to 16ins., very small ones were made as well as very large ones. Plate 84 shows an example of a very small clock. It has an overall height of 7½ins., a width of 3⁹/₁₆ ins. and the chapter ring a diameter of 3¾ins. The clock is particularly interesting in that it has a date circle on the inside of the chapter ring and it is fitted with an alarm mechanism mounted on the back plate.

A few lantern clocks made towards the end of the seventeenth century were fitted with tick-tack escapements but these are very much the exception rather than the rule.

One or two specials were also made. One example shown in Plate 85 is of a very large carillon quarter striking clock having an overall height of 26ins. It is particularly noteworthy in that it has three finials, instead of the usual two on the front and sides and has three trains. It formerly had an alarm train and originally had a crown wheel and verge escapement with a balance wheel but now has an anchor escapement with a long pendulum. As would be expected from such a large clock it was made to stand on a bracket and was not suspended by means of a stirrup and spurs. The clock is unsigned.

Finally a most interesting lantern clock by George Graham and its original oak travelling case with compartments for the weights are illustrated in Plate 86.

It does not seem that any particular progression can be ascertained by considering the frets, finials and hands on various clocks. For example the late R.W. Symonds illustrates three lantern clocks by Thomas Tompion, the frets and hands being different in all three cases.[7] It can however be said that the crossed dolphin fret (see Plate 58) is a later rather than an earlier feature and became very common from the latter part of the seventeenth century onwards.

---

7.   R.W. Symonds, *Thomas Tompion, His Life and Work,* London, 1951, figs. 97, 98 and 98a.

Chapter IV

Clock Movements during the Architectural Period

Christian Huygens claimed that he made the first model of a pendulum clock on Christmas Day, 1656, and in the June of the following year a patent was granted to Salomon Coster, of The Hague, for making such clocks. In the September of the same year, John Fromanteel, the son of Ahasuerus Fromanteel of London, entered into Coster's service, it is presumed, to absorb all that he could of the principles and practice of making the new type of clock. John returned to London in May 1658 and by the 27th of October of that year, Ahasuerus was able to insert in *Mercurius Politicus,* the following advertisement.

> "There is lately a way found out for making of Clocks that go exact and keep equaller time than any now made without this Regulator (examined and proved before his Highness the Lord Protector by such Doctors whose knowledge and learning is without exception) and are not subject to alter by change of weather, as others are, and may be made to go a week, or a moneth, or a year, with once winding up, as well as those that are wound up every day, and keep time as well, and is very excellent for all House clocks that either go with Springs or Weights: And also Steeple Clocks that are most subject to differ by change of weather. Made by *Ahasuerus Fromanteel,* who made the first that were made in *England:* You may have them at his house on the Bank-side in *Moses* Alley, Southwark, and at the sign of the Maremaid in Lothbury, near *Bartholomew* Lane end, London."[1]

Very few examples indeed have survived which can with assurance be said to have been made within five or so years of this advertisement, and most of these are spring-driven clocks. The main changes which had been made in the construction of these clocks to enable them to be controlled by the pendulum were for the verge to be altered from the traditional vertical position to the horizontal, and for the balance to be replaced by a lever. This lever had a forked end which was bent through an angle of ninety degrees. This lever is known as the crutch and the fork embraces a thickened portion of the pendulum rod, called the impulse block. The upper end of the pendulum rod was formed into a hook to engage a loop of silken thread suspended from a point in line with the verge pivot. The lower end of this pendulum rod

---

1. In *Antiquarian Horology, Vol. VI, pp. 614-626, Ernest Edwardes advances the opinion that the pendulum was used in England before 1658.*

Plate 87. *A timepiece by Salomon Coster, said to be the proto-type pendulum clock of 1657. The hinged dial supports the movement which has square pillars and cycloidal cheeks.*
Rijksmuseum, Leiden, Holland

Plate 88. *The velvet covered dial of the Coster clock in Plate 87.*

had the weight or 'bob' attached to it. Contemporary drawings show this bob as a sphere; but it is more likely that it was lenticular. In the prototype timepiece made by Coster (Plates 87-88) and also in other early Dutch clocks, the silken loop was quite long and oscillated between curved strips of brass, called cycloidal cheeks. The purpose was to make the pendulum bob describe a cycloidal arc during its swing by means of shortening the effective pendulum length as it reached the extremity of its swing, to attain isochronism or unequal arcs in equal time. It would be logical, there-fore to expect Fromanteel to have employed the same system in the first clocks which he made.

About 1940, the remains of an old spring-driven timepiece movement were dis-covered (Plates 89-91), which had engraved on the back plate the words "A. Fromanteel London Fecit 1658". This would appear to be the earliest English time-piece. In many ways it is very similar to the Coster prototype, but it is larger and very sturdy. It would also appear that both makers had such faith in the timekeeping properties of their pendulums that they could dispense with the use of fusees, for both have going barrels. There is stopwork on the barrel cap of the Fromanteel time-piece and it is significant that, like the Coster example, it has square pillars which are riveted into the back plate. This movement has a duration of eight days.

This important timepiece was restored by Mr. Charles Hobson, who replaced everything above the contrate pinion in the style of the Dutch work, with a hori-zontal crown wheel and verge. There remained just sufficient of the original dial to indicate what that had been like and a new dial was made similar to the original by Mr. J.W. Parkes (Plate 91). The engraver working on the chapter ring, having been given an authentic Dutch ring to copy, copied it too exactly, with the result that the figures 0 to 60 appear twice, quite incorrectly for this piece. The restoration of this movement has been proved by more recent research to have been correct, with the pendulum suspension following closely the Dutch method.

Since the case of this timepiece is lost, the method which was adopted for holding

Plate 89. Timepiece by Ahasuerus Fromanteel, dated 1658. It has square pillars riveted into the back plate. The date is not placed centrally, thus giving the impression that it was an afterthought.

Plate 90. The side view of the timepiece in Plate 89 showing the bridgeless motionwork and the stopwork on the barrel cap.

Plate 91. The replacement dial and new case of the timepiece in Plate 89. The chapter ring has been erroneously engraved 0-60 twice. The hands are original.

Plate 92. *The dial of a timepiece by Ahasuerus Fromanteel, with original hands, fine corner mounts and gilding. There is no gilding round the edge of the mock pendulum aperture, indicating that it is a later addition.* R.A. Lee

it in its case is not known but it may reasonably be assumed that, like the Coster example, the movement was suspended from the dial and that the dial was in all probability hinged to the case. The case itself may well have been also like the Coster case.

The timepiece movement illustrated in Plates 92-94 which like the previous one is of eight-day duration, is also very similar to the Coster timepiece but with the distinctive English difference of being heavier, with the larger wheels and thicker plates. This timepiece is suspended from the dial but has the addition of a fusee. It has had considerable modification through the years but in spite of this, it is possible to read from the stopped holes just what the original movement was like. There was a fixed potence, the evidence for this being a square filling in the back plate. The top of the crown wheel pinion had been supported in the Dutch manner, similar to that of the reconstructed dated example, by a bridging piece projecting into the front plate which also held the front verge pivot. It is not clear how the back pivot was supported; it has at the moment a knife-edge, but the stopped holes in the back plate in the area around the back cock suggest that several alterations have been made

Plate 93. The movement of the Fromanteel timepiece in Plate 92. The two top pillars are secured by screws which may be contemporary.

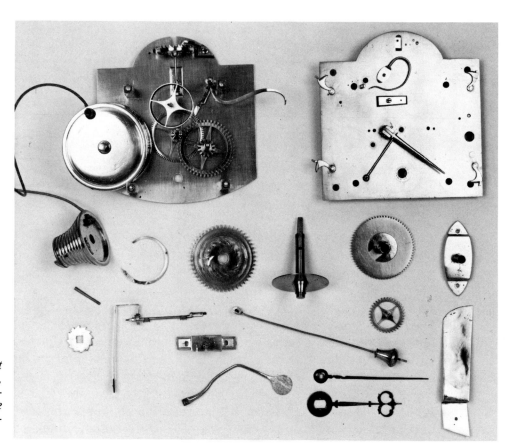

Plate 94. The movement in Plate 93 dismantled, showing the square pillars, the bridge for the motionwork and the replacement verge.

Plate 95. *A three-train weight-driven striking clock by Ahasuerus Fromanteel with an unmatted dial and foliate mount in the centre. The chapter ring has upright numerals, and alternate quarter-hour divisions blacked in. The minute hand makes a revolution every fifteen minutes. (The case is shown in Plate 213.)*

Fogg Art Museum, Harvard University

Plate 96 (above right). The side view of the clock in Plate 95, showing the square pillars and dial feet with the signature on one pillar, intermediate wheels and pinions, the count wheel engraved with the hours. Above the dial are a ball which indicates the phases of the moon and discs which show the age of the moon, the hour and day of the month.

Plate 97. The clock in Plate 95 showing the split front plate with original latches and bridged motionwork.

Plate 98. *A weight-driven striking movement by Ahasuerus Fromanteel, with square pillars and a vertical hammer arbor fixed to the front plate. Originally made with verge escapement, it now has an anchor escapement with 1¼ seconds pendulum. The interesting anchor pallets are shown in Plate 172. (The movement in its case is shown in Plate 218.)*
R.A. Lee

there, and it is at least possible that this, like the previous timepiece, may originally have had a silk suspension for the pendulum.

The shaping of the plates of this piece is unique and it has been suggested that they were originally rectangular. Some credence is given to this idea by the fact that while the bottom pair of pillars is riveted into the back plate, the upper pair is screwed on with screws which may be contemporary. This does not necessarily prove that the pillars have been moved nor that the theory is correct, for all the pillar and dial-foot latches are original, in good condition, and appear to be in their original positions.

The fusee, which has eight turns, and the main-wheel assembly are unusual (Plate 94). The winding arbor has a large steel disc recessed into the back of the main-wheel at the wheel end. Permanently pinned to the inside of the wheel is a fourteen tooth ratchet and recessed into the back of the fusee is a click pivoted on a double-shouldered screw. The click spring, which is shaped just as it might have been had it been recessed into the main wheel, is positioned by three pins and removable for knotting the line. The fusee cone is held in position on the winding arbor by a cross pin and its hook is held by two screws. The barrel, which is deeply flanged, has a snap cover in the back. The back end of the barrel arbor is squared, which must have been to enable it to be held in a vice while inserting or removing the spring or for setting up. The distance between the plates is 2 ins. As in the previous example, the pillars are square.

The use of square pillars may correctly be regarded as preceding turned pillars and there are two further examples known of their use in Fromanteel clocks. One is the weight clock shown in Plate 98, while the other is the astronomical clock in the Fogg Museum (Plates 95-97). These two square-pillared spring timepieces must be regarded as the earliest examples of English pendulum clocks known to the authors. It is of interest that all these square pillared clocks employ intermediate wheels between the main wheel and the centre pinion.

The little clock which is illustrated in Plates 99-103 must have been made at very much the same time as the previous one and has many significant and interesting features. This is certainly in the Dutch style throughout but a very English interpretation of it. It is the only example that has remained from this early period of the use of the Dutch style of case which may well have been used for Fromanteel's earliest clocks. It will be seen that the movement is suspended from the dial, which in turn is hinged to the case. This clock is of three-day duration. Its four symmetrically turned pillars are all retained by latches. The power is provided by two going barrels positioned on a vertical centre line, the going train barrel being above the dial centre and the striking below. The going train main wheel runs into the centre pinion and the centre wheel into a third pinion, the third wheel into a contrate pinion. This can be seen in Plate 101. All of this train is placed on the left-hand side of the movement as one looks at it from the front. There is then a long pinion driven by the contrate wheel with the crown wheel at the top, which is set at an angle of 25° from the vertical to enable the verge arbor to be at the centre of the top of the movement. This is the earliest example of a third wheel and pinion being used in a pendulum clock and was made necessary by the use of a pendulum which was only about 4 ins. long. The back cock is built up of three pieces and one of the joins is clearly visible in Plate 102. The present pallet arbor, which is not the original, is pivoted in this and the pendulum rod is fixed directly to it. There is, however, a rectangular hole in the top of the back cock for which there is now no purpose (Plate 101). This may well have been for an additional cock for silk suspension.

Plate 99. A small
three-day striking
clock by Ahasuerus
Fromanteel, London,
made very much in
the Dutch style. The
design of the dial
corners forms part of
that of larger corners
popular later in the
century (Plate 315).
The initials in the
engraved cartouche
above the chapter
ring are a later
addition. (Other
views of this clock
are shown in Plates
185-186.)

Plate 100. The side view of
the clock in Plate 99,
showing that the move-
ment is supported on the
hinged dial and has turned
pillars and dial feet.

Plate 101. *The clock in Plate 99 partly dismantled, showing the vertical hammer arbor with the bell below the movement, the angled crown wheel and pinion, motionwork bridge and also the latch from the door. There is an unused rectangular hole visible in the back cock.*

Plate 102. *The back view of the clock in Plate 99. The joins in the back cock are visible. The steelwork is blued.*

Plate 103. *A view of the back of the chapter ring of the clock in Plate 99, showing how the overlaid silver ring is fixed.*

The striking train is planted upwards from the lower barrel through the usual wheels and pinions. (The striking train is described in detail in relation to weight clocks on page 116.) The bell hammer in this clock strikes the blows horizontally in the manner followed by the Dutch makers who needed such an action since they placed the bell outside the case. The bell in this instance is, however, inverted below the plates inside the case.

It is more than three centuries since this clock was made and some parts have, of course, been replaced. There is, however, no reason to suppose that this was for any other reason than wear. The pin pinion is one of the replaced parts and it can be seen in the illustration that the repairer has turned away an unnecessarily large amount to release the collet rivet of the previous one. It is worth noting that the locking pinion is of seven leaves, not six, and thus there are seven teeth between the pins of the pin wheel.

Such a large amount of this clock has the remains of gilding, including the wheels, that it was all evidently originally gilt, this even applies to the bell nut. The arbors and other steelwork, apart from the pinions, have been reblued in recent times, the old blueing having been largely worn away. The bridge is made of such thin material that the steady-pins have to be retained in the front plate. The shaping of the feet of this and also of a number of the cocks, is very decorative.

Whether or not the two clocks just described were originally made with silk-suspension pendulums, the second one certainly now has a pivoted verge arbor at the back with a fixed pendulum rod, which would appear to date to the early 1660s and which suggests that it was the method to which Fromanteel turned first in preference to silk suspension.

The clocks which have just been discussed are all by Ahasuerus Fromanteel. No examples of pendulum clocks by any other maker are known which can be said to have been made much before about 1665. These Fromanteel clocks are all English versions of the Dutch prototype. The English makers had, however, their own well-established traditional methods of construction and when other men started making the new pendulum clocks, some of them were slow to abandon these methods. Chief amongst these traditionalists was Edward East, but there were others, such as John Hilderson, Edward Stanton, John Farmer and Henry Jones. For some time, therefore, there were two schools of practice in the design of spring clocks in particular.

Examination of the early work of these traditionalists will reveal a close affinity of method and finish with that of the earlier watches, horizontal table clocks and lantern clocks. What in the watch or table clock was the pillar plate, in the pendulum clock becomes the front plate with the tulip-shaped baluster pillars riveted to it, which is the reason why these spacing pieces between the plates are still called pillars (Plate 106). In the new style of movement favoured by Fromanteel, however, the pillars are symmetrically turned and are riveted into the back plate. There is a further difference between the two types in that the distance between the plates of these traditional clocks is usually 1⅝ins. or 1¾ins. as against 2ins. or 2⅛ins. in the case of the modern school. The earliest examples also do not have a centre pinion, thus again continuing the practice of the past.

Like Fromanteel, East seems to have been content to use going-barrels at first and to make his clocks of short duration with no intermediate wheels and pinions. The timepiece shown in Plates 104-107 is one such, with a duration of only three days and this piece, like the previous ones, is suspended from the dial. It has oblong plates

Plate 104. *The engraved dial of an alarm timepiece by Edward East, with a single hand with decorated alarm pointer and a slot in the dial for starting the pendulum, similar to that in the Coster clock in Plate 87.*   R.A. Lee

Plate 105. The front plate of the alarm timepiece in Plate 104, showing the lugs for the dial feet and the pin fitting into the hour wheel key for alarm lifting off.

Plate 106. The side view of the alarm timepiece in Plate 104, showing the tulip-turned pillars riveted into the front plate.

Plate 107. The back plate of the timepiece in Plate 104 with gilding almost intact and nicely engraved knife-edge keep, but with no gilding on the back cock.

Plate 108. *The side view of a spring clock by Edward East, showing the tulip-turned pillars riveted to the front plate and dial feet without bosses. This clock in its case is shown in Plates 200-201.*

Plate 109. *The back view of the clock in Plate 108. The movement is supported on the dial which has latches to hold it in the case. The back plate is plain with engraving on the count wheel and knife-edge keep.*

Plate 110. *The dial of the clock in Plate 108, punch matted all over except for a narrow band round the edge, a Tudor rose in the centre and a single ring round the winding holes.*

with four boldly contoured baluster pillars riveted into the front plate. This piece was evidently not intended primarily for showing the time, but as an alarm, for it has only one hand.

The barrels are positioned so that the winding squares are low down in the dial and equidistant from the dial centre. The clicks and the click springs are on the front plate (Plate 105) and the barrels were originally made, as were those on other early clocks of the traditional school, with the cap pinned on through six lugs. The holes in the lugs in this instance have been broken away and the lugs hammered over. The going train — traditionally known as the watch train — consists of a main wheel driving a pinion running in the centre of the movement which revolves once an hour, anticlockwise. A forward projection of this pinion carries a six leaf pinion which drives a wheel of seventy-two, the arbor of which carries the single hour hand. Frictionally fitted to this hand arbor is a socket with the 'lift-off' or 'let-off' piece, to which is fitted, under the hand, the alarm setting dial. This dial may be rotated to enable the time setting for the alarm to come in line with the pointer on the tail of the hand. The arbor of the anticlockwise pinion carries the wheel which drives the contrate wheel and pinion and this in turn drives the crown wheel and pinion. The verge arbor is in this instance supported by a knife-edge on the back cock. There is a finely engraved 'keep' over the back cock to prevent the verge from being lifted out of the crown wheel and by allowing the train to run free, to damage the crown wheel teeth when the verge drops back. The pendulum extends well below the plates and the bob is a patterned sphere.

The alarm train consists merely of a very shallow going barrel, with the main wheel running directly into the crown wheel pinion, driving a verge to which the bell hammer is fitted. There are four plates riveted to the front plate, extending radially from the corners, to accommodate the dial feet. This is another instance of the original case being lost. The night clock by John Hilderson described in Chapter XI also has an alarm train.

Another example of a short duration clock, also supported from the dial, can be seen in Plates 108-110. This is a striking clock and it goes for four days. These are two early clocks with the knife-edge pendulum suspension which ultimately was used by all makers for many years, including Fromanteel. They would soon have discovered that a weight of any kind suspended from a pivot working in a hole, would very quickly wear. The knife-edge was proved to be the answer to this problem but who it was that solved it, we do not know. Most of these early traditional type clocks have oblong dials with no spandrel corners, while most of the Fromanteel clocks have square dials which are mounted.

The knife-edge was not the only method of suspension that was tried and used at this early period, however, and examination of another, the roller suspension, will be of interest. Four examples of it are shown here, the first being the Ahasuerus Fromanteel longcase clock in the Museum of History of Science in Oxford (Plate 111). The movement of this clock is in very good condition and the back pivot of the verge swings on a pair of rollers. The pendulum bob, which appears to be original, is light and of unusual shape, very similar to the rating nuts found at the end of the following century.

The second example (Plates 112-113), also a longcase clock by Fromanteel, was at one time in the Iden collection. Mr. Walter Iden had the clock restored and the clockmaker replaced the verge with a knife-edge, but without the customary back cock as there were two short round brass studs in the way. These were of about

Plate 111. *The back view of the longcase movement by Ahasuerus Fromanteel with a roller cage.*
Museum of the History of Science, Oxford

Plate 112. *A longcase clock movement by Ahasuerus Fromanteel, London, with intermediate wheels and pinions. The extended hammer arbor and bell stand is for striking the bell outside the case. (The movement in its case is in Plates 216-217.)*

Plate 113. *A closer view of the movement in Plate 112, showing dial feet without bosses, the early date work on a disc mounted on a large 31 toothed date wheel and the reconstructed rollers and cage.*

⁵⁄₁₆ in. diameter, riveted to the outside of the back plate, and were drilled and tapped at the exposed end. These he considered to be for a plate on which to suspend the verge and used them for this purpose. It is extremely fortunate that he did this without destroying vital evidence, for the rollers on the clock just described are housed in a small cage or frame, oval in shape, which is screwed to two similar short studs. It is obvious, therefore, that this clock also was originally fitted with rollers which have since been restored.

The third clock is not by Fromanteel but by Edward East and is also in very good condition (Plate 114). Fortunately the very small but conventionally shaped bob has in this instance survived. This clock has never been converted to recoil escapement and the back cock is a roller cage which is riveted, not screwed, to the sides and feet of what is otherwise a normal back cock. This cage has however three rollers, whereas the Oxford Fromanteel has only two. The verge arbor, which is not the original, had been made to swing in a pivot hole in the back roller plate. As will be seen in the illustration, the rollers have now been restored.

The last of the four examples is the thirty-hour musical spring clock (Plate 115) which is fully described in Chapter XI. It is a clock which was many years in the making and one of the early features is a roller cage for two rollers. However, when the clock was finally completed this was not used. Problems must have arisen with roller suspensions for they were never widely used.

The dial which Salomon Coster used on his first pendulum timepiece (Plate 88) was rectangular rather than square and covered with velvet, the only mounts being the signature curtain and the chapter ring. As with other details of his clocks, Fromanteel did not slavishly copy Coster although what remains of the dated example (Plate 91) suggests that he may at first have retained the oblong shape and mounted it with just the chapter ring. It was not however covered with velvet but the surface was covered with decoration achieved by the wriggling of a narrow chisel uniformly over the entire area, except for that part occupied by the signature. This type of 'matting' is to be found on another early Fromanteel clock, the long duration timepiece which is described in Chapter XI (Plate 741). So far as is known, this is the only dial of this type made for a spring clock by Fromanteel, the nearest in style being that shown in Plate 99, which has no matting outside the chapter ring but spandrel mounts which are original. It is another sign of the initiative of Ahasuerus Fromanteel that he was not content with these dials, but almost from the very beginning made his dials square with the central zones matted and the spandrel spaces plain with corner mounts.

Edward East and his following, on the other hand, were more conservative in this matter, as in others, and throughout the first decade almost exclusively used the taller dial and usually without any mounts apart from the chapter ring. They were normally matted over all visible surfaces with an engraved Tudor rose at the dial centre (Plate 110). Occasionally they were further ornamented by the addition of a band of engraving within the chapter circle (Plate 137). All of the foregoing remarks apply specifically to spring clocks, for longcase clocks hardly appear in the first half of the decade and, when they do, the dials were usually square.

It may be of interest to describe the different methods of matting used at this period. The traditional makers normally used a matting punch which was made from a piece of ¼in. square steel about 3ins. long with the end finished perfectly square and flat and in which six or seven parallel cuts were made in each direction, probably

Plate 114. *A spring clock by "Edwardus East, Londini", with tulip pillars riveted to the front plate and a cage for three rollers riveted to an ordinary back cock foot. The hammer and fly are shaped as in a lantern clock. It has flanged barrels with pinned caps. (The clock in its case is in Plate 202.)*

Plate 115. *A thirty-hour striking and musical clock by Ahasuerus Fromanteel, showing the unused roller cage. The clock has a snail for regulation and cranks for winding. The bells and hammers are on a platform latched to the top. This clock is fully described in Chapter XI.*

with a cold chisel, producing 49 or 64 minute pyramids. This was then hardened and tempered. When the dial plate had been well prepared by filing and scraping, the centre was marked and the chapter ring area inscribed. The plate was then placed on a flat surface such as an anvil, to which it had to be firmly held whilst working, probably by an assistant. Then, starting in one corner with the punch held upright and quite square, it would be struck one sharp blow with a hammer, moved to the next position close to the last and the process repeated and continued in a straight line. This might be done either vertically or horizontally until the whole area is covered. Occasionally it will be found that the chapter ring has been surrounded with a ring of matting, in which case a union between the circular and the straight lines of punching will be visible. The best effect was obtained however when the punching was all done in one direction. When a Tudor rose or other engraving is on the dial, there is usually a line of matting following the edge of it. After the plate has been fitted into the case, a parallel plain band would be made on the outside edge with a scraping tool.

This matting process distorts a dial and makes it necessary for it to be flattened afterwards. The dial feet were usually riveted into the area covered by the chapter ring and positioning them in this way sometimes made it necessary to provide lugs on the front plate of the movement in order to accommodate them (Plate 105). The chapter rings on these dials were usually about 1 in. wide and continue the lantern clock practice of having wide Roman figures which are fairly crude and not always symmetrical. There is a minute ring outside the chapters, with every fifth minute numbered as a rule, and with quarter hour divisions on the inside of the ring. Although the engraving is not of the finest, the general effect is usually quite attractive.

Fromanteel's treatment of his dials made a new departure. His matting was achieved by the use of rollers which resulted in a more refined finish. Although he also usually sited his dial feet beneath the chapter ring, with the different type of matting and plain corners this was less important. The tool used for the matting consisted of a steel disc about ¾ in. in diameter and ¹⁄₁₆ in. thick, the edge of which was bevelled to about 90° and serrated to produce a series of spikes round the edge. When hardened and tempered, two of these discs were usually mounted in a holder with a thin shim between them and rolled over the surface of the dial under pressure to produce the matting. The best appearance was obtained by rolling in all directions until the whole area was evenly covered. The plate then needed to be flattened. The diameter of the tool which has been used, and the spacing of the teeth, may be determined by examining any over-run marks under the chapter ring, for normally the teeth are slightly irregular and the distance between peculiar indentations will determine the circumference of the disc.

An example of a dial which has been matted by rolling up and down only, is the dial by Joseph Knibb in Plate 457 which also shows how the makers economised in the use of gold by not gilding beneath the ring.

The chapter rings are normally dry silvered but Fromanteel, in a number of instances at this early period, faced his rings with silver, a practice which very few other makers followed. The method which he used for fixing the silver facing is interesting. The foundation ring is brass and has a number of fairly large holes in it, the holding pegs being riveted to it, a thin ring of silver, slightly overlapping the brass, was then made. It would appear that the ring was then placed face down on a flat surface and lead pellets inserted into the large holes in the brass which was then heated until the lead melted to provide a firm bond. There is no sign that a flux was used. These holes are clearly visible in the ring seen in Plate 103. It was evidently the intention that the chapter ring of the clock shown in Plate 147 should have been so finished for the holes for the lead are there, but have been filled with brass. Fromanteel's chapter rings are well divided and well engraved.

The usual spandrel mount during this decade is the simple cast angel head, but it is dangerous to be dogmatic about the evolution of such decorative features for there are variations to most. For instance, the clock in Plate 99 has a simple acanthus motif and that in Plate 218 has the winged head engraved. A further variation in dial design is seen in Plates 216-217 which has no matting in the central zone but an elaborate mount of acanthus scrollery. An almost identical mount is to be seen on the clock in Plate 95.

Fromanteel signed his clocks at first in a panel within the matting but soon adopted the practice of signing along the bottom edge. The traditional school did not, as a rule, sign their dials at all during the first decade, but relied on the bold script signature in an arc on the back plate of the movement. Fromanteel also signed his back plates but not usually in an arc. Dial plates were in all cases fire gilt, right up to, but not under, the chapter ring and often not under the spandrel mounts. The plain areas outside the chapter rings were always fastidiously finished before gilding, a practice which was not followed by all makers later in the century. The corner mounts were well finished castings, unchased but also fire gilt. These were carefully positioned on the dial, often numbered to ensure correct placing, and occasionally even with steady pins to prevent moving.

Variations to the traditionalists' dial practice will be found in Plate 104 which has floral engraving over the whole dial and this is seen again on a later clock (Plate 299) made at a time when the traditionalists were adopting the square dial and coming more in line with the new practices introduced by Fromanteel. Plate 125 shows a dial which is of interest on account of its peculiar construction. It is made of two very thin plates riveted together by a large number of pins. The inside surfaces of the plates are just as they came from the foundry. Only one of the dial feet is riveted through both plates, the other three being riveted into the back plate only, with the result that they have become loose. This had to be corrected by pins through both plates into the foot bosses.

The spring clock by Fromanteel, shown in Plates 116-118, demonstrates a further stage in the development of the pendulum clock. It is probably the earliest example of a striking clock employing the striking mechanism which ultimately became the standard for many years, and which has indeed never been entirely superseded. The movement is solidly constructed and is not suspended from the dial but is solidly seated on a base board. The front plate is split into two halves for easy assembly of the trains, the one half containing the going train and other the striking train. This is the earliest use of this very practical device which was much used afterwards. Fromanteel had not at this time introduced the firm locking between the two plates which he later employed, keying them together and latching the pillars across the division, but there were, however, two devices used to assist in keeping the two halves together. There were of course four pillars in each half but there were also two steady pins in the foot of the bell standard, one in each half, and the motionwork bridge spanned the division between the plates. This motionwork bridge was made of very thin metal which had been bent to shape with the pipe soldered in. The thinness of this metal made it necessary for the steady pins to be riveted into the plates

Plate 116. An eight-day spring clock by Ahasuerus Fromanteel, with split front plate, flat brass shutters riveted to cannons, and a maintaining power spring of round steel. The date pinion is screwed to the hour socket and the striking lift is from the cannon wheel. (The case is seen in detail in Plates 187-190.)

Plate 117. The clock in Plate 116 with the striking half plate removed and showing the small fusee and the crowded striking train and round wire hammer spring. A repair piece is visible dovetailed into the plate.

Plate 118. The back plate of the clock in Plate 116. This is unseen when in its case and has, therefore, been left plain.

with clearing holes in the bridge.

It is of interest to note that there is a large piece dovetailed into the going side half plate of this clock, which demonstrates one of the problems with which the makers had to cope with regard to the supply of metal in those days, making such a repair necessary. This piece, which takes the pivots for the centre pinion, the contrate pinion and the front verge pivot, has at some time worked loose and has had to be secured with lead solder.

The going train of this clock is very much like that of the Fromanteel timepiece described earlier (Plate 94) but it now is the fully developed English clock. It has not as yet attained the standard layout which would ultimately survive, but it has discarded all the typically Dutch features.

For instance, the Dutch practice of striking the bell horizontally is abandoned and the hammer is drawn directly from the pin wheel pins. The barrels and main wheels are very large, in fact, they occupy four-fifths of the movement frame and the winding squares are equidistant from, and in line with, the dial centre. Little space remains for the remainder of the trains. Both main springs are of great age and would appear to be the originals, that for the going side being half an inch shallower than the space in the barrel would allow. It was evidently realised that the striking train would require more power than the going train. There are $13\frac{1}{3}$ turns on the fusees and a full wind takes five turns of the barrels. Since there are nine turns in the springs, three setting-up turns provide ample power.

The main wheels have ninety-six teeth, the pin pinion eight leaves and the pin wheel eight pins for drawing the hammer; thus there is one blow for each tooth of the main wheel. Since there are $13\frac{1}{3}$ turns in the fusee, there are $96 \times 13\frac{1}{3}$ (1,280) blows with one winding. This provides adequately for the required 156 blows each twenty-four hours, for eight days. The wheel numbers and fusee turns are, however, unusual. The going train, on the other hand, will run for just nine hours short of the eight days. There is a value in this since the striking train will not cease to function while the clock is still going and cause the strike to be out of phase when it is rewound.

The main wheels are slightly larger than the barrels. The strike side one had to be a little smaller than the other in order to clear the centre pinion. There are large recesses in the sides of the main wheels with visible clicks, and the click springs are made of steel and shaped just as is that on the earlier timepiece. Each click spring is secured by two screws, giving a very positive and noisy action.

The number of wheels and pinions in the striking train is the same as in the earlier Dutch type of mechanism, but has to be confined within the top left hand corner of the plates, which makes it necessary for the hammer arbor to be pivoted in a cock over the locking wheel and for the hammer tail to be shaped like the reverse of a 'G' in order to work over the locking pinion. The centre boss of the left hand top pillar has had to be cut away also for two-thirds of its thickness in order to accommodate the hammer stem when it is drawn back.

This rather awkward planting of the train members gives a strong impression of the mechanism being laid out for the first time. There remain, however, a few of the older features. For instance, the hammer spring is long and round in section, running into a rectangular section at its foot; the acting end is splayed out and shaped to fit over the pin in the hammer arbor. Also the hammer counters on a fixed pin in the front plate but the spring-like stem permits a clean blow to be delivered.

This clock has maintaining power which is original, the shutters being made of flat brass. The spring is made in two pieces and acts on a small platform behind the right connecting arm, it is made of steel, round in section, hardened and tempered. The arc of action and the rest position are determined only by the pin on one arm and the slot in the other. There is no stop pin.

The hour socket and assembly is an updated interpretation of the previous lantern clock practice; the boss or flange replaces the star wheel (which was used for lifting off the strike) and the hour wheel, which lies upon it, is retained by a small key. This is covered by a sixteen tooth wheel which engages the thirty-two tooth date wheel and this sixteen tooth wheel is secured by two screws diagonally opposite. The bottom of the appropriate teeth are made deep to accommodate these two screw heads. This clock is in original condition with the exception of the escapement which was converted to recoil at some period and its verge replaced in 1959.

In the clock shown in Plates 119-122 a third train has been added for the sounding of the quarter hours. It is probably the earliest spring clock to include this

Plate 119. The 8¼ins. square dial of a three-train spring clock by Ahasuerus Fromanteel. The chapter ring is faced with silver and the spandrel mounts are also silver. The minute hand is a replacement. (Views of the case are in Colour Plate 6, page 142, and Plates 191-192.)
Christie Manson and Woods Ltd.

Plate 120. *The front view of the three-train movement of the clock shown in Plate 119, showing the split front plate and the bars for the dial feet.*

Plate 121. *The back plate of the movement in Plate 120 showing the count wheel and the cocked centre wheel. The pendulum is a later replacement.*

Plate 122. *Fromanteel's signature on the back plate shown in Plate 121.*

mechanism. The dial, which is 8¼ ins. square, and the hour hand are of the highest quality. The central zone of the dial plate has been roller matted from the cardinal points and the whole gilded. The chapter ring is faced with silver and the spandrel mounts are unchased silver castings. The date ring is also gilded and consequently the figures are unwaxed. Although the basic design of the hour hand is the same as on other Fromanteel clocks, it has more pronounced bevelled ornaments below the loops. The original minute hand may also have been slightly elaborated.

The pendulum is not the original nor are the verge and centre pinion. The three-armed centre wheel is probably original as the crown wheel and contrate wheel also have three arms and are certainly correct, as also is the back cock. The centre wheel is bridged to enable the full depth of the frames to be used for the fusee and main wheel and also for the spring barrel. These latter items account for almost four-fifths of the available space with only one-fifth being available for the striking and quarter work.

A steel cock on the left hand front plate extending over the hour wheel (Plate 120) has on its end a short spigot projecting forwards. Presumably a four-armed piece was mounted on this, three arms of which carried the shutters for the winding holes and the fourth connecting with the lever from the main arbor of the maintaining power with the customary pin and slot. The coil spring for this is still in position on the inside of the plate. A small hole in the right hand side of the case, level with the bottom of the dial, may have been used for a pull-string for this, but since the whole side of the case opens there may have been a hand lever for the maintaining power.

This clock is now just a quarter clock but must originally have been a grande sonnerie striking clock. Apart from a badly made replacement warning pinion, the quarter work seen on the left in Plate 120 is practically untouched since made. The count wheel, mounted on the pin wheel arbor has gaps for one, two, three and four blows. The pin wheel makes one turn an hour which, with a ratio of 12:1 between the main wheel and the pin pinion, gives us a fairly straightforward train with fourteen turns for a week. The hour train, seen on the right in Plate 120, now has its own lifting piece. The twelve-hour count wheel with its seventy-eight toothed wheel is moved by a gathering pallet on the locking pinion which is a replacement. However there appears to be four times the number of blows available in the train than are now used and they are provided by the wheel mounted under the triangular sub-plate screwed to the right hand front plate. The pinion on which this wheel is mounted engages the main wheel and this wheel itself drives a pinion, the back pivot of which has a projection formed into a four pin lantern pinion for driving the original count wheel. Just above the maintaining power arbor hole (Plate 120) and towards the centre of the plate, is an unused stud with a spring and stop pin which would appear to be part of the release mechanism for letting off the hour from the quarter side.

In this clock we see what is probably the first use of bars screwed to the front plate to enable the dial feet to be conveniently placed beneath the chapter ring. All the pillar and dial latches are remaining and the double-ended latch placed in the centre at the top is particularly interesting. The existing screws are numbered and their heads may best be described as flattish cheese heads with rounded edges.

Although this clock has suffered a good deal through the years there are many traces of gilding. The bright parts amongst the finger marks in Plate 122 are gilding and all the engraving retains its gold. There are traces on pillars, so all would have been gilded. The fusee on the quarter side is very much like that in the musical clock

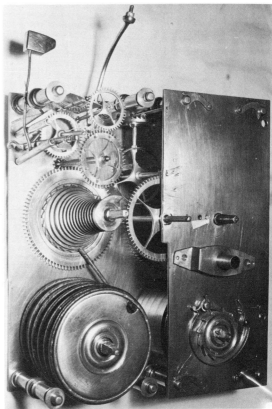

Plate 123. *An eight-day spring clock by William Knottesford, with split plates, wider than those in Plate 116. The barrel ratchet springs are of brass. There is a round hole for the warning piece. The striking lift is from the minute wheel. The steady pins for the bridge are fixed to the plates. It has no maintaining power.*

Plate 124 *(right). The clock in Plate 123 with the striking half plate removed showing the improved layout of the striking train compared with that in Plate 117. Note also the turning on the barrel cap.*

Plate 125 *(left). A side view of the clock in Plate 123 showing the large main wheels and small fusees. The construction of this dial is discussed on page 95.*

Plate 126 *(right). The back plate of the clock in Plate 123. It is plain but the count wheel has Arabic numerals and a rosette which is normally covered by the key, here shown removed. The bottom potence for the crown wheel is riveted in.*

described in Chapter XI. The hammer springs can be seen screwed to the front plate (Plate 120) working through slots and the hammers countering on stout pins, the rivets of which can be seen by the slots.

The next stage in the evolution of the spring clock is well illustrated by that shown in Plates 123-126. This clock was made by William Knottesford and has survived unaltered. It has the touch of Fromanteel throughout, the pillar latches being particularly in his style. Like that in Plates 116-118, this movement is quite undecorated except for an engraved Tudor rose in the middle of the count wheel which is, however, not seen because it is covered by the holding key. The awkward arrangement of the various parts of the striking train seen in that clock, has in this instance been overcome and we now see the standard layout established. There is a 12:1 ratio between the main wheel and the centre pinion, sixteen turns on the fusees and seventy-eight teeth on the strike side main wheel. The various component parts of the striking mechanism, such as the lifting arbor, are in the place where one would expect to find them with the hammer arbor below them. The hammer countering is still rigid; in this instance, it is done on the edge of the rectangular hole in the front plate that takes the stout pin on which the hammer spring acts. The hammer spring is made of coiled round steel wire, hardened and tempered, and it is prevented from revolving by a pin in the plate and an adjacent screw.

The fusees are very well cut and, that this was done free-hand, is indicated by the line of centre punch marks along the tops of the grooves. They are floating fusees and so well made that even now, after more than three hundred years, they will still pop when pulled apart. The main wheels still look big for the fusees but the click springs are now brass and are riveted into place. This clock is not quite so well finished as is that in Plates 116-118 and there is no maintaining power. The barrel ratchets and clicks are the same but the click springs are not of steel; they are of brass and are nicely shaped. Unlike the clock in Plates 116-118 the bottom potence for the crown wheel is riveted into the plate instead of being screwed and the crown wheel pinion is of five leaves instead of six. There are no signs of any alterations nor any stopped holes. The verge has knife-edge suspension and it and the pendulum are complete; the bob is quite small and has a wide arc of swing.

The little clock illustrated in Plates 127-128 would have been made about the same time as that just considered. The hammer is placed between the plates and while it now delivers its blow by gravity, it originally had a coiled spring and the countering is on a fairly solid piece of brass pinned across an aperture in the front plate. It has going barrels and was made with a duration of two days. About fifty years ago it was altered to eight days by simply reversing the barrels and inserting intermediate wheels and pinions of 4:1 ratio. It seems strange that a two-day clock should be made at this time.

There were quite a number of clockmakers working in London in the middle 1660s but where are their clocks today? Remarkably few exist and most of them are of eight-day duration. Is it that these clocks have been saved because they were the few eight-day productions, while the majority, because they were of shorter duration, have not survived?

We now turn to two clocks which may be considered together because they are almost identical, not only in regard to the movements, but also because the cases are alike. Both were evidently made or at the very least started by Ahasuerus Fromanteel, but whereas the one was signed by him, the other bears the signature of

Plate 127. A short duration clock by Ahasuerus Fromanteel, now converted to go for eight days by the reversing of the barrels and the adding of intermediate wheels and pinions. The striking train is beneath the going train.

Plate 128. The side view of the clock in Plate 127, showing the going barrels, the contrate and third wheel and pinion.

Plate 129. Back view of an eight-day Dutch striking spring clock by Ahasuerus Fromanteel with tall bell stand and hammer mounting fixed to the plates and high count wheel as in Plate 141. The signature is in a straight line. (The clock in its case is in Plate 193.)

Samuel Knibb. These clocks are illustrated in Plates 129 and 130-136. The one signed by Fromanteel (Plate 129) would appear to be the first that was completed as it lacks some of the refinements which one might have expected. It is very probable that these clocks were made about 1667, that the second was not completed when Ahasuerus Fromanteel left England for Holland in that year, and that it was subsequently finished by Samuel Knibb. Both clocks are identical in the striking train except for one particular, the Samuel Knibb has a five-leaf fly pinion.

Mr. Ronald Lee has said of the Fromanteel clock,[2] that it was found in a very sorry state of Victorian 'improvement' and that a few of the parts which had been removed at the time when the changes were made, were found in a tin on a clockmaker's workshop shelf. They were the warning wheel and pinion, the hammer-tail block and the warning arbor. The most significant feature of these two movements is that they strike the hour on the smaller of two bells at the half-hour and are the earliest English clocks to do so. This method of striking is usually referred to as Dutch striking for it was very commonly used by Dutch makers for many years. It ceased to be used in this country however, after about 1700 except on clocks that

---

2.   Ronald A. Lee, *The First Twelve Years of the Pendulum Clock,* London, 1969.

were made for the Dutch market. The bells and hammers are on long extensions in the cupola, which is fret-cut for the better outlet of the sound. The Knibb clock, which is illustrated here in Plates 130-136, has these extensions mounted on a horizontal plate fixed across the top of the movement by latches (Plate 132). The Fromanteel, which one presumes to be a little earlier, does not have this plate.

The hammer springs are still round in section, hardened and tempered, and the hammers still counter on sturdy fixed pins, relying upon the elasticity of the hammer stems for a clean blow. The hammers are drawn by connecting rods or links formed into pins at each end with spring covers; the hammer tails, which contact the pins in the pin wheel, are contained in a block which is free to move back and forth between the frames. It is moved by a forked piece attached to it which embraces the minute wheel, on either side of which is a face cam. There are pins on both sides of the pin wheel and the hammer tail is in contact with the pins on one side, but on the other side is clear of them. This back and forth action is referred to as 'pumping'. Within a decade or so it became the practice to spring-load one end of the hammer-tail block and to pump the other end from a cam on the minute wheel.

These clocks have maintaining power, as do the Fromanteel clocks previously mentioned, but in this instance it is operated by depressing a rod projecting through

Plate 130. The dial of a clock similar to that in Plate 129 but signed "Samuel Knibb Londini fecit" with silver chapter ring having each minute numbered and with quarter minute divisions. (The case is shown in detail in Plates 194-199.)

Plate 131. The back view of the movement of the clock in Plate 130 showing the count wheel divided for Dutch striking and with Arabic numerals and engraving on the key.

Plate 132. The rear view of the movement of the clock in Plate 130 showing the platform latched on pegs in the plates. The bell hammer mounting is screwed to this in one piece. The hammers counter on stout pins. On the left is the push rod for maintaining power.

Plate 133. The front view of the clock in Plate 130.

Plate 134. The front view of the movement of the clock in Plate 130 with the striking half plate removed showing a standard train from the pin wheel onwards. The movement has been gilded and the steelwork blued. The barrel ratchets and springs are like those in Plate 116. The hammer-tail block is below the warning wheel.

Plate 135. *The movement of the clock in Plate 130 with both half plates removed showing the pillars.*

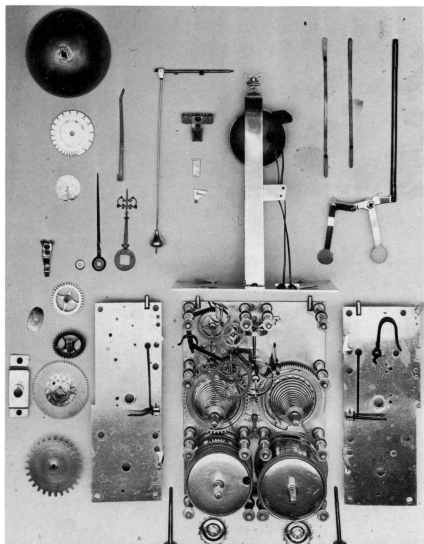

Plate 136. *The movement of the clock in Plate 130 partly dismantled showing the hammers connected to the tails by links.*

the top of the case. It is of interest to note that the hammer springs are round in section. Flat leaf springs were not used at this time by the progressive school of makers.

So far as we know, these two clocks are the last work of Ahasuerus Fromanteel to come to light. In less than a decade he had introduced the pendulum into English clocks and he had quite revolutionised the layout and making of spring clocks in particular. He had established the good width between the plates, had introduced the centre pinion in the centre of the movement and laid down the standard of two turns a day for main wheels. In other words, he had provided the standard for the English eight-day spring clock.

Reference has been made earlier to the clocks made by Edward East and others to whom we have referred as belonging to the traditional school and we found that these clocks were shallower, with pillars fixed to the front plate, that the motion work was floating and that the going train was wound anticlockwise. The clock illustrated in Plates 137-138 shows how the motion is transferred from the anti-clockwise pinion to the hands. A pivot on this pinion, which extends through the front plate,

Plate 137. The dial and hands of an eight-day Dutch striking clock by Edward East. The dial is punch-matted and has an engraved circle and central rose. (The clock in its case is shown in Plates 203-204.)

Plate 138. The front view of the movement in Plate 137 with friction drive to floating motion-work (here removed) from the minute wheel on the first pinion of the train which gives lift-off to the strike. Face cams on the third minute wheel rotate the stand supporting two bells, and bring each into the way of the hammer as required. The barrels are set up in opposite directions.

109

has, frictionally mounted on it, a wheel of forty teeth driving another of similar size and of the same count, on an arbor pivoted in the front plate in such a position that it is in the centre of the dial. This arbor, which carries the minute hand, runs in the hour socket, which in turn carries the hour hand and to which is keyed the hour wheel. (This is seen removed in Plate 138.) Over the hour socket is placed a distance piece, acting on the back of the dial, in which the socket runs precisely as in a lantern clock. This motion work is said to be floating. A further wheel, of the same count as the other two, is mounted on the front plate to carry the minute pinion and in some instances in clocks of this type, the lifting pin.

The clock in Plate 138 shows an advanced form of striking, which was used by this school. Fromanteel had introduced the striking of the hour at the half-hour on a small bell. The traditional school used a small bell to record the quarters, striking once at the first quarter, twice at the half hour and three times at the third quarter, the hour being struck on the larger bell. This was done quite simply. The two bells were mounted vertically and close together on a single perpendicular bell stand, which was pivoted. The third minute wheel, previously mentioned, carried a face cam — in some cases another is mounted on the back of the wheel — a fork-piece embracing these is made to move as the wheel turns, slightly rotating the bell stand, bringing the second bell into line with the single hammer for striking the hour. The wheel and pinion numbers of the striking train had to be altered in order to provide for the extra seventy-two hammer blows. Fromanteel had re-introduced the intermediate wheel and pinion to provide for his half-hour strike.

The time honoured practices are to be seen in the striking trains of the clocks by the traditional school. It had long been the custom in lantern clocks for thirteen pins to be in the pin wheel, which was the main wheel of the clock, with a driving pinion of six leaves driving a wheel of seventy-eight teeth, upon which the count wheel was mounted. The main wheel would thus make six turns in twelve hours. This is just what the the traditionalists did in their spring pendulum clocks (e.g. the clock shown in Plates 139-140) with thirteen pins in the pin wheel driving a pinion of six and so on, but they mounted the count wheel on a stud high up on the back plate.

The provision of springs for these clocks must have proved quite a problem; their size necessitated such large barrels and, since it was the rule that the main wheel should be the same size as the spring barrel, these clocks have large main wheels also. The consequence is that the remainder of the train is crowded into the upper part of the plates, making it necessary for the winding squares to be placed above the dial centre (Plates 137-138). The caps of the spring barrels are of larger diameter than are the barrels, thus forming flanges back and front and these are held in position by six or more lugs on each side, which are pinned. Another peculiarity of these clocks is that both barrel and fusee turn in the same direction. The lantern clock tradition seems to have been continued in the shape and sturdiness of the hammers of these clocks and also in the heavy springing and counter springing, which is only slightly modernised.

In due course the traditional clockmakers discarded the floating motionwork by introducing a bridge on the front plate. At the same time they planted the previously anticlockwise pinion at the dial centre, made it revolve clockwise and carry the minute hand. Then it became necessary for the going train to be wound in a clockwise direction. This also reversed the direction of the crown wheel, which had revolved clockwise. Later, the crown wheel cock was removed from the front plate and mounted on the back plate, which resulted in the contrate wheel being reversed to make the crown wheel rotate clockwise again. In due course the pillars were fixed

Plate 139. *The back plate of an eight-day spring clock by Henry Jones, London, whose work resembles that of Edward East to whom he was apprenticed.*

Plate 140. *The side view of the clock in Plate 139, showing pillars differing from those in Plate 114. The crown wheel and pinion are mounted on the front plate. It has floating motionwork, a friction mounted minute wheel on a front extension of the first pinion on which the second wheel of the going train is mounted, flanged barrels with pinned front cap and narrow frames.*

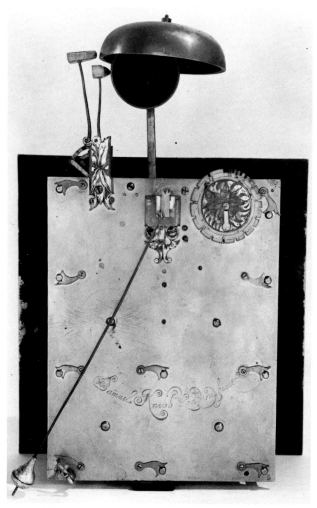

Plate 141. *The back view of a large Dutch striking clock by Samuel Knibb, with eleven pillars riveted to the front plate. The back plate is plain with engraved fittings. Stoppings in the plate indicate that alterations have been made. (The clock in its case is in Plate 212.)*

Worshipful Company of Clockmakers

Plate 142. *The front view of the movement in Plate 141. The hammer-tail pump is positioned as in Plate 134 and the hammers counter on a spring. There is no maintaining power. The barrel ratchets and clicks are as those in Plate 117. The click springs are missing.*

on the back plate and thus conformed to the more modern practice initiated by Fromanteel.

The clock by Samuel Knibb illustrated in Plates 141-142 would have been made shortly after the cupola clocks and it incorporates some features of both schools of practice, for instance, pumping hammer-tail block and half-hour striking with remote hammers but with the pillars fitted to the front plate. It is, however, much bigger and heavier than most. The impression given is that a man who was brought up in the traditional school was trying his hand at making a clock in the new manner. The quality is not so high as in the clocks of the Fromanteel school and it lacks maintaining power. The present verge escapement is not the original and it has not so far been possible to discover from the stopped holes just what the original escapement was like.

The clock by Johannes Fromanteel illustrated in Plates 143-145 would have been made after Ahasuerus left London in 1667 and is, therefore, an example from the end of the decade. It is a striking clock which strikes the hours at the half hour on a smaller bell. Plate 145, which shows the under dial work and the back of the dial, illustrates the mechanism of the bolt and shutter work that was described in relation to the Fogg Museum Fromanteel (Plate 97). The shutters rotate round the centre hole in the dial and the action of the lever is determined by two pins knocked into the back of the dial. There is a coiled spring on the front plate. The dial has its original gilding and angel-head corner mounts precisely positioned by a small pin in the extreme top of each head. A sign that the design has slightly progressed from that of earlier Fromanteel clocks can be seen in the hands which are slightly more elaborate but the early 'J' form of the figure one is retained.

The hammer springs are of brass and they and the hammers have been slightly altered in position, presumably to take up wear. The hammer heads are quite heavy. The springs may have been intended to act as counters which did not prove satisfactory and the hammers now counter on fixed pins. The hammer stems are of wire, fixed into the arbors with sufficient flexibility to give a clean blow to the bell. The verge escapement is original and has the unusual feature of a seven leaf contrate pinion instead of six. The present back cock is a replacement and it is impossible to say exactly what the original was like from the numerous filled holes, but it was probably double-footed. The bell stand has been cut away, presumably to accommodate the foot of the cock.

Like most clocks made during this decade, the back plate is quite plain except for the maker's name. The engraving in this instance is quite shallow and the engraver has indulged in a little levity in the scrolling end of his 'J'. This ornamentation is also to be seen in the signature on the Samuel Knibb clock shown in Plate 141, thus suggesting that it was the work of the same engraver.

There is no doubt that there are no known weight-driven pendulum clocks which are as early as those which are spring-driven, which is remarkable considering the acknowledged advantage which is given by the even spread of power of a falling weight. The earliest weight-driven pendulum clocks are, however, the work of Ahasuerus Fromanteel. It would appear that the example illustrated in Plate 98 is the oldest known, while the three-train clock in the Fogg Art Museum, shown in Plates 95-97 probably belongs to about the same date. This latter clock has not been examined in detail but there are, nevertheless, a number of features common to it and the former, which can be seen in the illustrations and which indicate the early date. For instance, they both have the square pillars which we have seen in the early

Plate 143. *The dial and hands of an eight-day Dutch striking spring clock by Johannes Fromanteel with more detail in the hour hand. (The clock in its case is in Plate 239.)*
R.A. Lee

Plate 144. *The back plate of the clock in Plate 143, with a plain back and the name engraved in a straight line. The decorative feature in the tail of the 'J' is found also in the signature in Plate 141. The count wheel is now slightly larger.*

Plate 145. *The under dial work and split plate of the clock in Plate 143. Also the back of the dial showing the bolt and shutter work on the dial centre as on the clock in Plate 97.*

spring-clocks (Plates 89 and 94) and they both have intermediate wheels and pinions. Both of these clocks also are unusual in that the minute hand makes one revolution in fifteen minutes. The practice of making the minute hand revolve once in the hour was so well established at this time, that this peculiarity can have no relation to the fact that they may be the earliest weight-driven pendulum clocks. Why, therefore, was it done? The purpose must have been to indicate time with more precision at a period when the greater efficiency of the pendulum was making it possible. It is, however, confusing for us to read the time from this dial, although one is helped (Plate 95) by the alternate blacking-in of the quarter hour graduations on the inside of the chapter ring, for one must first read the appropriate quarter hour from this ring and the hour hand before reading the minutes from the minute hand. One wonders at the need for such accuracy in the early 1660s.

The dial of the first of these clocks (Plate 218) has the original gilding. It is matted in the centre, except for the central engraved Tudor rose and for the shaped zone at the bottom for the signature "A. Fromanteel Londini". The spandrel corners are also engraved, and the quaint little faces are beautifully executed.

This clock was constructed with a verge escapement but was converted to anchor escapement at an early date and since this is significant, it will be discussed further on.

The striking mechanism of the weight-driven clock evolved naturally from that of the lantern clock. The main elements are: the main wheel, pin wheel, locking or hoop wheel, warning wheel and fly with their respective pinions, and the count wheel which is sometimes called the locking plate or check plate.

The main wheel works in the pin wheel pinion, driving the pin wheel which normally carries eight pins. Each of these pins will cause the hammer to strike one blow on the bell. With forty-eight teeth in the pin wheel working in the next pinion of six leaves, the locking wheel will turn once for each blow of the hammer. This wheel normally has a hoop fixed to the back of it, with a gap in it into which the locking piece will fall after each hammer blow, thus locking the train. The locking wheel is also usually of forty-eight teeth or a multiple of six, provided that the next pinion, the warning wheel pinion, is of six leaves. This ratio will ensure that the pin in the next wheel, the warning wheel, stops in the same position each time, for if this is not done it makes for difficulties. The warning wheel carries a pin which is arrested by a warning piece when the train is unlocked just before the hour. During this early period, this wheel normally has forty-eight teeth unless the fly pinion has only five leaves, in which case the warning wheel has forty or forty-five teeth. The count wheel in the early clocks is usually quite small, often only 1½ ins. in diameter, and is keyed to a short stud of either brass or steel, high up on the back plate. It is mounted on a wheel of thirty-nine teeth, which is driven by a pinion of four leaves formed on the end of a large pivot of the pin pinion projecting through the back plate and which looks very much like four pins. There are some instances of these numbers being doubled, in which case the back pivot of the pin wheel is smaller and the projecting piece has a pinion of eight leaves squared on to it to drive a wheel of seventy-eight teeth. This is preferable as it results in one blow of the hammer for each tooth instead of only half a tooth, thus making for smoother movement of the count wheel and avoiding difficulties with counting and locking.

It was customary to mark all the parts, one tooth in each wheel being marked with a file. This marked tooth had to match up with a file mark on the leaf end of the appropriate pinion. Also there would be a line across the count wheel driving pinion and the end of the pin pinion pivot square and a mark on one leaf of the pinion, which, when everything was lined up, appeared through a hole in the count wheel. If these conditions do not exist in any clock with this type of mechanism, it usually means that some alteration has been made, such as shortening the hammer tail. When a clock is correctly assembled, the gap in the hoop wheel should be in a position to lock as soon as the hammer tail has dropped off the lifting pin and the count wheel is in place for the locking piece to drop in. There should be a third to half of a turn of the warning wheel before the warning pin is arrested by the warning piece. This does not only apply to the early clocks but to all striking work employing a count wheel.

The very small count wheel used on the early clocks was not retained for long. Very gradually they were being made larger and at the same time the main wheels were being lowered, thus providing for a larger amount of space in the upper part of the plates for the mechanism. Eventually the count wheel was mounted on to an extension of the main wheel pivot. In order to make this possible the main wheel arbor must be so constructed that it does not turn as the clock is wound. This was done by attaching the winding square to the front cap of the barrel only. The main wheel was then mounted on an arbor which passed through the barrel which is left free to turn. It is on the arbor that an extension was made at the back on which the count wheel was mounted. It is known as a floating arbor.

The clock discussed earlier and shown in Plate 98, has an intermediate wheel and pinion in the striking train as well as the going train. The hammer arbor is mounted vertically on the edge of the front plate and is tall enough to carry the hammer arm above the top of the hood, where this is squared on to it, to strike the bell in a horizontal plane. The bell standard, which is also tall, is mounted upon one of the square pillars. The frames are big and sturdy and in spite of the undoubted Dutch influence, this is a truly English clock.

The other clock which was mentioned (Plate 95) is a three train clock and has a dial with a similar chapter ring. The spandrel corners have, however, cast angel head mounts; there is no matting in the centre and surrounding the hand centre there is a symmetrical foliate cast mount which can be seen repeated on the dial of the clock in Plate 216. The motion work in this instance is very large, the minute wheel makes one revolution an hour and has four lifting pins, which perhaps in this clock, should be called depressing pins, for, as the wheel rotates anticlockwise, the let-off lever is drawn downwards and is spring-loaded to return it to the stop position. The bells of the quarter work are secured by screws with heads which are very similar to those used on the thirty-hour musical clock described in Chapter XI, and the bells are of the same shape. The first wheels and pinions are also similar and it seems reasonable to presume that both clocks were at least started at about the same time. The pillars of this clock are however square and one of them carries the signature, "A. Fromanteel Londini".

There are indications which are carried above the dial. One is a spherical moon. The moon's age is shown together with the hours, and underneath is the day of the month. The lead-off for this work is taken from the motion wheel which revolves once an hour by the use of a worm. There is also maintaining power, with shutters keyed to a hollow boss fitted to the inside of the centre hole of the dial, and standing proud at the back. There is a lever at the bottom of the dial, which, when moved to the left, will rotate the shutters from the winding holes by the projection at the upper end of the bent lever shown in the rest position in Plate 97.

Plates 112-113 and 216-217 show another Fromanteel clock which would appear to demonstrate the next chronological developments. It still retains the intermediate wheels and pinions, and the hammer arbor mounted on the side of the front plate, striking the bell above the top of the hood, but there are several new features. The plates are rectangular and the pillars are now turned in the manner with which we are familiar, with three bosses flanked by small fillets. In this instance there are eight pillars as the front plate is split in two. It is possible that this clock also includes the earliest use of the date indication shown through an aperture in the dial; certainly the mechanism involved in this is unusual. There are four short pegs riveted into the front plate, clearing the diameter of the hour wheel and mounted on these is a thin plate which has fitted to its centre a short stout tube through which the hour socket and minute pipe pass. The date numerals are engraved on the face side of a circular plate which is pivoted on this short tube and the plate has riveted on to its back a large thirty-one toothed wheel.

The dial plate is quite plain and has the maker's signature on the bottom edge which became the conventional position. The date aperture is between the winding holes which just clear the inside of the chapter ring and which is only about an inch wide. There are cast angel head mounts in the spandrel corners and the cast mount in the centre to which reference has already been made. This clock and that in the Fogg Art Museum are the only ones known to have this decoration. The hand collet is in this instance squared on to the centre pinion, presumably to increase the friction driving the hands.

This is the clock which was referred to on pages 88 and 91 which has had the roller cage for the back suspension of the verge restored. The crown wheel is above the top of the plates, making it necessary for the front pivot of the verge to be carried in a flat swan-necked cock on the front plate.

The clock which would appear logically to follow this is that illustrated in Plate 111 which was referred to on page 88 as having a roller cage for the back suspension of the verge pivot. The crown wheel, however, is not placed above the top of the plates in this clock although, like the last example, it has rectangular plates. It also has turned pillars and the hammer arbor mounted on the edge of the front plate, as well as maintaining power. Although the bell is now low down on the top of the plates, it is obvious from the construction of the case that this is another example of the bell being originally exposed above the hood, when both the bell standard and the hammer arbor would have been longer. The barrels in this instance are not grooved and the ratchet on the going train is not cut on the edge of the back barrel cap but between it and the main wheel. The main wheels lap over each other in plan and so are staggered in height; that is, they are at different distances from the plates. There is no date indication on the dial of this clock. We can see in this movement a distinct advance towards the standard layout of the traditional English weight-driven pendulum clock and for the first time we have a movement with no intermediate wheels and pinions.

The clocks which were made from the time when the last clock mentioned was made, normally conformed to a standard layout of the trains, which, apart from minor variations and developments, has persisted to the present day. One of the earliest clocks to be made to this standard layout is illustrated in Plates 146-147. The barrels in this clock are of more robust construction than before and are again grooved, while the main wheels are so positioned that they do not overlap. The main wheel clicks and springs have developed to delightfully simple and artistic shapes.

Plate 146. *An eight-day longcase movement by Ahasuerus Fromanteel with horizontal hammer and bottle-shaped plates.*

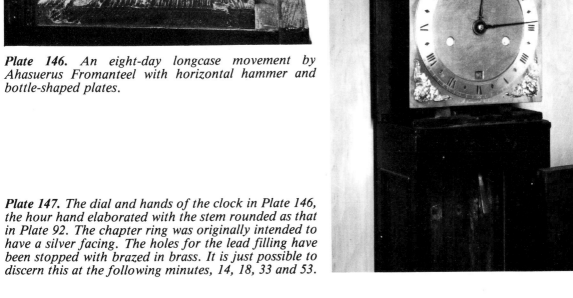

Plate 147. *The dial and hands of the clock in Plate 146, the hour hand elaborated with the stem rounded as that in Plate 92. The chapter ring was originally intended to have a silver facing. The holes for the lead filling have been stopped with brazed in brass. It is just possible to discern this at the following minutes, 14, 18, 33 and 53.*

Two of the more obvious changes are the removal of the hammer arbor from the front plate to the back and the making of the plates bottle shaped. Plates of this shape are not peculiar to Fromanteel but were used not only by Knibb and East but also by Clement. The apparent upward extension of the plates was not necessary for the accommodation of the crown wheel and pallets, for this had previously been done in the rectangular plates. It must therefore have been done to give the movement a more attractive appearance. The front plate is now made in one piece; consequently fewer pillars are required. It was the normal practice at this early stage for the movement to be set up on two wooden blocks which had fixed iron spikes engaging in holes in the centre bosses of the lower pillars to hold it in position. The hands of this clock are very sturdily made, the hour hand being slightly more elaborate than the other known examples of the same immediate period. Also the minute hand has been made with the scroll at the centre, the reverse way from normal.

The dial of this clock (Plate 147) has a matted centre and with the changed layout of the movement trains the winding holes are now in the position in which we are accustomed to find them and they are masked by shutters. The spandrel corners have the angel head mounts of the period. Later corner mounts, although more elaborate, were no improvement on these. There is a date aperture very low in the central zone but the mechanism for this has been much simplified. The disc has given place to a ring with internally cut teeth, which is mounted on rollers running on pegs in the back of the dial plate. This ring is made quite large in order to avoid the winding holes. The chapter ring here is worthy of note, the bold diamond-shaped half hour marks are unusual at this period, and a close inspection reveals a number of large stoppings in it, about twelve in number. This suggests that it was drilled for the addition of a thin silver face plate as were others of the period (page 94) but that it was not in the end done in this instance. It is remarkable that all these holes should have been filled in this way rather than make another ring. One wonders why such economy should have been necessary.

Another clock which has a chapter ring overlaid with silver is shown in Plates 148-152. This is a keywound clock with a duration of thirty hours and is probably the earliest of its kind. It has a verge escapement and was made by Joseph Knibb while he was still working in Oxford, that is, before about 1670. Thirty-hour clocks were made in some numbers in the seventeenth century for patrons of lesser means but most of these were made with pull-up winding as used in lantern clocks. In the middle 1930s, the going train was modified to go for eight days by the addition of a main wheel and barrel, an intermediate wheel and pinion and a pinion screwed to the back of the going main wheel to engage the intermediate wheel. This was in the shaped extension plates seen in the illustration which were attached to the bottom of the seat board. Thus, the only mutilation to the original movement was two screw holes.

This is a three-train ting-tang quarter chiming clock and is in quite exceptionally original condition. The workmanship throughout is of the best with the front plate split into three parts. It is constructed in the manner of an eight-day clock with a centre pinion and not a floating motionwork. The ratio between the centre pinion and the going main wheel must be 2:1, since there are sixteen turns on the barrel for the clock to run for thirty-two hours. The hour side fly is built upon a large and heavy blank wheel similar to those found on some Continental clocks. Both fly springs are end springs pressing the fly against the side of the pinion head for

Plate 148. *The dial and hands of a thirty-hour key-wound three-train ting-tang quarter longcase clock by Joseph Knibb, Oxon. It has a silver faced chapter ring and simple symmetrical hands with minimal bevelling. The corners are engraved with fruit, a dog rose and vine leaves.*

Plate 149. *The dial of the clock in Plate 148 with the chapter ring removed to show the roller matting from the cardinal points, and the way in which the gilding is strictly confined to the visible areas.*

Plate 151. *The quarter striking side of the movement in Plate 148 with the lifting pins in the main wheel to which the count wheel is attached. It has a single screw back cock, a knife-edge and bridged motionwork. Below the seat board is a modern attachment converting the going train to go for eight days.*

Plate 150. *The hour striking side of the movement in Plate 148 with the lifting pins in the main wheel. The fly is built on a disc with an end spring.*

Plate 152. *The lower portion of the dial of the clock in Plate 148 showing the signature and the over-running of the matting rollers, indicating that this has been done from the cardinal points.*

friction. The lifting pins are round the main wheel as are those in clocks with pull-up winding and the quarter side count wheel is also fixed to it. The hour count wheel is driven by a squared-on pinion and wheel on the outside of the back plate. As in lantern clocks both hoop wheels are fixed directly to their pinions. Oddly for a Knibb, the dial plate is exceptionally thick, particularly in the middle, and the gilding in good condition. The engraving is similar to that on a number of clocks of the period. One is by East in the Clockmakers' Company Collection, for instance. No two are exactly alike but all are full of character, pears being the predominant fruit depicted, with apples, pomegranates and so on.

Bottle-shaped plates with the horizontal hammer located on the back plate were used for a time by East as well as by Fromanteel and can be seen in the clock in Plates 153-155. The dial in this clock with its silver faced chapter ring is original but the hour hand is a replacement. The clock has been reconverted to a verge escapement and the stopped holes can be seen in Plate 154 which also shows the original shutters and the date wheel fixed to the hour socket by two screws. Plate 155 shows the different crossings on the main wheels and an original pulley.

Plate 153. *An eight-day longcase movement by Ahasuerus Fromanteel with a silver chapter ring.*

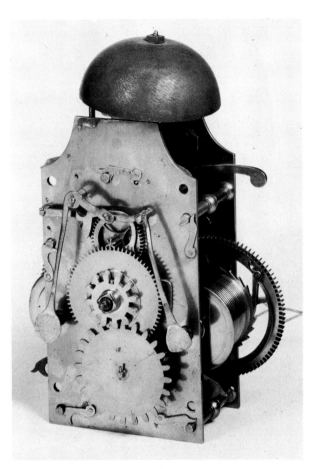

Plate 154. The under dial work of the clock in Plate 153 with the hour socket wheel screwed on, the hour wheel with the key beneath it. The shutter arms are on cannons and are of steel with brass shutters brazed on.

Plate 155. The back of the movement in Plate 153 showing the bottle-shaped plates with the arbor for the horizontal hammer on the back plate. The crossings on the main wheels differ from each other. The sturdy pulley has the pin cross-pinned.

Plate 156. A similar longcase clock movement to that in Plate 153, by Edward East.

Plate 157. A similar longcase clock movement to that in Plate 153 but in this case the hammer delivers its blows in the opposite direction to the other, by the reverse working of the levers. (The clock in its case is in Plates 221-223.)

125

Plate 158. *The dial and hands of an eight-day longcase movement by Joseph Knibb, Oxon, with what is possibly the earliest seconds dial, the ring having bold divisions. The hour hand is lightly engraved with dolphins and waves. It is the only Knibb dial known with loops below the wings on the angel corner mounts.*

The next and probably the most significant change to take place in the mechanism of the weight clock, was the introduction of the long pendulum, which it was realised would provide for vastly improved timekeeping. It has long been a matter of debate as to whom the invention of the anchor escapement should be credited, for there appears to be no positive proof. What is certain, however, is that there were a number of attempts to solve the problem of constructing a suitable escapement to control a long pendulum before the anchor escapement was perfected. Of the surviving examples of these attempts, the earliest would appear to be that made by Joseph Knibb, illustrated in Plates 158-161. This has a pendulum beating seconds, and was made by him while he was still working in Oxford, that is before about 1670. It has a most unusual escapement which is usually referred to as a 'crossbeat' because of its similarity to that made by Jost Burgi, and so named by Prof. Dr. Hans v. Bertele.[3] These however do not have a long pendulum but a pair of crossbeating counterpoised arms.

The escape wheel of this Knibb clock makes one revolution in sixty seconds and thus it is possible for the arbor to extend through the dial to carry a seconds hand. The escape wheel has thirty teeth of the usual shape but it is mounted the reverse way round from that which later became the norm and thus it has the radial faces of the teeth forwards. It is also thicker than the other wheels of comparable diameter in the

---

3. Hans v. Bertele, "Precision Timekeeping in the pre-Huygens Era", *Horological Journal,* December, 1953.

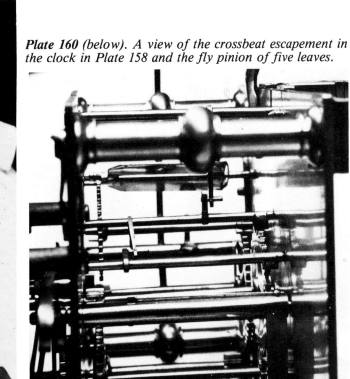

Plate 160 (below). A view of the crossbeat escapement in the clock in Plate 158 and the fly pinion of five leaves.

Plate 159 (above). A side view of the movement of the clock in Plate 158, which has rectangular plates. There is a hook for the pendulum suspension, a winged rating nut on top and a crutch of thin strip brass.

Plate 161. A closer view of the crossbeat escapement of the clock in Plate 158 showing the thickness of the wheel and that the radial faces of the teeth face forwards.

clock. The escapement consists of two arbors pivoted on an arc centred on the escape wheel arbor, one being on a line vertically above the centre and the other at an angle of about thirty degrees from it. Each of these arbors carries a pallet engaging the escape wheel and a short lever. These two levers, which are of equal length, are worked together by a slot and pin lever linkage in such a way that as one pallet escapes, the other arrests another tooth of the escape wheel until it in turn is pushed forward and escapes and the first pallet engages. When a pallet engages a tooth, the wheel is slightly pushed backwards and thus the escapement is a recoil escapement, with the attendant advantages and disadvantages. The pallet arbor above the escape wheel arbor has a further short lever attached, which engages a slot in a longer lever mounted on a third arbor carrying the pendulum crutch. The ratio of these last two levers being 9:2, greatly reduces the arc of swing of the crutch arbor, which nevertheless is greater than is desirable.

The back cock is also unusual and interesting, being made from sheet metal, bent to the required shape, with the feet bent over the top of the back plate and the knib squared and soldered in. While the shape of this back cock is in the main that which became a standard practice, it gives the impression that it was a trial piece which proved satisfactory in performance. The butterfly regulation for the pendulum is one which Knibb continued to use.

That Joseph Knibb was not the only maker to be experimenting with escapements for use with long pendulums, may be seen from the clock by Edward East shown in Plates 162-165. This clock now has a conventional anchor escapement, but it will be seen that there is an unused pivot hole on a clearly scribed radial line (Plate 163), also at an angle of about thirty degrees from the vertical. In this instance, however, there is no additional hole for a third arbor to carry the crutch, which must, therefore,

Plate 162. *The dial of an eight-day longcase clock movement by Edward East with a large seconds circle and with the signature off centre partly covered by one of the corner mounts.*

Plate 163. Part of the rectangular front plate of the clock in Plate 162 showing an empty pivot hole made in preparation for a crossbeat escapement and a large hour wheel key on top of the wheel.

Plate 164 (below left). The back view of the movement in Plate 162 showing the separate suspension for the pendulum and the back cock for the arbor pivot only. The count wheel detent is cocked.

Plate 165 (below). A view of the striking train of the clock in Plate 162. The hammer counters on a stout pin. The barrels are placed high in the plates.

Plate 166. The front plate and under dial work of an anonymous eight-day longcase clock which was designed for a crossbeat escapement. The unused pivot hole, by the right top pillar, is evidence. It has archaic features such as pillars riveted to the front plate, a lantern type hammer and a high number hour socket pinion fitted friction tight. There are steel shutter arms on cannons with brass shutters pinned on.

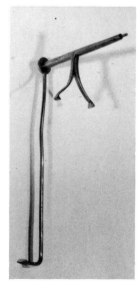

Plate 167. An angled view of the movement in Plate 166, showing the worm controlled rise and fall mechanism for the pendulum, the pillar latches, pinned dial feet and the leaf spring for the maintaining power.

Plate 168 (left). The recoil pallets from the clock in Plate 166, formed from a strip of steel, sawn down the middle and spread out. It is permanently fixed to the arbor.

Plate 169 (far left). A top view of the movement in Plate 166, showing the thick escape wheel with the radial faces of the teeth facing backwards but the reduced wheel collet indicating that it has been turned and that the faces had originally faced forwards. The hand collet is squared on. This movement is unconventional and may not be London made.

have been where the present one is. Although the suspension adjustment is fairly recent, the back cock itself is original and in its original position. The clock now has an anchor recoil escapement, but when made had two arbors in a similar position to the pallet arbors of the previous Knibb clock, one of which carried the crutch and both of which had long arms with pallets engaging a small escape wheel.

The anonymous clock, which is shown in Plates 166-169, is another example of a clock where the hole for this extra arbor can be seen, although in this case the inadequacy of the attempted escapement was evidently discovered before the movement was finished and it was never installed. The escape wheel, like that in the last clock, is thicker than the other wheels in the clock and there is indisputable evidence that it has been knocked off its collet and reversed, thus proving that this wheel originally had the radial faces of its teeth facing forwards.

In past years, other clocks have been found with empty pivot holes in this position for which no purpose was then known. They were consequently filled with the result that the evidence has now been obliterated. One in particular is remembered which also had a thick escape wheel which had obviously been reversed.

There are other details in the East clock (Plates 162-165) which should be noted in passing. Firstly, the locking arbor is cocked at the back in a similar way to that on the early spring clocks, then, the count wheel is situated on the main wheel arbor, but the hammer is still countering on a stout pin.

There seems to be conclusive evidence, therefore, that the long pendulum was applied to weight-driven clocks before the invention of the anchor escapement, that the 'crossbeat' escapement was the first to be used with any success, that the surviving example by Joseph Knibb which has short pallets and a crutch arbor is the sophisticated form and that those which have not survived had small escape wheels and long pallets in order to reduce the arc of swing of the pendulum.

It would have been obvious to the makers of crossbeat escapements that they would involve friction at a number of points which it would be most desirable to eliminate if possible. The most obvious would be connected with the second arbor situated at two o'clock from the escape wheel centre, with its associated pin and slot. This latter would be particularly vulnerable to either gumming up with dried oil or rusting up for want of it since it involved two steel faces working together. Since the pallet on the upper arbor rotates that arbor in an anticlockwise direction, some device was required to provide an impulse in the reverse direction and arrest the escape wheel. It might have seemed logical to the clockmakers at the time that, if they were to provide another lever and pad to engage the escape wheel on the other side, it must be below the horizontal centre line, in order to achieve the necessary outward thrust. This is, however, erroneous thinking but it may explain why the new escapement evolved as it did.

In Plate 170 may be seen a reproduction of an escapement which was found in an early longcase clock by Joseph Knibb.[4] Here it will be seen, the maker has added a second lever on to the pallet arbor with a pad engaging the escape wheel teeth below the centre line. It will also be seen that this entrance pad clears just one tooth below the centre and the exit pallet interrupts the escape wheel three teeth past the vertical centre line. This seems to be a logical step in the evolution of the anchor escapement. Below this illustration will be seen one of the remains of another pair of pallets which

---

4.   This escapement was made by George White, Esq..

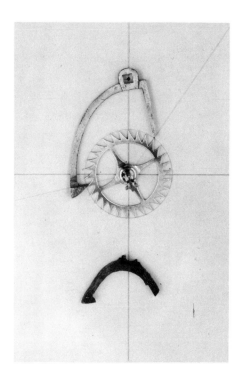

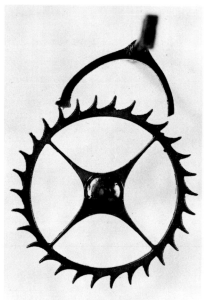

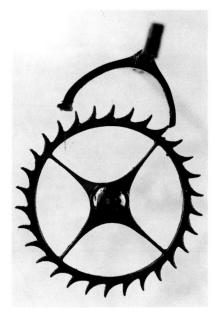

Plate 170. *A copy of the pallets found in an eight-day longcase clock movement made by Joseph Knibb which is probably the earliest form of anchor pallets. Underneath are the remains of a pair of pallets which were discarded from an unknown clock in about 1690.*

Plate 171. *The escapement in the 'Astrolabe' longcase clock by Thomas Tompion which is described in Chapter XI. The shape is nearer to that of an anchor. The exit side has no pad. The radial faces of the teeth face forwards.*

Plate 172. *The escapement of the movement in Plate 98 showing the small escape wheel of fifteen teeth with radial faces forward, riveted to the pinion head. The pallets are formed from a strip of steel, saw cut down the middle, made red hot and bent to form anchor-shaped arms. While the bending is taking place, metal falls away from the surface and this can be seen. Pads are formed on the ends of the arms which are almost of equal length.*

were recently found in the lead of a seventeenth century month clock weight, evidently discarded when improved pallets were fitted to a clock in near contemporary times. Similar pallets may occasionally be found where early long pendulum conversions have been made to lantern clocks.

The next illustration (Plate 171) is of the escapement in the 'Astrolabe' Tompion in the Fitzwilliam Museum and which is more fully described in Chapter XI. This escapement must date to the time when the anchor escapement was in transition. The escape wheel is mounted with the radial faces of the teeth forwards and they are slightly curved and under cut. The crossings are very slender, more so than the other wheels in the clock. The whole escapement is in original condition and the rivet has not been disturbed. The wheel train is so arranged that the escape wheel rotates in an anticlockwise direction when viewed from the front, which is to us the reverse from normal but might have been considered normal to a man familiar with crossbeat escapements. This escapement has proved to be quite satisfactory for it has functioned for more than three hundred years.

The pallets here are similar to the pair found in the lead weight (Plate 170). The exit pallet is merely the end of the arm, contacting the escape wheel at about 27° from the vertical, a slightly greater angle than is the case with the Knibb escapement (Plate 170). The entrance pallet is however at about 45° from the vertical, which is that normally found in anchor escapements. Thus the pallets embrace only six teeth and are much nearer in shape to the conventional anchor. On the end of the entrance arm of the pallets in the last two illustrations, we see for the first time a distinct 'pad'. Earlier pallets had no such 'pads'. The verge pads are in reality just short levers and the crossbeat pallets are longer but quite plain levers. Even the exit arm here has no pad.

Reference has been made earlier to the anchor conversion made to the early longcase movement by Ahasuerus Fromanteel and shown in Plate 172. This conversion was made very shortly after the clock was made and is very probably the earliest completely 'anchor' escapement to survive. It has a one and a quarter second pendulum. The diameter of the escape wheel is less than the distance between the escape wheel and the pallet arbor centres, has only fifteen teeth and the radial faces of the teeth face forwards. The anchor would appear to have been made from a piece of steel which was twice the width of one of the arms and has been sawn down the middle for some distance and the two arms spread outwards and fashioned to the required shape. The arbor hole has been drilled just above the end of the saw cut. Close examination will reveal evidence of some overrun of the saw cut. The pallets on the anonymous clock shown in Plate 168 were made in the same way. Although finished very differently, they must be almost as early.

It is of interest to note that both of the clocks which have been described as having these very early anchor escapements (Plates 162 and 168) have pendulums which beat more than one second. The Fromanteel beats 1¼ seconds and the anonymous clock 1⅛ seconds. Neither of these movements are, however, in their original cases. It may be suggested that the pendulum length had been calculated to take advantage of the extra width available in the base of the case for the swing of the pendulum. The Knibb clock with the crossbeat escapement, however, has a one second pendulum and its original case was made wider than cases of similar design which have verge escapements.

The final form of the anchor escapement is seen in the clock by John Fromanteel in Plates 175-176 and here the radial faces of the teeth are facing backwards. The

Plate 173. An eight-day longcase clock by Johannes Fromanteel, with the now conventional but small seconds ring. The finish to the hour hand is primitive, otherwise the appearance of the dial is as one by Ahasuerus Fromanteel.

Plate 174. The movement of the clock in Plate 173 with bottle-shaped plates but with a side extension for the new style of hammer with a long stem. The back cock is half a bridge with the pendulum support riveted in and the plate cut away for the insertion of the pallets. The count wheel is on the main wheel arbor.

movement is of interest also on account of the fact that only the pin wheel has a collet. All the other wheels are mounted on the pinion heads, which makes their positions different from the norm. There would be a considerable saving of both time and of materials in constructing the clock in this way; but it must have been very soon realised that there were objections to it, for it was not continued. Since both the wheels and pinions are close together on the back plate, much greater precision would be required in the making and it would be impossible to move the wheels slightly along the pinions to reduce the effects of wear as is the normal practice. One result of this may be seen in Plate 176 where the third pinion is deeply worn. All the parts of this movement are original and unaltered and it must be one of the earliest to be made with the fully developed recoil escapement.

It was at this time that the vertical hammer was replaced by one pivoted between the plates and we can see in Plate 174 that John Fromanteel had found it necessary to modify the shape of his plates in order to accommodate the hammer arbor. This may have been one reason for the return to rectangular plates as in the second clock.

The back cock on this clock (Plate 175) is similar to those used on clocks with verge escapements (Plate 150) but with a pivot hole in place of the 'V' and with the nib for the pendulum support riveted in. The crutch is fitted to the flat of the pallet arbor in a similar way to the pendulum rod to a verge arbor except that in this case the rivet does not pass through the flat but is above it. This clock, like that in Plate 95, has shutters pivoted on the dial centre and held in position by a very thin key. They are rotated by a pin in a lever from the bolt arbor. The front pivot of the maintaining power arbor is as large as the arbor itself and the shoulder is provided by a boss on the arbor.

The dial plate of this clock is made of copper and has its original gilding of very good colour. The hand bosses are very thick and the chapter ring is faced with silver. The spandrel corner mounts are also of silver.

These important escapement experiments and developments would all appear to have taken place at the end of the 1660s and in the Fleet Street area, where Knibb, Tompion and Jones were working and that Knibb, in particular, was associated with them. Certainly the anchor pallets on the Wadham College clock,[5] which are credited to Joseph Knibb and which must have been made about 1670, show no sign of being experimental but a perfectly mature piece of mechanism.

No attempt appears to have been made during these years, nor indeed for a great many years, to apply the anchor escapement to a spring-driven clock. Nevertheless, the clock by Samuel Knibb, which is shown in Plates 141-142, may have been intended to have an escapement based on the crossbeat. Otherwise the stopped holes cannot be adequately explained. The present escapement would appear to date to the 1920s, but the back cock and the pendulum bob have gilding which appears to be original. This is, however, the only clock known which is spring-driven which could have had this type of escapement. Nevertheless there were other experiments with these clocks at about the same time.

As early as 1673 Joseph Knibb had made a short duration timepiece to the order of the astronomer James Gregory for the University of St. Andrews (Plate 177). This clock does not have the normal verge escapement but one of a very different type

---

5.   Beeson, ''The Wadham College Clock'', *Antiquarian Horology,* June, 1957.

Plate 175. *The striking side of the movement of a long-case clock by Johannes Fromanteel which has a long hammer stem with counter spring. The wheels are riveted to the pinion heads and the count wheel is fixed to the main wheel. The dial is of gilded copper and has a silver faced chapter ring. (The case is shown in Plate 228 and Colour Plate 7.)*

Plate 176. *The going side of the movement in Plate 175. The escape wheel teeth have radial faces facing backwards and the pallets are in the shape of an anchor with both arms of almost the same length, the exit arm having a pad. It has a single screw back cock. The crutch head is slotted over the pallet arbor which is made of 'verge' steel. The shutters rotate about the dial centre and the maintaining power lever is behind the dial.*

which may have been an attempt to adapt the anchor type to a short pendulum. Although this type of escapement is particularly associated with Knibb, it was used by other makers and is to be found in the architectural spring-driven clock by Tompion, which must have been made shortly after Tompion's arrival in London, which is presumed to have been in about 1671 (Plates 178-180). Plates 181 and 182 show escapement parts taken from a clock made by Tompion of almost a decade later and Plates 475-477 and Colour Plates 18-20, pages 336-337, and Plates 478-479, are clocks by Knibb which are inscribed on the back plate "Joseph Knibb Invenit et fecit 1677" which have the same escapement. This escapement has become known as the 'tick-tack' escapement. One wonders what it was that Knibb was claiming to have invented. It is true that this clock has what is termed 'Roman strike' and this is certainly something that is peculiar to Knibb, but did he feel at that late date that a claim to the tick-tack escapement invention needed to be made? He certainly used it on some of his best clocks during that decade.

Plate 178. *The dial and hands of an eight-day spring clock with tick-tack escapement by Thomas Tompion with alarm. The chapter ring has no half-hour marks. (The clock in its case is in Plates 248-252 and Colour Plate 8, page 162.)*

Plate 179. *The under dial work of the clock in Plate 178, of sturdy construction, very much in line with the work of the Fromanteels, with barrel ratchets of 18 teeth and similar turning. The barrel clicks have an additional ball at the end of the tail and the click springs are similar to those on the clock in Plate 117. The shutters are on studs.*

Plate 180. *The movement of the clock in Plate 178 with the striking half plate removed showing the key in the plate under the centre pinion. There are large main wheels and small fusees. The striking train is similar to that in the clock in Plate 117 but with an improved layout. The hammer counters on a steel pin. There are ten pillars.*

Plate 181. *The tick-tack escapement from an eight-day spring clock by Thomas Tompion. The marks of the file from which the pallets are made can be seen. The shape of the entrance pad is very nearly on an arc from the pallet centre and the tops of the teeth almost touch the pallet arbor. On the left a tooth is clearing the exit pad. On the right a tooth is clearing the entrance pad.*

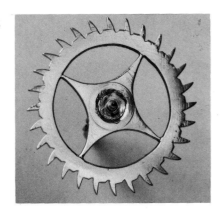

Plate 182. *A tick-tack escape wheel of the same period, with broader teeth for which the pallets must have had a longer exit pad.*

The pallets shown in Plate 181 have been made from an old file and the cross lines of the file teeth are clearly seen. In this escapement, as made by Tompion, the pallets embrace two teeth. Thus, when a tooth of the escape wheel is placed against the exit pad of the pallet, in the position to which it should drop, the toe of the entrance pad will just clear the tooth which is two removed from that first mentioned, causing the pallets to 'embrace' two teeth. The slender shape of the teeth of the escape wheel is necessary with this escapement, as is the very deep 'U' shape of the pallets on either side of the centre; as it gets very little impulse from the entrance pallet, it has to come from the exit pad. There is also a tendency that during recoil, the toe of the exit pad will be contacting the tooth for almost its entire length, with the consequent friction and drag of oil. These are two defects of this escapement which interfere with the free swing of the pendulum.

The above remarks apply particularly to the tick-tack escapement as made by Tompion. Joseph Knibb appears to have been more successful; at least more clocks made by him still have this escapement. His method was to allow more space between the top of the escape wheel teeth and the pallet arbor, which helped to eliminate the faults. A timepiece by Knibb with tick-tack escapement is shown in Plates 183-184.

The verge escapement remained the standard for all spring clocks for a great many

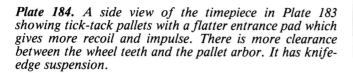

Plate 183. The dial and hands of a spring timepiece by Joseph Knibb. The dial has up and down roller matting with a date aperture top centre.

Plate 184. A side view of the timepiece in Plate 183 showing tick-tack pallets with a flatter entrance pad which gives more recoil and impulse. There is more clearance between the wheel teeth and the pallet arbor. It has knife-edge suspension.

years and changed hardly at all during its use.[6] The shape of the escape wheel teeth remained constant, except that they were sometimes under cut. The verge is normally made in one piece from a strip of rectangular steel, on which the knife-edge is made and which is slotted into the brass head of the pendulum rod. In the early 1670s, Henry Jones and some others twisted the steel strip at the back end into a horizontal line, into which the pendulum rod was squared. This allowed for only a very shallow knife-edge. The pallet pads were halved in thickness laterally below the arbor during the early period. Towards the end of the century this thinning was done by the simpler method of thinning the entire length of the pad across the arbor.

---

6.   W.J. Gazeley, *Clock and Watch Escapements,* London, 1956 and 1973.

Chapter V
Clock Cases during the Architectural Period

It was by a fortunate coincidence that the wooden clock case was introduced into this country at precisely the same time as was the pendulum invention to the clock. John Fromanteel, who was responsible for bringing that invention back from Holland, would have been familiar with the little box-like cases into which Salomon Coster had fitted his clocks. It would have been entirely natural, therefore, that the first clocks which were made by Fromanteel should have been similarly cased. We have no grounds for saying that they were not, for remarkably few clocks have been found which can have been made during the first two or three years after John arrived with the information about the new method and hardly any of these now have their original cases.

It has already been suggested in the previous chapter that the dated timepiece shown in Plate 89 may have had such a case, and that they were made may be confirmed by one example which is illustrated in Plates 185 and 186. This clock is certainly amongst the earliest wood cased pendulum clocks and it appears to be of Dutch design in almost every particular. The one door is hinged on the left, which is the Continental practice and the movement is suspended from the dial which is also hinged to the case on the left, and although it is a spring clock, provision has been made for it to be hung on the wall, which was also a Dutch practice. There is no back door and the whole of the interior is veneered and there is a small slide-up section in the right hand side to give access to the movement without swinging the movement out (Plate 100). In conformity with Dutch practice there are no key operated locks, but simple spring catches.

Simple cases such as this one would certainly have suited the taste of the Commonwealth leaders of the day. By the time that pendulum clocks were being made with more confidence, however, the Commonwealth austerity was over and the stage was set for the grand entry, for what followed was not merely a vastly improved timekeeper, but an entirely new furnishing item of great beauty. There were at that time many cultured men in the country, well versed in classical and Italian Renaissance art and its architecture in particular, who would require something far finer than the sober little box case when they were purchasing such an important new addition as a clock for their homes.

The study of the development of clock case design during the first decade of the pendulum clock in particular, is most fascinating. The specialist craft of clock case

Colour Plate 6. *A three train spring clock by Ahasuerus Fromanteel in an ebony veneered case of architectural design, with gilt metal mounts and pierced dome. Circa 1660-65. The finials are not contemporary. (Further views are shown in Plates 119-122 and 191-192.)*

Christie, Manson and Woods Ltd.

Plate 185. Ebony veneered case for spring-driven movement by Ahasuerus Fromanteel. Made in the Dutch style with the door hinged on the left, it is quite possibly of Dutch make. Circa 1659-60. (The movement is shown in Plates 99-103.)

Plate 186. View of the clock in Plate 185 with the door open showing the hinged dial and the latchwork to the front door.

maker did not, of course, exist and the skills and know-how had to be developed. Nor, indeed, was that of the cabinetmaker in existence when the clock case was first introduced. R.W. Symonds says that the craft was not introduced into England until the return of King Charles and his court in 1660, and that the first cabinetmakers to work for the crown were either Dutch or French.[1] It would appear that this was precisely the time when the first of the architectural clock cases was made. The majority of the furniture made here in the middle years of the seventeenth century was the work of joiners, was usually constructed of oak and was not veneered. By contrast, the new clock cases made from about 1660 onwards were without doubt the work of very experienced cabinetmakers, men who were able to work to rigid specifications. Who then were these men? We shall probably never know for sure. At first, understandably, there would have been few of them for very few clocks were being made but a close study of the cases suggests that there must have been at least two. We have one very good clue that Joseph Clifton was one of them and it may well be that John Gutch was another, for by April 1673 he was sufficiently established as such to be admitted as a brother of the Clockmakers' Company.

It is extremely difficult to place many of these early clock cases in strict chronological order purely on the evidence of their design, for in spite of the fact that some appear to be more mature than others, one has to realise that some, at least, of the differences in design and construction indicate the work of different men rather than different dates. The work of the man or men who made cases for the Fromanteels and Knibbs differed from that of East and Hilderson.

It is interesting, also, to conjecture on the identity of the man who was responsible for making working drawings in the first place, incorporating as they did such a wealth of architectural detail. It is highly unlikely that any of the clockmakers or the case makers would have had sufficient knowledge to have done it. Mr. L.L. Fabian has explored the possibility that Christopher Wren may have been involved in it, although he admits that it cannot be proved.[2] There were, of course, other men with the knowledge and someone must have given guidance to the case makers. However, once the standards had been set, there is no doubt that these men would have been quite capable of making such modifications as were required from time to time and for the evolving design over the years.

By the beginning of the 1660s the movements of spring-driven clocks were being made larger and heavier which made the suspension of the clock from the dial impractical. It was, therefore, necessary for the movement to be stood on a firm base. One of the first cases to be made for the more advanced movements is shown in Plates 187-190. Here is evidence of a new concept in the casing of a clock movement; one which allows adequate access for adjustment and at the same time provides stability for the movement. It would appear that the man who designed it still had its Dutch antecedent in mind while doing so, for there are many features in common. No back door has yet been introduced, indeed the back of the case is quite flat and unveneered. In addition provision has been made, as with Dutch cases, for the clock to be hung on the wall if desired or stood on a table. The movement stands firmly on the base and is fixed to the back of the case by a bracket. Access to it is achieved by

1.   R.W. Symonds, *Furniture Making in Seventeenth and Eighteenth Century England*, 1955.
2.   L.L. Fabian, "Could it have been Wren?" *Antiquarian Horology*, Vol. 10, pp. 550-570.

Plate 187. *Ebony veneered case for spring-driven striking clock by Ahasuerus Fromanteel. Made in the English architectural style. Circa 1660-65. (The movement is shown in Plates 116-118.)*

Plate 188. *Side view of clock in Plate 187 showing the earliest form of fret panel, the fabric panel in the sliding top and the suspension hole in the unveneered back.*

Plate 189. *Right side view of clock in Plate 187 with both doors open showing the latch-work and the sliding panel on the top.*

Plate 190. *Detail of the clock in Plate 187 showing the side mount and the cast Corinthian capital, which should be compared with that in Plate 252 which is built up.*

146

the entire right hand side of the case being made to swing back and in addition the top panel will slide off backwards (Plate 189). The front frame surrounding the dial is still hinged on the left in the Continental manner and there are no key operated locks used. Unfortunately much of the original latch work was missing when the clock was found, but sufficient remained to allow a reconstruction to be made. Both doors are released by a turn of one knob working through a hole in the right hand side door. The original hasps on the doors can be seen in the illustration in Plate 189. The whole of the entablature of the case is securely fixed to the back of the case, as the very flimsy ebony dial framework provides it with very little support. The case is ornamented with architectural features in gilt brass which include Corinthian capitals and bases. The ball finials are however replacements. The front and the side door are both hinged on pins in the capitals and bases. In the side door is seen the early fret design which is intended to be functional rather than decorative.

An almost identical case is illustrated in Plates 191-192 (it is also shown in colour on page 142), but this case has the rather surprising feature for the period, of a rectangular pierced gilt metal dome. This feature will present a problem to some, because domes are associated with the cases of a decade or so later. However there is one other case of this period with a wooden dome which may be seen in Chapter XI and is illustrated in Plate 744. The design of the piercing on this dome is not normally on clock cases before the late eighteenth or early nineteenth century when cast frets of a similar design were common. However, such pierced designs are to be found on English silver from about 1597 and so this is not a valid argument against dating this dome in the 1660s. It should be noted that the ends of each loop in the design are shaded with engraving. The dome is constructed of thin cast brass, pierced and bent to shape, mostly in one piece with the exception that one end is a separate piece of metal, and brazed together. Close examination convinces one that it is undoubtedly of early date. However the method of fixing it to the case is very elementary; indeed it is hardly really fixed at all. It stands on a very simple ebony faced plinth, positioned only by four little tongues of the metal fitting into slots in the wood. It is just the rod from the figure of Father Time which holds the whole down.

The top of the case has been so constructed that it was quite evidently intended for some such superstructure but even the aperture in the top appears to have been modified and the plinth on which the dome stands extends to the back of the case which the dome does not. However, such modifications have to be accepted on early clocks and the inclination is to accept this as correct. There is another spring clock case at present in a private collection, which also had a pierced brass dome which was removed during restoration in the 1930s in the belief that it was incorrect. Today this clock has a panel over the aperture in the top. Plate 240 shows a spring clock by Joseph Knibb which would have been made only a few years after this clock which has a somewhat different cast brass dome. The finials on the Fromanteel case are not the originals and there is evidence that there have been four wood blocks ⅞in. square as pedestals for the finials.

The decorative mounts on the rails of the case are ribbon-tied swags secured by screws through the case. These are quite conventional mounts but the little winged angel head mounts applied to the frieze are quite unique.

As in the case illustrated in Plates 187-190 the back is quite plain and unveneered and although there are holes in it which may have been used to fix it to a wall, there are none for the purpose of hanging it up. The doors open in exactly the same way as

Plate 191. *A spring clock case veneered with ebony for a three-train movement by Ahasuerus Fromanteel, with gilt metal mounts and pierced dome. Circa 1660-65. (See also Colour Plate 6, page 142. The movement is shown in Plates 119-122.)*
Christie Manson and Woods Ltd.

Plate 192. *The case shown in Plate 191 with the doors open.*

those in the last and the latches are similar. The large hole in the right hand side door for operating the catch on that side is however in this instance in the top rail. In the illustration in Plate 192 the hole is not visible but a narrow slot in line with it may be seen into which the hasp on the front door will slide when both doors are closed. Thus a hook, which is unfortunately missing, pivoted in the hole in the rail, will in one operation secure both front and right hand side doors. Inside the left hand side door, at the extreme bottom, will be seen the catch for that door, which has a tapered nib at its end which should snap into a catch in the case. There is, however, no evidence of anything having been fitted for this purpose nor for any releasing device.

Another example of a case that was made about the same time, although the

Plate 193. Ebony veneered case for spring clock by Ahasuerus Fromanteel with elaborately mounted cupola. Circa 1666. (The movement is shown in Plate 129.)

movement was finished later, is described in Chapter XI. In that case we again see latchwork used but later removed. However, the hasp on the front door can be seen in Plate 746 and, like the last example, the reconstructed spring catch is operated through a hole in the side of the case, although in this instance by the winding key. It is another example of a case designed to go against the wall, if not hung from it, for the back is unveneered and there is no back door. Access to that movement is obtained by sliding the case upwards from the base, it being fitted with a groove at the back into which the back board fits. It is in fact very similar to lifting the hood from a longcase clock.

Yet another clock which is dealt with separately in Chapter XI is in this group of cases fitted with spring catches; it is the Fromanteel long duration longcase clock which is of quite unique construction. The illustration of the inside of the trunk-cover in Plate 743 shows what evidence remains of the original latchwork. The later wooden frame round the dial would need to be removed were it to be replaced.

The best examples of latchwork in original state are to be found in an almost identical pair of spring clocks, and one of these by Ahasharus Fromanteel is illustrated in Plate 193, while the other, which bears the name of Samuel Knibb, is illustrated in Plates 194-199. These cases show a considerable advance in design and yet the Continental influence is still evident, not only because of the latchwork but also because the front doors are hinged on the left. It has to be said that this is of some advantage since winding is normally done with the right hand and will not be impeded by the open door. The latches on these clocks operate the back and front doors independently through rods extending through the top of the case which have to be depressed to open the doors. The hasps at the bottom of each door may be seen in Plate 197. The complete assembly is shown in Plate 199. These cases have gable-end pediments both back and front and are probably the earliest cases to have the back elevation treated almost as the front. The heavy base is in this case a fixture, for turntable bases had not been introduced at the time when these clocks were made.

The tall metal cylinder supporting the cupola is pierced to allow for the bells to be heard and it will be noted that it is done to the same design as we saw in the side frets in the clock in Plate 188. Access to the movement is achieved here in a different manner from the last clock, by lifting off the top board or, if necessary, the entire entablature. This is made necessary by the tall bell stand. Pendulum adjustment is simple, however, since a back door has now been provided. This door is hinged on the right and is the earliest example of a glazed back door. All the mounts are of cast brass and are fire-gilt.

The cases just described would all have been made by the man who first made cases for Fromanteel and all demonstrate a high degree of craftsmanship and the evolution of the case from a rectangular box into the refined architectural work of art in half a dozen years or so. By the middle sixties there were a number of other clockmakers making pendulum clocks and other clock case makers were being involved. It is not possible, however, for the next decade to associate any particular style of case with a particular clockmaker, largely because the men making the cases were not making them exclusively for one clockmaker. It was not until the output of the leading clockmakers had risen to the point where they could command the total output, or at least the major part of the output of a particular case maker, that one can in any sense identify the maker of a clock from the design of its case. That it was the case makers who were ultimately responsible for the case design and not the clockmakers, is strongly supported by the fact that even cases made to the designs which are particularly associated with such makers as Tompion or Knibb are to be found with movements by other makers. It may well be that the clockmakers would choose the superficial embellishments such as handles and keyhole escutcheons and they would, of course, have dealt with the men whose work and designs most pleased them.

Clock cases were normally constructed of mild wainscot oak of about half an inch in thickness. Pine was used for the backing of the mouldings and for other non-structural parts but only very rarely for main construction in the early period. All the very early cases were veneered with ebony although pear wood, stained and polished black, was sometimes used later for the backs of the cases and there are one or two fairly early cases veneered with this wood which were probably made for less wealthy clients or for humbler positions in a house. The mouldings in each case were made up of thin strips of the surface wood backed up with pine, the facing wood being in most cases no more than about an eighth of an inch in thickness. The thinness of this wood made it necessary for the mouldings to be made to a very shallow profile.

Plate 194. *Ebony veneered case for spring-driven clock signed by Samuel Knibb with elaborately mounted cupola. Circa 1666. (The movement is shown in Plates 130-136.)*

Plate 195 (above). Rear view of the clock in Plate 194 showing the back completely veneered and with mouldings as the front.

Plate 196 (above right). Right side view showing the flat top of the clock in Plate 194.

Plate 197. Right side of the clock in Plate 194 with the top removed and the doors open showing the latch hasps.

152

Plate 198. The case of the clock in Plate 194 dismantled.

Plate 199. Cupola and front door of the clock in Plate 194 and the latch release mechanism removed.

153

When the requirements of the architectural precedent being followed made it necessary for the moulding to have more pronounced features, this was done by making the moulding up in several sections. The mouldings, which were often very fine, were made with a tool known as a scratch which consisted of a thin piece of steel filed to the reverse of the moulding profile desired. This is then fitted into the scratch stock and used in a similar way to a spoke shave, until the desired profile is achieved. This method of making small mouldings is most satisfactory with even grained hard wood such as ebony, but is less satisfactory with softer woods and quite impossible with many.

Probably one of the earliest wood cased spring clocks not made by Fromanteel to survive complete, and made to the design which is most associated with the early period, is that illustrated in Plates 200-201. It shows very well the basic features of the design of the late 1660s; the gable-end pediment with the top roofed in, the front door hinged on the right and the back door unglazed. The carved valance below is unique on a spring clock and forms the front of a small drawer made to hold the

Plate 200. *Ebony veneered case for spring-driven clock by Edward East with key drawer beneath. Circa 1660-65. (The movement is shown in Plates 108-110.)*

Plate 201. *Rear of the clock in Plate 200 showing the plain back veneered with pearwood over the moulding ends.*

Plate 202. *Ebony veneered case for spring-driven clock by Edward East with Corinthian columns. Circa 1663-65. The escutcheon is a later addition. (The movement is shown in Plate 114.)*

winding key. There are on this clock key operated locks to both front and back doors. The finials on the clock are those particularly associated with the maker of the clock. The case has no columns and although this is a feature of many early cases, it does not necessarily follow that the case is an early one. In some cases it may have been so made to satisfy a client requiring a less expensive clock but even if this were the case, it was not reflected in the quality of the workmanship, which was never allowed to suffer. The feet, which are original, are unusual at this period. This particular clock was stolen from its owner in 1975.

Plates 202 and 203-204 show more mature cases of this type which have columns with the normal cast brass Corinthian capitals of the period. It should be noted that half columns are placed at the rear. By the end of the architectural period, the Corinthian capitals were being made up of a number of separately cast pieces giving them a more delicate appearance than those on this clock. The capitals and bases are usually held in place by brass metal threaded screws from the inside of the case (Plate 372) or in some cases as in the clock in Plate 189, by wood screws through a brazed-on strap. Early cast mounts were not, as a rule, chased or tooled over but were fine castings just well trimmed up and fire gilded. Mounts were always used discreetly and no early clock was over decorated. Even on the cupola clocks, the mounts are very carefully chosen. All were in keeping with the architectural inspiration of the

Plate 203. *Ebony veneered case for spring-driven clock by Edward East with Corinthian columns. Circa 1665. (The movement is shown in Plates 137-138.)*

Plate 204. *View of the back of the clock in Plate 203 showing the early form of fret in the back door, suspension hole and below, holes for wall spikes.*

design and were often faithful copies from Italian originals. The ball-and-claw feet seen on these clocks are found on a number of clocks by Edward East at this early period.

The backs of these early clocks are usually severely plain and quite unrelieved by any mouldings or mounts. They were normally veneered, frequently with pearwood, and the back doors were unglazed. The glazed apertures in the front and sides of cases now frequently have the rebates formed by overlaid fine ebony mouldings. An indication that the makers were still thinking that the clock might be required to hang on the wall can be seen on the back of the example in Plate 204, where the wall hook hole has obviously been used. There are also four holes in the case which were probably used for spikes to hold the clock steady. This clock has a back door which is framed up with two fret panels of the usual early design and is hinged on the left.

It cannot be too strongly emphasised that the high quality of workmanship employed in these cases was not confined to the exterior. We owe it to the skill and integrity of the men responsible for making them, that so many early cases have survived to the present day in the condition that they have. The foundation work was well done, the wood for the carcases well chosen, well seasoned and well finished. The main carcase of the conventional spring clock case was usually dovetailed together, with the pins on the top and bottom members. The insides of the back doors were often veneered, the front doors always. The hinges on both doors were identical, of the back cock type about ¾ in. square, and made of thin cast brass. They were fixed by flat-headed, handmade nails. If screws are found in a hinge of this type, they are without doubt later necessary additions once the original nails have been withdrawn. It is not unusual to find that the knuckles of the hinges, and sometimes the whole hinge, have been gilded. The locks on the front doors are made throughout of brass, including the spring. They were in reality, key operated latches, used in conjunction with a staple in the dial frame. An illustration of one of these locks is shown in Plate 616. There is very little doubt that there were specialist craftsmen making fittings such as these locks and hinges, as they were standard on all clock cases from an early period. The back door locks are the simple and conventional iron cut-in locks of the period. The addition of mock panels to the tops of these architectural cases is usually regarded as an indication of slightly later date (Plate 208) but should not be relied upon. The inset quadrant beads around the glazed or fret apertures do not appear on the earliest cases.

The fitting of frets to clock cases at this period was the exception rather than the rule; indeed, they were not generally used until much later. The makers were, however, aware of the value of providing an aperture for the outlet of the sound of the bell, although some of the measures adopted were rather crude. Just two holes have been made in the back of the case of the Stanton clock shown in Plates 205-206. Although these holes might have been intended as a means for hanging the clock on the wall, as the case has a back door it is more likely that they were for the sound of the bell. An early attempt at decorative fretwork is seen in the other Stanton clock in Plate 207, where the carcase has been cut away at the back of the gable and the covering veneer cut in a series of holes and slits which are backed with fabric. The back of the Hilderson clock in Plates 208-209 may well have been finished in the same way, for the moulding around the glazed aperture is not contemporary and in any case, a glass window in that position is purposeless. Not all of the cases made at this period had these gable tops, quite a number had tops which were flat. One of these is illustrated in Plate 210.

Plate 205. *Ebony veneered case for spring-driven clock by Edward Stanton. Circa 1665-70.*

Plate 206. *Rear view of the clock in Plate 205 showing the fabric covered holes made to let the sound of the bells out.*

158

Colour Plate 7. *The upper part of an ebony veneered longcase for a clock by John Fromanteel, with twist columns to the hood. Circa 1670. (Further views are shown in Plates 175-176 and 228.)*

Plate 207. Rear view of a clock by Edward Stanton showing more ornamental fretwork in the back of the carcase. Circa 1665-70.

Plate 208. Ebony veneered case for a spring-driven clock by John Hilderson. Circa 1665-70.

Plate 209. Rear view of the clock in Plate 208 showing the glazed aperture which may originally have been covered with fretted veneer.

Plate 210. Ebony veneered case for a spring-driven clock by Edward East. Circa 1665-70. The feet are later additions.

Plate 211. Ebony veneered case for a spring-driven clock by Edward East. Circa 1665-70. The escutcheon is a later addition.

Plate 212. Ebony veneered case for a spring-driven clock by Samuel Knibb. Circa 1665-70. (The movement is shown in Plates 141-142.)
Worshipful Company of Clockmakers

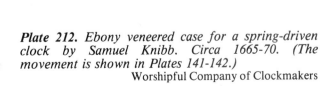

161

Colour Plate 8. *Case for a spring clock by Thomas Tompion. It is veneered in olivewood with olivewood and ebony mouldings and stands on a restored turntable base. Circa 1673. (Further views of the clock are shown in Plates 178-180 and 249-252.)*

Reference has been made to the fact that cases were to hang on the wall if required. It has been claimed that the earliest English weight-driven pendulum clocks were, like many of their pre-pendulum predecessors, also hung from the wall and that the first cases made for them were a bracket covered by a hood. There appears to be no example extant of such a clock which can be regarded as pre-dating the known early longcases, to justify this claim. There do exist, however, two longcase clocks which are quite early and appear to have started life as hooded wall clocks. These are the Fromanteel clock which is in the Fogg Museum and is shown in Plate 213, and more particularly the clock in Plates 219-220. With regard to the former, it is obvious that the trunk is of later date than the hood, while the latter shows strong evidence that the trunk is by a different hand from the hood and would appear to be a contemporary afterthought. It is veneered with pearwood while the hood is of ebony. When these two clocks were first made, they may well have looked more like the two hooded clocks shown in Plates 214 and 215, which are of slightly later date than that in Plate 213.

As is the case with the spring clocks, the earliest known, weight-driven pendulum clock has lost its case. Nevertheless, there are a number of quite early clocks in their original long cases and examination of those illustrated here will demonstrate how many of the details of the design, in particular with regard to the trunk, show signs of immaturity. With the exception of the clock in Plates 216-217, all of the very early longcases we have illustrated have no mouldings mitred around the top of the trunk. The mouldings seen at this point are all fixed to the hood and where they overhang the trunk, the overhang is relieved by the use of brass drop finials. These were of course liable to drop off and in no case are those shown the originals. The clocks in Plates 218 and 219-220 have in addition little carved valances to the front of the hoods. The first of these clock cases is attributed to Joseph Clifton and one is tempted to speculate as to whether this feature is peculiar to his work. It is also to be found on the spring clocks in Plates 200 and 238. By way of contrast, the case in Plates 221-223 has no mouldings on the hood but all the mouldings on the trunk.

The seat boards for the movements of these early longcases rest directly on to the top of the trunk and the movement is raised up to the required height on two wooden blocks. Several of these cases have a moulding mitred round the trunk just above the long door, making a kind of frieze below the hood which gives the case the general appearance of a rectangular column supporting the clock (Plates 218 and 224-225). The hinges that are used on the long doors are the conventional iron strap hinges of the period (Plate 226), although the method of fitting them varies. In some instances it is the butt end which is cranked as in the clock in Plate 232, while in others it is the strap which is cranked as in Plate 230, and the latter method was widely adopted.

The design of longcase hoods is almost identical with that of the standard spring clock case — compare 200 with 222. The framework round the dial and of the sides is as narrow as is consistent with strength and both the front and the sides are made of half-lapped frames with no door to the front. The tops of the early hoods are in all cases flat, with gable-end pediments at the front only. There are at least two instances of the hoods being made in such a way that the bell can be positioned above the top of the case. The effective top of the case in these instances is fixed to the back board, thus allowing the hood to slide upwards without disturbing the bell assembly. One of these clocks is shown in Plates 216-217 and the other is in the Museum of Science at Oxford. It is quite possible that others were so made and if so it would have been in line with the Dutch practice in the seventeenth century. The

Plate 214. *Ebony veneered hooded bracket for a movement by Ahasuerus Fromanteel. The gilt metal mask on the valance hides the keyhole of the lock holding the hood shut. Circa 1665.*

R.A. Lee

Plate 213. *Case of an elaborate clock by Ahasuerus Fromanteel, the upper part veneered with ebony and said to have been originally a hooded wall clock. Circa 1660-65. (The movement is shown in Plates 95-97.)*

Fogg Art Museum,
Harvard University

Plate 215. *Ebony veneered hooded bracket for clock by Edward East. The finials are replacements. Circa 1665.*

164

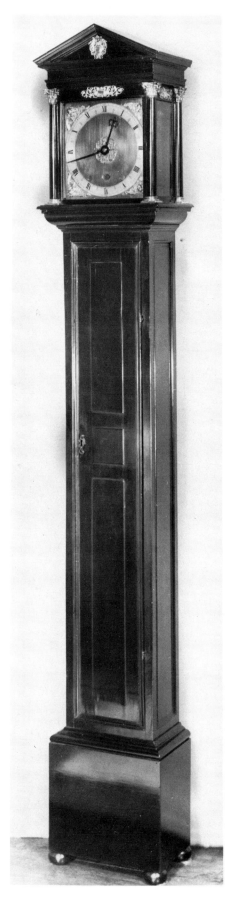

Plate 216. *Ebony veneered longcase for clock by Ahasuerus Fromanteel. Showing the half columns placed at the back of the hood. Circa 1665. (Views of the movement are in Plates 112-113.)*

Plate 217 *(left and below). Views of the upper part of 216, showing how the bell and bell hammer is accommodated above the hood.*

Plate 220. *Upper part of 219, showing the trunk with no moulding at the top but a carved valance at the front.*

Plate 218. *Ebony veneered longcase now with a movement by Ahasuerus Fromanteel. Joseph Clifton's token was found embedded in this case. Circa 1665. (The movement is shown in Plate 98.)*

Plate 219. *Longcase clock by Ahasuerus Fromanteel, the hood veneered with ebony, the trunk a contemporary addition. Circa 1665.*

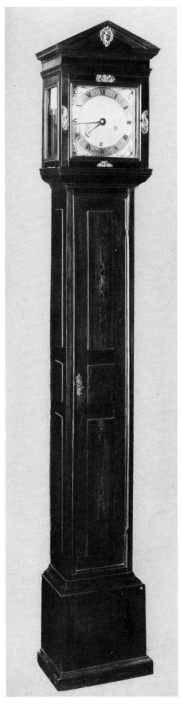

Plate 222. Upper part of 221, showing how the long door extends up to the top moulding of the trunk.

Plate 223. Upper part of 221, showing that the mouldings are on the trunk and not at the bottom of the hood.

Plate 221. Longcase veneered with brown ebony for a clock by Ahasuerus Fromanteel. Circa 1665. The skirting round the base is a later addition. (The movement is shown in Plate 157.)

Plate 224. Ebony veneered longcase for clock by Ahasuerus Fromanteel. Circa 1665.
Victoria and Albert Museum

Plate 225. Upper part of 224. The trunk has no moulding at the top and no valance at the front.

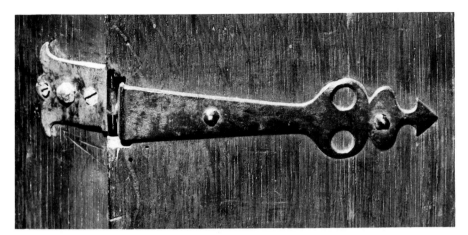

Plate 226. Wrought iron strap hinge used on early longcases.

Plate 227. Keyhole escutcheon as used on longcases during the first two decades or so.

sides of all hoods are grooved at the back to enable them to slide up and down a tongue on the back board. For winding and minor adjustments to the movement, the hood may be held in a suitable raised position by a spring-operated hooked lever, usually high up on the right hand side. The hook is as a rule made of brass and the leaf spring of steel. A wrought iron bolt will also lock the hood down by leverage on its lower end as the long door is closed. These fittings can be seen on several of the clocks illustrated and in detail in Plate 372.

The veneers with which the cases are covered are rarely mitred, although there are exceptions, some of which are shown in Plates 218, 233, 234 and 235. The rail veneers are butted up to those on stiles, giving the appearance that they are integral with the construction of the case. The side timbers of the trunk extend right to the extreme bottom of the case and the base is built round it. Bases at the early period are usually quite plain, but there are instances of the base being stepped as in the clock in Plate 218. The moulding which is mitred round the trunk just above the base is as a rule broken ogee, with the profile of the convex member almost a semi-circle. The longcase at this period and indeed almost throughout the rest of this century, does not have a plinth or skirting to the base, but stands on four bun feet. Unfortunately, most cases had a plinth added in later years when such a feature was the rule on newly made cases, and considered more correct. In many cases this addition has preserved the foundation and its removal exposed the holes for the feet. A view of the bottom of a Knibb case, showing the feet holes is shown in Plate 338. Most of these first longcases had the long door fitted between the trunk sides without any strip of wood down the inside of the trunk to give extra width to the framework round the door. There was however a very thin framework overlaid on the sides, about an inch in width which added to the width of the front frame and formed a

Plate 228 (*far left*). *Ebony veneered longcase for a clock by John Fromanteel, with twist columns to the hood. Circa 1670. (Also shown in Colour Plate 7, page 159. The movement is shown in Plates 175-176.)*

Plate 229. Ebonised longcase for a clock by John Fromanteel, with no columns to the hood. Circa 1667-70.

Plate 230. Upper part of 229 showing how the long door covers the front of the trunk with the strap of the hinge on the trunk.

Plate 231 (left). Ebonised longcase for a clock by Joseph Knibb, Oxford, with no columns to the hood. Circa 1667-70.

Plate 232 (above). Upper part of 231 showing how the long door covers the front of the trunk but with the strap of the hinge on the door.

sunken panel on the sides. Around this panel was mitred a shallow scratch moulding. A similar moulding was mitred round the long door and since this moulding did not overhang the framework as in later clocks, the door was also a sunken panel, decorated with three smaller panels of raised veneers. There are one or two instances of early longcases which have been made with the long door made the full width of the case. Two are shown here in Plates 229-230 and 231-232. These cases also have no panels on the sides of the trunks and may be the work of a different case maker.

Decorative fretwork does not appear to any extent on longcases during the 1660s and during this decade the dials are normally about 8⅝ ins. square.

With the introduction of the long pendulum a wider trunk became necessary and a proportionally larger dial. On Plate 228 and Colour Plate 7, page 159, we see such a case which has a 9 ins. dial. It is also one of the few longcases with silver mounts.

Plate 233. *Ebony veneered case for a spring-driven clock by Henry Jones, with quarter columns at the rear and a key drawer below the dial. Circa 1670.*

Towards the end of the '60s a number of spring clocks were being made whose cases were proportionately taller than those previously made. The change was made by the addition of a pedestal or dado to the columns. This may have been prompted by a desire to provide a receptacle for the winding key and door keys, for this could then be done by making a drawer below the dial, and this is illustrated in Plates 233, 234 and 236. Two of these cases also show a further innovation, the introduction of twisted columns, which rapidly became normal practice. At this period many dials are larger than before. The cartouche seen in the tympanum on the Edward East clock in Plate 235 is of the design particularly associated with that maker while that on the clock in Plate 234 is seen more on clocks by Fromanteel. Here also we see quarter columns at the backs of the cases set against barge boards. The change from

Plate 234. *Ebony veneered case for a spring-driven clock by Edward East, with twist columns, quarter columns at the rear and a key drawer below the dial. Circa 1670.*

Trustees of the British Museum

Plate 235. *Ebony veneered case for a spring-driven clock by Edward East, with twist columns, and quarter columns at rear. Circa 1670. The escutcheon is a later addition.*

the earlier half columns takes place about this time on both longcase and spring clock cases.

The clock illustrated in Plates 236-237 has a case of more unusual construction. This clock and another made by Edward East,[3] are the only known examples of the entablature being made to lift off to enable the movement to be withdrawn upwards from the case. Making the case in this way has made possible a smaller case, for both movements are too large for them to be removed through the back door. The dial is made to slide down a groove in the dial framework. In this case also we see an early example of a decorative fret being inserted in the frieze. Whether the frets were designed and cut by the clock case makers themselves or by specialist craftsmen we do not know. It is most likely to have been by the same men who were soon to be cutting marquetry. Most frets, for a decade at least, were limited in design to a very few patterns. This one consisting of a reciprocal evolute scrolling design with stylised fruits or flowers at the terminals of the scrolls, is probably the most common.

---

3.   H. Alan Lloyd, *The English Domestic Clock,* 1938, figs. 12 and 12a.

Plate 236. Ebony veneered case for a spring-driven clock by Joseph Knibb, with decorative fret in the frieze, straight columns and a key drawer below the dial. Circa 1670-75. (The movement is shown in Plates 473 and 474.)

Plate 237. The case shown in Plate 236 showing the drawer and how the entablature is removable for the movement to be withdrawn upwards.

Plate 238. *Walnut veneered hooded bracket for a spring-driven clock by William Clement, which may be hung on the wall or stood on a table. Circa 1670. The metal finials are probably a later addition.*

176

Plate 239. *Ebony veneered case for a spring-driven clock by John Fromanteel, with twist columns, quarter columns at the rear and a small key drawer below the dial. Circa 1670. The finials and their blocks are replacements. (The movement may be seen in Plates 143-145.)*   R.A. Lee

By about 1670 the dials of most spring clocks were being made much larger and often were as much as 10 ins. square. By this time also quite fundamental changes in the design of the cases were beginning to take place. Probably the most noticeable was the demise of the gable-end pediment which had been an almost essential feature from the beginning. It was discarded in favour of a flat top, giving to most cases a somewhat squatter appearance. At first they were still unadorned at the back but most cases now have glazed back doors. The changes in spring clock case design are parallel to those in the design of the longcases. Compare, for instance, the clock case in Plate 240 with that in Plate 334. Both have the same general proportions, the same long windows, the twist columns with Corinthian capitals and bases are the same, and both have the same gilt brass swag on the rail above the dial. It is true that the spring clock has no quarter columns at the back but it is more than likely that it had them originally. The case brass dome on this spring clock is however a very unusual feature as are the feet at this period. The finials here are probably unique. Although of similar outline to others of the period, they are not cast solid but built up of separate cast pieces, giving them a more delicate appearance. One method of

Plate 240. Ebony veneered case for a spring-driven clock by Joseph Knibb
with fire-gilt cast brass dome and built-up cast brass finials. Circa 1670-73.
The Leicester Museum

Plate 241. Detail of the finial from the clock in Plate 240.

Colour Plate 9. *Ebony veneered case for a spring-driven striking clock with alarm by Joseph Knibb, which has mouldings all round and silver mounts. This case has its original turntable base. Circa 1672-75.*

Plate 242. *Olivewood veneered case for a spring-driven clock by William Knottesford, with key drawer on top. Circa 1670-73.*

decorating the tops of these flat topped cases may be seen in Plates 242 and 243-244. So far as is known, however, these are the only cases which have the bible-back moulded addition to this central panel, made to contain a drawer for the keys. The usual case is seen in the clocks in Plates 245-247 and 248-252. The taller panel, almost an inverted bell, seen in Plate 239 is unusual.

It was at this period that more decorative veneers were introduced. These cases are veneered with olivewood with some of the mouldings and the columns of ebony with no metal capitals and bases.

What may be regarded as the final stage in the evolution of the architectural spring clock case arrived when the makers applied the mouldings to the backs of their cases as well as the fronts, thus making both front and back almost identical. In some the

Plate 243. Olivewood veneered case for a spring-driven clock by William Knottesford, with some of the finer mouldings made in ebony and with a key drawer on top. Circa 1670-73.

Plate 244. Rear view of the case shown in Plate 243 showing the key drawer on top.

Plate 245. Ebony veneered case for a spring-driven clock by Thomas Harris, with architectural mouldings front and back and with reconstructed turntable base. Circa 1670-73.

back door completely covers the back, as the front door does the front of the case and, therefore, the columns are set into the corner of the door. This may be seen in Plates 249 and 253-254. The glazed aperture in the doors is, however, smaller at the back. The more usual method of making the back door, and probably slightly later since it is the method which continued to be used, is that seen in Plate 246. Any decoration applied to the fronts of these cases in the way of mounts is frequently also applied to the backs.

Plate 247 shows the top of one of these cases where, in addition to the four elaborate urn finials on low blocks, the case has a fine moulding decoratively mitred round. The silver mounted Knibb clock in Colour Plate 9, page 179, has a heavier moulding similarly added with five finials and taller blocks. The Tompion case in Plates 248-252 (also shown in Colour Plate 8, page 162) has five finials but the little

Plate 246. Rear view of the case in Plate 245 showing how it turns on the turntable.

Plate 247. Detail of the top of the case in Plate 245.

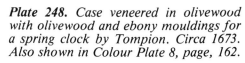

Plate 248. Case veneered in olivewood with olivewood and ebony mouldings for a spring clock by Tompion. Circa 1673. Also shown in Colour Plate 8, page, 162.

Plate 249. Rear view of the case in Plate 248 showing the back door extending the full width of the case.

Plate 250. The side view of the case in Plate 248 showing how the case will revolve on the turntable.

Plate 251. View of the bottom of the case in Plate 248 showing the central pivot hole for the turntable. Two non-contemporary holes may be seen for fixing the movement and alternative holes for the bolt and shutter pull-string. The light patches at the corners are where later feet have been fixed.

Plate 252. Detail of the cornice of the case in Plate 248 showing the Corinthian capital and finial.

Plate 253. *Walnut veneered case for a spring-driven clock by Joseph Knibb with mouldings all round. Circa 1670-75. The top member of the cornice moulding is missing and has been replaced by veneer.*

moulding mitred round them does not have the extra feature in the centre as found in Plate 247 and Colour Plate 9, page 179. Many of these cases decorated on the back and also some of the flat back type, were originally fitted with turntable bases. Unfortunately most of these have been discarded during the three hundred years since they were made. That a case was originally fitted with a turntable base can be ascertained by a glance at the bottom, for it will have a large hole in its centre. Colour Plate 9, page 179, shows one case which still has its original turntable. It is one of the finest cases of its period, with silver mounts throughout. Most of these clocks are quite heavy and large and there is no doubt that these bases were fitted to enable the clock to be turned round for any necessary adjustments to the movement without occasioning damage to the surface of the piece of furniture upon which it stood.

Plate 254. Rear view of the case in Plate 253.

Plate 255. Rear view of the case shown in the frontispiece.

Plate 256. *Pearwood veneered case for a spring-driven clock by Joseph Knibb, with japanned finish decorated in the Chinese manner. The twist columns are set in rebates. Circa 1675. The handle is a later addition and it is most likely that the original finials would have been made of wood.*

Japanned finishes are very rare in these early days and the case in Plate 256 is the only one known to the authors. The recessing of the columns into the corners is also unique for the period.

The case of the clock by Jeremie Gregory which forms the frontispiece of this book and the back view of which is in Plate 255, is quite exceptional. It illustrates the danger involved in expecting a clock to exactly conform to a design associated with its period. The mounts in this instance are peculiar to this clock and include a

Plate 257. *Ebony veneered case for a spring-driven clock by Henry Jones, with repoussé silver fret and mounts and a cornice moulding that does not conform to architectural design. Circa 1670-75.*

cartouche containing an intricate cipher which has been deciphered to read, GEO(rgius) REX D(ei) G(ratia) A(ngliat). Translated as, George by the Grace of God King of England. This would suggest that the cipher was added to the case some decades after the clock was made. It can however be deciphered to read, CAROLUS II REX DEI GRA(tia). Charles II by the Grace of God King would be more in keeping with the date of the clock which is circa 1670-75.

We can regard the end of the architectural period of spring clock design as coming when the case makers ceased to adhere strictly to the architectural principles and details. Probably the first sign of this was the abandonment of the architectural design of the cornice moulding and its replacement by one with a simpler profile. Such a case can be seen in Plate 257. This clock also shows the early use of a convex dome and the early use of decorative repoussé work is seen in the frieze. The handle on this clock cannot have been used for carrying the clock which is quite heavy, and may well have been added at a later date when a handle was deemed to be the correct finish for a spring clock.

Chapter VI
Later Weight-driven Movements

In the year 1673, the records of the University of St. Andrews suggest Joseph Knibb supplied to that University the pair of timepieces whose movements are illustrated in Plates 258 and 259. By that time the use of the anchor escapement had become firmly established. Both Knibb and Tompion had made it a practice to cut an aperture in the back plate to the shape of the pallets used, in order that they could be withdrawn without dismantling the movement. Thus, a good guide to the shape of original pallets may be gained from this where the cut-out has not been interfered with. The method of making anchor pallets adopted by the Knibbs at this period was to bend the bow from one piece of metal, making a pad at each end and then to dovetail the pallet arbor into the underside. Thus, in some instances at least there was very little clearance between the escape wheel teeth and the pallet arbor. If one looks at the cut-out in the back plate of the movement in Plate 259, one will see that it is so shaped as to accommodate the pallets with the arbor in that position and that the present pallets must, therefore, be a replacement.

That method of attaching the anchor to the arbor was later abandoned and the arbor was dovetailed into the top of the pallets. Later still the pallets were made with more metal in the centre through which the arbor passed and were usually fixed in position by pins. The practice of pinning the pallets was not satisfactory, for in time the motion of the pendulum caused the pin to wear with consequent movement of the pallets on the arbor. They were subsequently frequently soldered.

Although the anchor escapement was soon generally adopted, not all makers immediately used it and some who did also made clocks with the old escapement. One such is shown in Plate 260, a clock by Edward East which must have been made in the middle '70s. We have already seen that at least one clock which was made with a verge escapement was converted to anchor at quite an early date.

In Plates 261-263 are seen views of a longcase movement by Joseph Knibb which is fairly early and which has a seconds hand and maintaining power. Many of Knibb's later clocks not only have these features but also features which suggest that they did not originate from his workshop. For instance, they have quite ordinary back cocks without Knibb's refinements. Unfortunately, however, because the clocks bear Knibb's name, many of these have since been 'improved' by having back cocks fitted with the rise and fall mechanism associated with Knibb. When seconds hands and

Plate 258. *One of a pair of longcase timepieces supplied to St. Andrews University in 1673 by Joseph Knibb. (The case is shown in Plate 330.)*

Plate 259. *The second of the timepieces supplied to St. Andrews University in 1673 by Joseph Knibb. (The case is shown in Plate 331.)*

Plate 260. *A longcase striking clock by Edward East of about 1670-75, yet still made with a verge escapement.*

Plate 261. *The under dial work of a longcase movement by Joseph Knibb with the shutter arms of steel on brass cannons.*

Plate 262. *A view of the striking side of the movement in Plate 261 showing the early type of seat board extending the full depth of the case.*

Plate 263. The underside of the dial of the clock in Plate 261.

maintaining power are found on a clock of undoubted Knibb workmanship, it is usually a particularly fine example such as that in Plate 277. Maintaining power does not appear to have been considered necessary at this time for a domestic clock.

When maintaining power is used at this period it is normally associated with the winding hole shutters and is referred to as 'bolt and shutter maintaining power'. It provides sufficient power to keep the clock in motion while the power provided by the weight is removed by the process of winding. The motive power for it is a leaf spring seen pressing on the right hand shutter arm in Plate 261. It is brought into operation when the shutters are opened by the lever on the right being depressed. The right hand shutter arm is squared on to an arbor, known as the bolt arbor, to which is fixed the operating lever and an arm extending downwards towards the centre wheel and bent at right angles with a square hole in it. The bolt lies along this arm. It is square at its lower end to slide through the square hole and round at its upper end to slide through a hole in the bolt arbor. A light spring along the bolt arbor passes through a hole in the bolt to spring load it downwards, bringing its lower end, which is chamfered, into contact with a tooth of the centre wheel when the operating lever is depressed. Thus sufficient power is applied to the train to keep it in motion for about three minutes, at the end of which time the centre wheel has rotated to a point where the bolt becomes free from the teeth and the shutters will have closed. The bolt is visible in Plates 258 and 259.

195

Plate 264. *The dial and hands of a longcase clock similar to that in Plates 261-263. It was once owned by Admiral Byng. This design of hour hand was used by makers such as East and Stanton.*

In Plate 262 may be seen the back cock used in connection with the butterfly rise and fall mechanism favoured by Joseph Knibb, a number of illustrations of which appear later. There is a square hole in it through which the square brass head of the suspension spring will slide. This has a screw protruding from its top for the butterfly nut which raises or lowers the pendulum. The variation of the effective length of the pendulum is achieved by the suspension spring passing through a slot in a small fixed cock. In early examples of this type of suspension, a slot is made in the back cock to enable the suspension spring to slide through for the removal of the pendulum, but this was soon simplified by fitting a hook to the end of the suspension spring and making a hole in the impulse block to receive it (Plates 271, 272 and 273). This made it unnecessary to have the crutch open-ended.

Another early feature of the clock in Plates 261-263 is the steel hammer spring. A piece of steel is fixed across the end of the hammer arbor, providing a flat surface for the spring. It is slightly rounded at the top where it works on the spring and its lower end counters upon it. Most of Joseph Knibb's clocks have hammer and counter springs, both of which are of brass and both of which work on a steel pin projecting from the hammer arbor.

It would appear that this movement was made before pressures for a greater output of his clocks forced Knibb to skimp on some of the details of his work, for here the hammer stem is dovetailed into its arbor and not just a steel wire driven into a hole. Also while the motionwork is not bridged, the early type of hour socket is employed with the wheel of fourteen teeth being retained by two screws over the key and the wheel.

We have not illustrated the dial of this clock but Plate 264 shows one which is very similar with a seconds ring, maintaining power and Knibb hands having only a minimum of bevelling. It may well be that hands which were pierced but unfinished were obtainable by the clockmakers, for this pattern was used by a number of makers, including East and Stanton on both spring-driven and weight-driven clocks, each finishing them to their individual standard. As was usual at this period, the date aperture is placed low and the bevels are narrow.

Plates 265-267 show a clock by Henry Jones which may have been constructed with the intention of giving it a verge escapement. It is an eight day, two train, quarter striking clock. There are two variations of quarter striking, the one striking the quarters on the smaller of two bells, as in this case, one blow at the first quarter, two at the second and three at the third. The other is similar but striking ting-tang on two bells, usually at an interval of one third. In either case the blows are produced by putting more pins in the pin wheel than in a normal striking clock and by increasing the ratio between that wheel and the great wheel so that provision is made for the striking of 150 blows in each twelve hours. The count wheel is also divided into 150 with notches to regulate the delivery of the blows (Plate 265). There is a separate hammer for each bell, remote from the hammer tails which are pivoted in a hammer-tail block, pumped by face cams on the minute wheel. There are pins on both sides of the pin wheel with one hammer on each side. In a clock striking the quarters ting-tang, both bells are struck in succession, the higher followed by the lower. When pumping takes place at the hour, the hammer for the higher pitched bell is moved out of the path of the pins and the hour is struck by the other hammer on the lower pitched bell. These bells are usually fairly large, the hammers are also large but lightly sprung and lift easily. A weight of about 16 lbs. is usually required.

Plate 265. *The back view of a two-train quarter striking longcase clock by Henry Jones.*

Plate 266. *The under dial work of the clock in Plate 265.*

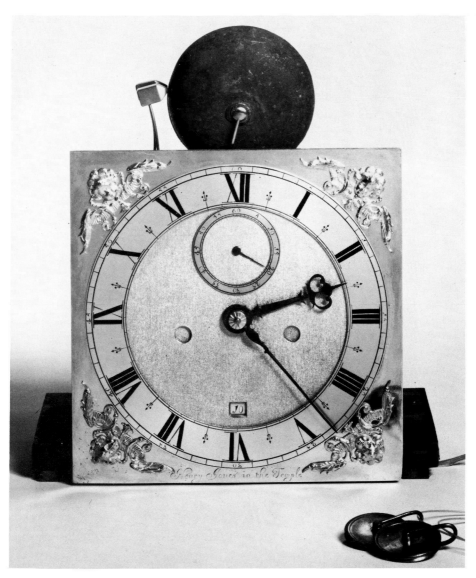

Plate 267. The dial and hands of the clock in Plate 265.

It will be seen from the illustration that the hammers are connected to the hammer tails by pieces of wire. It is most probable that there were originally spring links here. Plate 265 shows the back plate with its large count wheel, the drop-in piece which works through a slot in the plate. The back cock is interesting, for the nib support for the pendulum is riveted into a wedge-shaped piece which slots into the back cock. This latter is of similar shape to many found on spring clocks of the same date and is also used on longcase clocks fitted with rise and fall mechanism.

The 10ins. dial of this clock in Plate 267 is of quite early appearance with the narrow chapter and seconds rings (the latter is quite large). It has the early 'J' in place of the figure 1 and angel corners with the scrolls tight against the chapter ring. The hands are slightly more decorative than those used in the previous decade. While the general design of hands remains much the same over the period, there are subtle and quite significant changes in just a few years. This illustration also includes a pair of original pulleys.

Plate 268. The striking side of the movement of the month petite sonnerie longcase clock No. 3 by Tompion, showing the large count wheel.

Plate 268 is of a month longcase movement by Tompion which has petite sonnerie striking. That is, it strikes the quarters on a small bell and the hours on a larger at each quarter except at the hour when it strikes just the hour. To strike the hour four times an hour for twelve hours requires 312 blows of the hour hammer and to strike the quarter blows requires 72 blows. Thus provision has to be made on the count wheel for 384 blows, hence the very large wheel. The toothed wheel, which is attached to the count wheel and driven by the pin pinion, has engraved upon its face in an outer ring the quarters and on an inner ring the hours. The pointer seen indicates the last quarter struck which in the photograph is the second quarter past ten o'clock. In order to pump the action from the quarter hammer to the hour hammer another count wheel is attached to the back of the first upon which rides an arm with an angled end to drop into the slots. Both wheel and angled arm are just visible in the

Plate 269. The dial and hands of the clock shown in Plate 268.

photograph. While the arm is riding on the circumference of the wheel the hours will be struck and when it drops into the slots the quarters will strike. Thomas Tompion's method of doing this is for the hammer tail to be on a small horizontal arbor pivoted in a frame on the main hammer-tail arbor, it is spring-loaded and has a short projection at right angles to the hammer tail. An inclined plane working on this projection transfers the up and down motion of the count wheel arm into a horizontal movement of the hammer tail which will carry it either into or out of the path of the lifting pins. The long wire with a loop at its end, seen at the back of the movement, is in reality a long pin for securing the pendulum suspension.

The dial of this clock, seen in Plate 269, has inset into the dial plate, just within the chapter ring, a circle of iron the purpose of which is not known. Otherwise this is a typical Tompion dial with a border of wheat-ear engraving with the signature in square script in a panel at the bottom. The matting is very fine, which is not always

Plate 270. *A longcase clock by Thomas Tompion of one month duration and with Roman striking, seen in its case in Plates 370-371.*

the case on Tompion's dials for some are coarse and uneven. When this is the case it indicates that it has been done with rollers consisting not of a series of pyramidical spikes, but of sharp ridges requiring much greater pressure. The date aperture on this dial has a much wider bevel than the previous dial illustrated. Maintaining power was normally fitted to Tompion's clocks.

Plate 270 gives a view of the only known longcase clock by Tompion which has both a skeleton dial and Roman striking, features usually associated with the clocks of Joseph Knibb. Strangely, and unlike Knibb, he has used a square-edged bell for the higher pitched note and a domed one for the lower. Another square-edged bell is used on which a single blow is struck at the half hour by a hammer lifted by a pin in the cannon wheel. A hole in this bell strongly suggests that it was intended for a watch and the hole was to take the winding key. This photograph shows the normal method adopted for securing movements to their cases with a pair of brackets screwed together, the one being fixed to the back board and the other to the back plate of the movement. From earliest times, holes had been drilled in the centre bosses of the lower pillars to take iron pegs fixed in the seat board. Later the holes in the pillars were threaded for bolts through the seat board.

A clock with Roman striking, but by Joseph Knibb, is shown in Plate 271 and shows his method of adjusting the length of the pendulum by the use of a winged nut and also the hook to which the impulse block is attached. On this clock the square edged bell is the larger of the two. These features can also be seen in Plate 272 which is Roman striking but of three months' duration. This clock has, however, a number of unusual features apart from the shaping of the plates, some of which may be the result of restoration work. For instance, the pallets, which can just be seen through the aperture in the back plate, have a neck, which is wrong for the period and also the crutch is over long. The larger hammer here has a steel spring which also acts as a counter while the smaller has a separate counter spring. The pallet cock, although correct, has screwed under it a cast cock to hold the suspension spring. The more usual cock here is bent up from a strip of brass with the tip of the foot forming a steady pin, as in Plate 271. This, and the slightly elaborated wing nut on a modern thread, suggests a renewal.

We have described earlier a petite sonnerie clock by Tompion with a two-train movement. A full grande sonnerie clock however needs to strike 312 hour blows and 120 quarter blows every twelve hours and requires a very considerable output of power. There would also be a great disparity between the trains if the hours were to be provided by one train and the quarters by another. In the clock in Plate 273 we see an ingenious compromise made by Joseph Knibb, where he has adopted the 'double-six' method of striking which is found in some Italian clocks, for the hour indications at the quarters. In this, when the quarters are sounded until a quarter to seven, the hour which is struck following is the normal hour but after seven o'clock the next three quarters are followed by one hour blow, after eight o'clock by two blows and so on, but the correct hour is always struck at the hour. This method of striking at the quarters makes a considerable saving of power but must be very confusing to the uninitiated. No doubt one gets used to it. The train on the left in the illustration provides for the striking of the hours only at the quarters on the 'double-six' principle, while that on the right provides for the quarter hour blows and for the correct blows at the hour. Therefore, there are no quarter blows at the hour.

The dial of this clock is shown in Plate 274 and it demonstrates both the exquisite artistry of Knibb's dials and hands but at the same time how slipshod he could be in

Plate 271. *The movement of a longcase clock by Joseph Knibb of one month duration and with Roman striking.*

Plate 272. *The back view of a longcase clock by Joseph Knibb of three months' duration.*

Plate 273. The back plate and count wheel of a three-train, eight-day longcase clock by Joseph Knibb. The unusual striking mechanism is described in the text.

Plate 274. The dial with skeleton chapter ring of the clock shown in Plate 273.

so insecurely riveting the dial feet into the plate that they have loosened. He could also have placed them beneath the chapters where they could not be seen.

A clock signed by Knibb but not of his workmanship is seen in Plates 275-276. It is probably an example of a movement bought in a partly finished state and completed in his workshop, for the dial (Plate 275) is in the best Knibb tradition. The movement is without the rise and fall provision usually made by Knibb and the pendulum is supported by a very simple cock riveted into the back plate. The pallet arbor is pivoted in a plain cast single foot cock with a quite inexplicable sliding wedge, while Knibb would normally have used a bent up cock. In this clock there is a pumping hammer-tail block and connecting links. The hammers are positioned low down and the two sliding pins of the hammer-tail block may be seen protruding through the back plate just above the count wheel.

It is by no means unusual to find a Knibb clock with features so unlike his normal work. Unfortunately, however, a great many of these have been 'corrected' over the years, removing much valuable evidence of the trade practices of the seventeenth century. Back cocks in particular have appeared in many forms, some made from

Plate 275. *The dial with skeleton chapter ring of an eight-day quarter striking longcase clock signed by Joseph Knibb.*

Plate 276. *The movement of the quarter striking clock in Plate 275.*

Plate 277. *The dial with skeleton chapter ring of the month longcase clock by Joseph Knibb seen in its case in Plates 333-334.* Fitzwilliam Museum, Cambridge

motionwork bridge castings. In the clock illustrated, the dial feet latches differ from the normal as seen in Plate 261, the aperture in the back plate to receive the pallets is in the form of a figure eight and the hammer arbors pass through a piece of steel from which both the hammer stem and the drawing lever are formed. The count wheel has been elegantly crossed out. The crutch is made from a strip of brass and is not open ended. The movement of the miniature longcase clock shown in Plate 345 has a very similar movement.

In Plate 277 is seen the dial of an extremely fine month clock by Knibb which is an example of a clock with a seconds dial but with no maintaining power. As will be seen from the illustrations of the complete clock in Plates 333-334, it is a clock which one would expect to have this refinement, which is included on much less important eight-day clocks.

One of Daniel Quare's better quality clocks is shown in Plates 278-279. All of the parts, with the possible exception of the shutter arms, are made of quite substantial metal. The crutch arbor is squared and the crutch is then riveted on to it without a large shoulder. When this is done the crutch will tend to work loose. It will be seen that the pallets are of an anchor shape, that the pulley is well finished and decorated

Plate 278. *The dial and hands of an eight-day longcase clock by Daniel Quare. (The clock in its case is shown in Plate 383.)*

Plate 279. *The movement of the clock in Plate 278 with the back cock, pallets and a pulley.*

with rings and that the nib of the back cock also has decoration. This is often found on Quare's best clocks as is the recessing of the holes in the front plate for the dial feet. The dial is of interest; it is the first to be illustrated in this chapter which has rings round the winding holes. This decoration is generally regarded as a late feature but it is not necessarily so, and while in some instances these rings detract from the aesthetic appearance of the dial, it is not always the case. This 10ins. dial is very attractive with its snake minute hand.

The clock by William Coward, which is shown in Plates 280-282, is of interest on account of the fact that much of the work in it has an affinity with that of Thomas Tompion. A great many of the component parts are shaped in a similar way to those of Tompion but lack the refinement and finish of Tompion's work. This is particularly true of the feet of the hammer, counter and maintaining power springs, the bell stand, the hammer head and stem, the latter being heavier than Tompion would have made it. The way in which the crutch is attached to the arbor and the type of bevelling on the bridge are all reminiscent of Tompion's work as are the main wheel click springs and the shape of the aperture in the back plate for the pallets. The hour hand is certainly of a pattern extensively used by Tompion. The single screw back cock is, however, more in the style of John Fromanteel as is the method of operating the shutters as can be seen in Plate 282.

Plate 280. *A partially dismantled eight-day longcase clock movement by William Coward.*

Plate 281. The dial and hands of the clock in Plate 280.

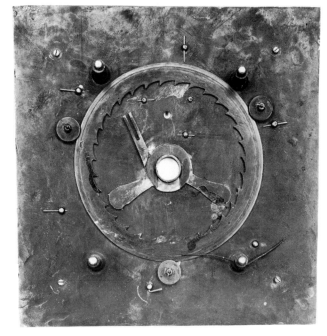

Plate 282. The back of the dial of the clock in Plate 280.

A clock made in Ashford in Kent by Richard Greenhill is shown in Plates 283-286. The design of both the dial and the case of this clock (Plates 347-348) suggest that it is a provincial attempt to reproduce the London work of about 1680 at least a decade later. The movement is however the work of a lantern clock maker. The plates are quite large, it has an enormous bell stand and counter spring and the hammer and lifting arbors are square. Only the escape wheel has a collet, the other wheels being shouldered on to the pinion arbors. In Plate 285 can be seen the twenty-four hour wheel, the back of which still has the scribe marks from the dividing plate for the teeth. The shape of the back cock is also reminiscent of that on a lantern clock although fitted the reverse way up. The barrels were cast in halves and brazed or soldered up. The hands are well executed but the oval boss suggests provincial origin. The maintaining power is a replacement. When this clock was made, Ashford would have been a very small market town and more than fifty miles from the specialist craftsmen of London, yet one is inclined to see in the workmanship of the dial in particular a skill which would have had little chance of developing in an agricultural community.

Plate 283. *The under dial work of an eight-day longcase clock by Richard Greenhill of Ashford, which can be seen in its case in Plates 347-348.*

Plate 284. *The back plate of the clock in Plate 283.*

212

Plate 285. The partly dismantled movement of the clock in Plate 283.

Plate 286. The engraved dial of the clock in Plate 283.

213

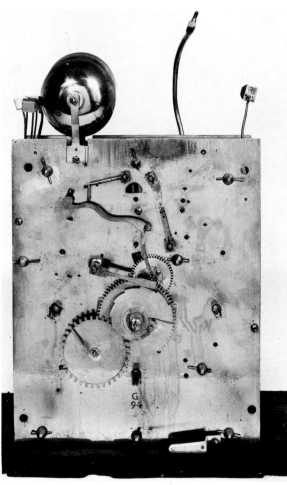

Plate 287. *The under dial work of a three-train eight-day longcase clock by Christopher Gould, which can be seen in its case in Plate 398-399.*

Plate 288. *A view of part of the movement of the clock in Plate 287.*

In Plate 287 may be seen the front plate of a three-train grande sonnerie longcase clock by Christopher Gould, shown in its case in Plates 398-399. The minute wheel cock which has been removed, can be seen on the seat board and the levers on the front plate are seen more clearly. The quarter train has been planted on the left of the movement and the hour striking train on the right. This has the advantage with intermediate wheels and pinions for the hammers can be drawn outwards. Three of the lifting pins in the minute wheel are visible in the photograph and these operate the lifting piece. Warning is obtained by a piece riveted to the end of the lifting piece passing through a slot in the plate. The lifting piece also lifts the 'L' shaped lever above it which is squared on to the quarter rack hook arbor. The quarter snail is behind the minute wheel. Squared on to the front end of this arbor is the lever seen just above the minute wheel. This has at its end a spring-loaded piece which will pass the lever above it when moving to the left, but will move it to the right when moving in that direction in the last gather.

The arbor on which this last lever is squared is the hour rack hook arbor, seen in Plate 288. By moving to the right, this unlocks the hour rack which is pivoted to the left of the minute wheel and the rack arm can be seen squared on to the end of the arbor. The pin which stops on the snail is fixed into the long thin spring screwed to the front of the rack arm. This permits the end of the pin to ride over the snail in the event of a malfunction and will not stop the clock as a rigidly fixed pin would.

The strike/silent mechanism is operated from the dial. It will be seen that the minute wheel cock, which has been removed, has a spring screwed to it which will press on the end of the minute wheel pinion and force it back so that the lifting pins will miss the lifting piece, thus effectively silencing the clock. There is a double-ended lever pivoted behind the front plate on the screw seen just below the semi-circular aperture. This has at its lower end an inclined plane which will carry the minute wheel pinion forwards for the pins to engage the lifting piece. It is moved from the dial by a piece inserted in a fork at its upper end.

Ahasuerus Fromanteel claimed, in his advertisement in 1658, that he was able to make clocks that would go for six months or a year with one winding and yet none are known to have been successfully made by him although that described in Chapter XI may have been one of his attempts. It would appear that it was not until a good deal later that this duration was achieved and not until towards the end of the century that such clocks were made to any extent. Those which Thomas Tompion made to the order of Sir Jonas More for Flamstead's new observatory at Greenwich in 1676, were probably the first satisfactory timekeepers to be made which went for a whole year (Plate 289). Tompion achieved this very largely by giving the movements long pendulums swinging at two seconds intervals and thus doubling the duration which the train would have had if fitted with the normal pendulum length of one second. Both of these timepieces have since been altered to take a one second pendulum.

The clockmaker, and Knibb in particular, had no difficulty in making clocks which went for one month and even clocks of three months' duration could be made by using intermediate pinions of eight leaves instead of the more normal twelve or fourteen and by having heavier weights. To obtain a duration of six months or a year, two intermediate wheels and pinions were required and the upper part of the train had to be much lighter. The illustration in Plate 290 shows the lightness of all the work above the first intermediate wheel and pinion, and one can see that all above the centre pinion has been shortened by the insertion of an internal cock. It is

Plate 289. *The movement of a year timepiece made for the observatory in Greenwich in 1676 by Tompion.*

Plate 290. *The side view of a six month longcase timepiece by Daniel Quare, seen in its case in Plate 390.*

Plate 291. The side view of a year longcase timepiece by Daniel Quare, seen in its case in Plates 407-408.

very important that these arbors should not be long for it is very difficult to turn long thin arbors true, and perfect poise of each wheel is essential to reduce the moment of inertia to a minimum. The greatest degree of stability has been assured by the sturdiness of the internal cock.

This timepiece is a good example of Daniel Quare's best work. The pallet arbor has had a boss turned on the back end beyond which it is squared. The crutch is fashioned from a single piece of steel, the upper part being finished as a short tube into which the squared arbor fits and is secured by cross pinning. The length of this tube is sufficient to prevent any play developing.

A year timepiece by Quare is shown in Plate 291. This also has two intermediate wheels and pinions and again the upper parts are shortened, in this case by the use of a subframe on the back plate, as were the timepieces made by Tompion for Flamstead. Here, however, the centre pinion is shortened but not the pallet arbor. It will be seen also that the plates are of much heavier gauge metal than the former timepiece and that the pillars are more robust. Also that, unlike the former, the motionwork has a bridge and the minute wheel is cocked. Neither of these timepieces has a seconds hand.

Plate 292. *The side view of a year calendar and equation longcase timepiece by Daniel Quare.*

Plate 293. *The year timepiece in Plate 292 in its case. (Further views of the case are shown in Colour Plate 15, page 283, and Plates 409-411.)*

Plates 292-293 illustrate another Quare year timepiece which is basically very similar to the last with only minor variations but with the addition of a seconds hand and a remote dial placed in the long door, indicating the date and the equation of time. This movement has the same heavy plates and sturdy pillars, the subframe and the shortened centre pinion. Differences are that the first intermediate wheel is riveted to its pinion head and that the pallets have a long neck, which, by increasing the distance between the centres of the escape wheel and pallet arbors, reduces the arc of swing of the pendulum without loss of efficiency. The calendar and equation dial is operated by a wheel mounted on the front plate carrying a pinion which works in a contrate wheel at the upper end of the rod which extends downwards to the motionwork of the calendar dial where there is a worm working in a worm wheel. There is a wheel making one revolution a year, the arbor of which carries on its front end the calendar pointer and on the other end the equation kidney. The calendar is engraved round the outer edge of the dial, within which, in the upper half, are engraved thirty minute divisions. The figure 0 is in the centre and on either side the minutes 5, 10 and 15 are numbered. Between these figures are engraved the words SUN TOO SLOW on the left hand side and SUN TOO FAST on the right. The equation hand, in the form of a sunburst with a pointer, is controlled by the equation kidney. It will be seen that the hour and minute hands are very elaborate and that the minute hand is counterpoised, which is normal on long duration clocks. The dial corners on this timepiece appear to be quite unique. The engraved rings to be seen on the pendulum bob should be noted for they are a feature of Quare's clocks.

Plate 294. *The dial of a year longcase timepiece by Edmund Wright. The hand is a replacement. (The clock in its case is shown in Plate 401.)*

There is no doubt that the finest of the year longcase timepieces are those made by Thomas Tompion. There are two in the Royal Collection and these are described in R.W. Symonds' book on Tompion.[1] One of these has many similarities to that which we illustrate in Plates 295-298. This clock was for more than two centuries at Drayton House. In these year timepieces, Tompion has very sensibly reversed the layout of the train, planting the barrel arbor at the top of the movement.

This is an elaborate calendar and equation timepiece and indicates, in addition to the time, the day of the week with its appropriate god in the central zone, while above the dial, but not visible when the clock is in its case (Plates 405-406), the day of the month and the day in the zodiac. Plate 295 shows the dial which has a twenty-four hour chapter ring engraved for the minute hand to make one revolution in two hours. This ring shows "Equal time" or, as we would say, Greenwich mean time. Outside this ring is another narrower ring which, like the main ring, is engraved with minutes for two hours, and is marked "Apparẽt time". This by moving forwards and backwards throughout the year will indicate the time by the sun. Thus, the illustration shows the dial indicating mean time as 9.38½ p.m. and solar time as 9.50½, showing that on October 5th mean time is indicated as twelve minutes behind the sun.

A view of the right hand side of the movement is given in Plate 297. This shows the massive construction of the barrel, main wheel, first intermediate wheel and pinion and the plates in which they run, which are high up and at the rear. There is nothing further between these plates except the bolt arbor for the maintaining power. These plates are so shaped that they will sit on to metal plates on the ends of the high sides of the case and the front plate extends downwards to carry the rest of the movement on cocks. In this low forward position is the escapement with the pallets engaging the underside of the escape wheel and there is an extremely long crutch reaching to the top of the long door.

With the calendar situated in the top of the dial, the take-off rod extends upwards behind the dial with a single lead worm at its top end. This worm engages a wheel, the arbor of which carries the calendar disc and the equation kidney. This kidney has a slot running round its outside edge in which a roller rides which is at the top end of a rod having at its lower end a rack. This rack engages a wheel which rotates the apparent time ring of the dial forwards or backwards according to the position of the roller on the kidney. The pendulum bob is made in two parts and the bob is backed by a plate engraved in degrees from a centre line and with two adjustable markers to enable the arc of swing to be checked.

The reputation of the London clockmakers is justly based on their high quality productions, and yet most of them, even the more famous, also made clocks of lesser importance. These were in the main weight-driven clocks of short duration, made in accordance with the tradition of past decades. That is to say, the construction was based largely on that of the lantern clock, although not necessarily with all the decorative features associated with that type, such as pillars and finials. The clock by Andrew Prime which is illustrated in Plates 299-301 is a fairly early example but since it has a fully developed anchor escapement it cannot have been made much before 1675. Like the pre-pendulum clocks it is constructed with a top and bottom plate with four corner posts or pillars. Between these plates are mounted three narrow strips of brass, one centrally at the front, another towards the back and the third

---

1.   R.W. Symonds, *Thomas Tompion, his Life and Work*, London, 1951.

Plate 295. *The calendar and equation dial of the year longcase timepiece by Thomas Tompion, formerly in Drayton House and now in the Fitzwilliam Museum, Cambridge.*

Fitzwilliam Museum, Cambridge

Plate 296. *The calendar timepiece in Plate 295 in its case. Further views of the case are in Plates 405-406.*

Plate 297. *A view of the right hand side of the movement in Plate 295.*

Plate 298. *A view of the left hand side of the movement in Plate 295.*

Plate 299. *The dial and hand of a posted frame thirty-hour weight clock by Andrew Prime.*

Plate 300. The right hand side of the clock in Plate 299.

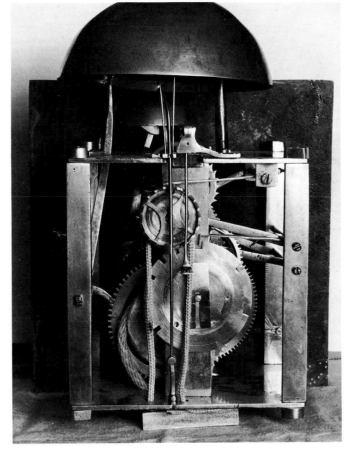

Plate 301. The back of the clock in Plate 299.

Plate 302. The dial and hand of a posted frame thirty-hour weight clock by Edward Clement. (The case is in Plate 734.)

between them. The going train is mounted between the front and middle strips and the striking train between the middle and back strips. The power on each train is provided by a weight of about five or six pounds suspended on a line or rope of woven cotton, passing over a spiked pulley which is free to rotate on its arbor to enable the weight to be pulled up. It has a spring-operated stop working on the arms of the main wheel of the train fixed to the arbor to provide the driving power to the train. Separate weights for each train were necessary in pre-pendulum times as regulation was done by varying the driving weight. Since this clock has a long pendulum, which is adjustable in length, two weights were not necessary. It has to be wound twice a day as the duration is not much more than twelve hours. It has an alarm mechanism and indicates the half-hours on a small bell by a single blow. Like most short duration weight clocks, it only has one hand but a very attractive dial.

A somewhat similar posted movement is shown in Plates 302-304. It is a typical example of the more humble majority of thirty-hour clocks with long pendulums. Since with these pendulums regulation is not achieved by altering the weight, both going and striking trains can be driven by one weight if it is increased to about ten pounds and this done by the use of an endless rope drive with the weight on one loop of the rope and a small lead ring of about half a pound weight on the other to keep it in tension and in contact with the pulley spikes.

Even Tompion was not above producing such clocks and that illustrated in Plates 305-306 is one example. He has used a lantern clock frame which has never been drilled for frets or for a suspension hoop and spurs, nor has there ever been a finial on the top. The turning of the pillars and finials is good but not fine and the making

226

Plate 303. The right hand side of the clock in Plate 302.

Plate 304. The back of the clock in Plate 302.

Plate 305. *The dial and hand of a posted frame thirty-hour weight clock by Thomas Tompion.*

Plate 306. *The side view of the clock in Plate 305.*

is generally good. The dial is quite beautiful with engraving of excellent quality, as are the corner mounts.

The clock by Christopher Gould shown in Plates 307-309 is also a thirty-hour clock but in this case the trains are set between plates as were many of the later short duration clocks. This one is quite exceptional in that it has quarter repeating work on four bells and, while most of the short duration clocks are housed in quite modest cases, this one is in an exquisite miniature longcase (Plate 402). The movement also is of high quality and sturdily made. It was evidently made for a Spanish client for the 7½ ins. dial has "Suona" and "Non suona" engraved by the strike/silent lever. All the engraving is of the highest quality and the gilding on the dial plate and the corners is intact.

The design of longcase clock dials develops considerably during the last three decades of the seventeenth century, increasing in size from 9 ins. or 10 ins. square to 11 ins. and then 12 ins. Their features also change. The chapter rings, which in earlier

Plate 307. The dial and hands of a plated thirty-hour repeating weight clock by Christopher Gould.

Plate 308. The repeating side of the clock in Plate 307.

Plate 309. The striking side of the clock in Plate 307.

years were quite narrow, are during this period wider and by the end of the period much wider. It may be useful to define the various rings which are normally found on a chapter ring. There may be five of these, an inner ring indicating the quarter hours, a wider one containing the chapters, beyond this a ring with the minute divisions, then the minute numerals and on the outside an outer ring. As will be seen in Plates 310 and 311, not all dials have five rings.

These two dials which are on clocks by different makers, are very similar to each other and bear many signs of having been made in the same workshop. They were made about 1680. For instance, the fleur-de-lis half-hour marks terminate in heavy black dots with similar dots in the minute rings and these contain the minute numerals at five minute intervals as well as the minute divisions. The two dials are not, however, identical and it will be seen that the Henry Jones example is not engraved with a minute mark where the single figure five is engraved. This is quite

Plate 310. A 10 ins. dial of a striking clock by Henry Jones. Circa 1680.

Plate 311. A 10 ins. dial of a striking clock by William Clement. Circa 1680.

Plate 313. The 10 ins. dial of a striking clock by Thomas Tompion. Circa 1680.

Plate 312. A 10 ins. dial of a striking clock by Thomas Tompion. Circa 1680.

normal practice, but on the Clement dial there is a minute mark and the figure five has been engraved beside it. Occasionally a dial may be found which has had the figure superimposed over the minute mark.

The date apertures in both dials are strictly rectangular and quite plain with narrow bevels. Although they are on clocks by different makers, both dials have features associated with Henry Jones, such as the curled ends of the figures 3 and 5 and also the black dots. Being individually engraved they also differ in other respects such as the signatures, one of which is in square script, the other is sloping.

The two dials on clocks by Tompion in Plates 312 and 313 are almost as early as those in Plates 310 and 311 but in these instances the minute numerals are outside the minute circle which is narrower than in the previous examples. The engraving of the numerals is typical of Tompion's style with the abbreviated curl of the figures 3 and 5 and the triple arrow half-hour decorations. There are no half-quarter marks in the minute circle. It will be seen that the hour hands are not identical. The minute hand in Plate 312 is a typical Tompion hand but that in the other illustration is not. The 'S' scroll at the centre boss is longer than usual and the pointer is on a radius of the circle at its outward end. The more correct hand in Plate 312 has the scroll extending past the foot of the pointer. Also, it is not Tompion's practice to drill recesses in the scroll ends as has been done in Plate 313. This is the kind of error that some restorers make, the over ornamentation of their work. Tompion made his seconds hands with a hole in the centre of the boss and they had a split brass tube silver soldered to the back to fit on to the seconds pinion end protruding through the dial. On these dials we also see the slightly different spandrel mounts used by Tompion. The wings are

Plate 314. The 10 ins. dial of a striking clock by Henry Jones. Circa 1680-85.

bent downwards to almost touch the chapter ring as do the scrolls. Sometimes one can see on the back of these corners where they have been cut to facilitate bending and have been soldered up.

The date apertures in the dials have a wider bevel. It was Tompion's custom to drill small holes in the date ring between each date into which a pin could be inserted when the date needed to be altered. In some instances he filed a little nick in the bevel to give better access to these holes. Both of these dials have the wheat-ear engraved band round the edge with the signature in a panel at the bottom. In at least one instance Tompion used the little central feature at the top for stamping the clock number and on his clock No. 49, which has a similar dial, the number is stamped across the signature.

Another dial by Henry Jones is shown in Plate 314 and it has features which are early and corner mounts which are often mistakenly regarded as late. The hour hand is similar although heavier than that in Plate 310 but the minute hand is of an entirely new design.

The spandrel corner mounts of this design were used much earlier than is generally realised, certainly in the '70s, but many of these have been removed largely because early writers on the subject, notably Cescinsky and Webster,[2] only refer to and illustrate dials with the small angel corners and narrow chapter rings, as early dials.

---

2.   Cescinsky and Webster, *English Domestic Clocks,* 1914, reprinted 1976.

The larger foliated corners are quoted as belonging to the latter years of the century. Most of the dials which have had the corners changed can, however, be identified by the existence of filled or unused holes in the dial plate. The design may indeed have existed long before the '70s for, if one glances at the Fromanteel clock in Plate 193, one will see the feature which is at the apex of the corner of the Henry Jones dial used as a frieze mount, while the small corner mounts on the even earlier Fromanteel clock in Plate 186, which appear to be original, consist of this same feature plus the scrolls below it. This cannot be a coincidence, either the design of these early mounts was incorporated into the later corner or the design was in existence complete quite early. It is however true that this type of corner was more frequently used towards the end of the century and often on dials which really were too small for them and in some cases they overhang the edge of the dial plate.

The dial in Plate 315 is an example of about 1690, it is a 10 ins. dial with the foliated corners and is signed by Daniel Quare. The workmanship of the movement however suggests that it was not a clock made in Quare's workshop but probably by John Wise.

Plate 315. *The dial of a striking clock with alarm by Daniel Quare. Circa 1690.*

The dial in Plate 316 belongs to the last decade of the century and shows the foliated corner mount used on a much larger dial where it is really too small. It is on a three month clock by Joseph Saer and it is difficult to imagine a dial with more decoration. It has ringed winding holes, engraved banding round the edge and inside the chapter ring, as well as decoration surrounding the calendar apertures.

The next dial illustrated (Plate 317) is a 12 ins. dial by Quare which belongs to the early years of the eighteenth century and it has corners of a new design. It has been said that they were designed to commemorate the accession to the throne of Queen Anne. Whether or not this is so, they began to be used at about that time and particularly by Quare. On this dial we see the wider chapter ring of the period with half-quarter marks in the numeral ring and engraving on the dial plate between the corners. The signature is on the chapter ring.

Plate 316. *The elaborate calendar dial of a clock by Joseph Saer. Circa 1690-95.*
Antiquarian Horological Society

Plate 317. *The dial of a striking clock by Daniel Quare. Circa 1705.*

236

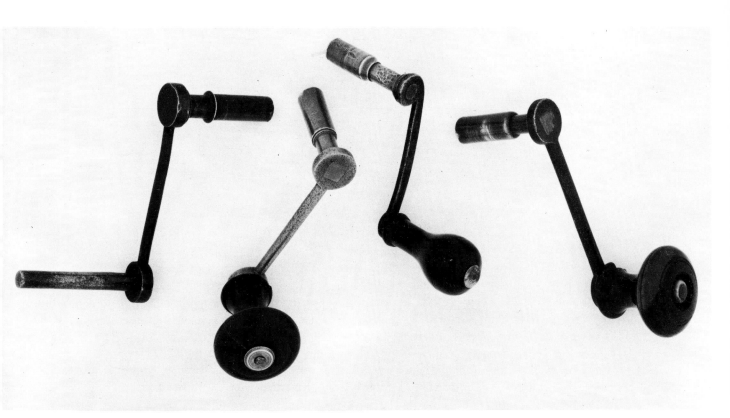

Plate 318. *Seventeenth century crank winding keys. The simple pear-shaped handles are the earliest, later they become more shapely.*

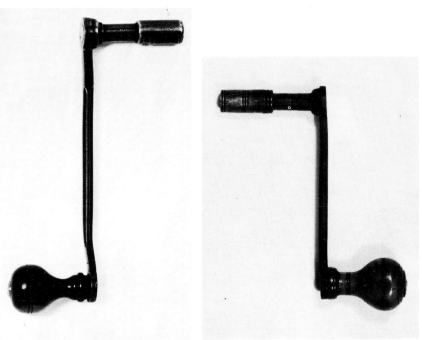

Chapter VII
Later Longcases

We have referred to the first twelve or so years of the domestic pendulum clock case as the 'architectural' period; but it is only really with regard to the cases for spring clocks that we can say that the architectural style was discarded at the end of that period. In the years that followed, the design of the longcase continued very largely as before, while that of the spring clock case very rapidly changed. It is very easy to discern the influence of the principles of classical architecture being followed in the design of longcases almost throughout the eighteenth century. There were many reasons for the changes which took place. Fashions were rapidly changing in the furnishing of mansions following the restoration of the monarchy, the cabinet-makers were learning new skills, new woods were being introduced and new ways of exploiting their potential being tried.

Probably the most obvious change which we notice was that in the size of the clock, for the dial in the '70s was usually 10 ins. square. This larger clock was only partly due to the advent of the anchor escapement, which required more space within the trunk for it to swing, for we see that the spring clocks were being made much larger at the same time. In spite of the larger size, the general design of the longcase was little changed. Consider, for instance, the clock by Hilkiah Bedford shown in Plates 319-320 and compare it with that in Plate 225. The general outline is the same, but somewhat simplified since the more decorative walnut veneer renders the addition of panels to the long door unnecessary. The use of the softer wood also required the elimination of the finer details from some of the mouldings. These nevertheless remain basically as before, particularly that round the long door. There are, however, two innovations, one being the glazed aperture in the door for viewing the pendulum bob. This feature is usually octagonal at this early period. The other new feature is the twist columns which were introduced about 1670 and remained popular for most of the remainder of the century.

Similar clocks, but which have had the frieze to the trunk omitted, may be seen in Plate 325 and Plates 321-322, which is veneered with lignum vitae. Here it will be seen that the veneers used on many parts have been cut at an acute angle from small limbs in order to obtain the greatest effect from an otherwise straight-grained wood. It was, of course, possible to include the fine detail in the mouldings with this very hard wood but great difficulty was found in turning it for twisted columns. There is no applied ornamentation on this case. It will be seen from the illustrations that a number of cases were made in the '70s which still had the gable-end pediment. In the illustration of the clock in Plates 323-324 quarter columns can be seen at the back of the hood. This became common practice. During the previous decade the back columns were normally half columns.

Plate 320. *The upper part of the clock in Plate 319. The mounts are replacements.*

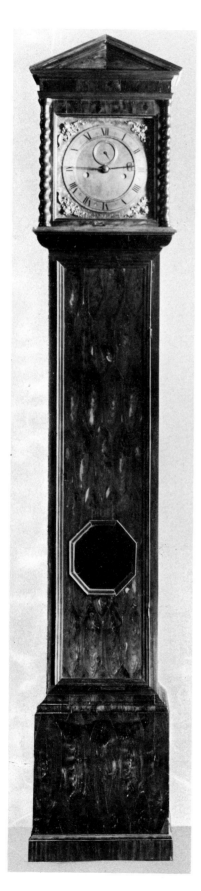

Plate 321. *Longcase veneered with lignum vitae for a clock by Edward East with a one second pendulum. Circa 1670-73. The skirting is a later addition.*

Plate 322. *Detail of the arrangement of the veneers on the long door of the case in Plate 321, showing the conventional large octagonal pendulum aperture and the early type of moulding round the door.*

Plate 323. The upper part of a longcase veneered with walnut for an anonymous striking clock. Circa 1670-75. The mounts are replacements.

Plate 324. The side view of the case in Plate 323.

It is unusual to find longcases at this period without columns at all but one is shown in Plate 326. The case is very like those of the previous decade in every respect except that now ebony is not used but ebonised pearwood.

While the case makers were using the hard woods such as ebony, lignum vitae and cocus (Plate 327), they would have had very few problems in obtaining a good finish to their work. These woods, if well cleaned up, can be very satisfactorily polished by applications of wax, while the softer woods now being used like olivewood and more particularly, walnut, require very different treatment in order to fill the grain and satisfactorily protect the surface with a hard skin. This now had to be done with applications of varnish. Fortunately Stalker and Parker, in 1688, left us an account of how this was done. They describe the method of making and applying "Seed-Lacc-varnish" as follows:[1]

"Take one gallon of good Spirit, and put it in as wide-mouthed a bottle as you can procure; for when you shall afterwards strain your varnish, the Gums in a narrow-mouthed bottle may stick together, and clog the mouth, for that it will be no easye task to separate or get them out. To your Spirits add one pound and a half of the best Seed-Lacc; let it stand for the space of 24 hours, or longer, for the Gum will be the better disolved: observe to shake it well, and often, to keep the Gums from clogging or caking together. When it hath stood its time, take another bottle of the same bigness, or as many quart-ones as will contain your varnish; and your strainer of flannell made as aforesaid in this book, fasten it to a tenter-hook against a wall, or some other place convenient for straining it, in such a posture, that the end of your strainer may almost touch the bottom of your Tin-tunnel, which is supposed to be fixed in the mouth of your empty bottle, on purpose to receive your strained varnish. Then shake your varnish well together, and pour or decant into your strainer as much as conveniently it will hold, only be sure to leave room for your hand, with which you must squeeze out the varnish; and when the bag by so doing is almost drawn dry, repeat it till your strainer being almost full of dregs of the Gums, shall (The moisture being all pressed out) require to be discharged of them. Which faces or dregs are of no use, unless it be to burn, or fire your chimney. This operation must be continued, till all your varnish is after this manner strained; which done, commit it to your bottles close stopt, and let it remain undisturbed for two or three days: then into another clean empty bottle pour off very gently the top of your varnish, so long as you perceive it to run very clear, and no longer; for as soon as you observe it to come thick, and muddy, you must by all means desist; and again give it time to rest and settle, which 'twill do in a day or two; after which time you may attempt to draw off more of your varnish, and having so done you may lay it up, till your art & work shall call for its assistance."

These writers went on further to describe the application of this varnish to olive-wood:

"To begin with Olivewood which for Tables, Stands, Cabinets, &c, has been highly in request amongst us; that which is cleanly workt off, void of flaws, cracks, and asperities is a fit subject for our skill to be exercised in. Having rushed it all over diligently, set it by a weak fire, or some place where it may receive heat; and in this warm condition, wash it over ten or twelve times with Seed-Lacc-varnish, that remained after you had poured off the top for better use, with a pencil (brush) proportioned to the bigness of your table or stand or the like; let it thoroughly dry between every wash: and if any wroughness come in sight, rush 'em off as fast as you meet with them. After all this, welcom it with your rush until 'tis smooth, and when very dry annoint it six several times with the top or finest part of aforesaid Seed-Lacc-varnish. After three days standing call for Tripolee scraped with a knife; and with a cloth, dipt first in water, then in

1.   John Stalker and George Parker, *A Treatise of Japaning and Varnishing*, Oxford, 1688.

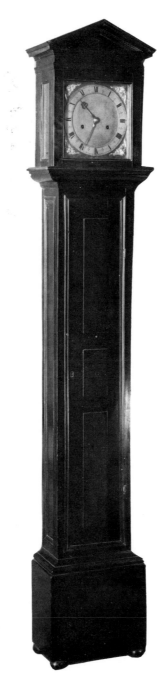

Plate 325. *Longcase veneered with walnut for a clock by Henry Jones, with most of the mouldings made in a straight grain wood and the early moulding round the long door. Circa 1670-75. The skirting is a later addition.* R.A. Lee

Plate 326. *Longcase veneered with pearwood, stained and polished black, for a clock by Joseph Knibb, with early type panelling on sides of the trunk and the door. Circa 1670-73.*

Plate 327. *Miniature longcase veneered with cocus wood for a clock by Edward East, the long door and base with geometric panels of oyster pieces and with the early style of moulding round the door. Circa 1670-73.*

powdered Tripolee, polish and rub it till it acquire a smoothness and gloss: but be circumspect and shie of rubbing too much, which will fret and wear off the varnish that cannot easily be repaired: if when you have laboured for some time, you use a rag often wetted, without Tripolee, you will obtain a better gloss. Then wipe of your Tripolee with a sponge full of water, the water with a dry rag: grease it with Lamblack and oyl all over; wipe off that with a cloth, and clear it up with another ... If after all this pains your work look dull, and your varnish misty, which polishing before it is dry, and damp weather will effect; give it a slight polish, clear it up, and that will restore its pristine beauty....

"... I ... desire you to observe the same method exactly for varnishing Walnut, ... also for all sorts of wood, that are of a close, smooth grain such as Yew, Box, the Lime-tree and Pear-tree &c."

Neither walnut nor olivewood is as suitable for the making of fine scratch mouldings as is ebony or pearwood. The consequence of this is that cases veneered entirely with these former woods have less detail in their mouldings and this may have been one of the reasons for the continuing use of ebony and ebonised pearwood for some of the mouldings on cases veneered with olivewood. We have seen that on the early walnut veneered longcase in Plates 319-320 the case maker has endeavoured to use the traditional mouldings. One can also see that these have been made with the grain of the wood running lengthways. This was usual at this period and will be seen on other clocks illustrated (Plate 325). It was soon realised however that both walnut and olivewood would show their grain to best advantage on mouldings made cross-grain. It is not practical to use a scratch on cross-grain wood nor indeed are mouldings with any fine detail possible as a rule. The result was, therefore, that new or at least very much modified profiles had to be used which eliminated much of the detail. We find that the new mouldings tend to be more prominently convex and this is particularly seen in the moulding round the door which becomes a simple shallow convex. This moulding in particular, once adopted, remained in use not only on walnut and olivewood cases, but also on black ones for the remainder of the century.

The cases made at this time with mouldings of straight grain walnut were also veneered with fairly plainly figured wood but the cabinetmakers were fast learning how to select and cut their veneers and also learning the art of matching and quartering their veneers in such a way as to get the best decorative results.

In Plates 330 and 331 we see two longcase timepieces which stand in the Library of St. Andrews University and since they are known to have been purchased from Joseph Knibb fairly certainly in 1673[2] they identify other products of that period. They are fortunately in good original condition and are probably the only pair of clocks still in their original ownership. They are not truly domestic timepieces, having been supplied for the purposes of the University's observatory and it is probably for this reason that the hoods have no side windows. Each hood is finished not with a gable-end pediment but a carved pediment, usually today referred to as a carved cresting, which is a good example of the earliest type. It consists of a carved repeat of the top member of the cornice moulding as a pair of introverted scrolls terminating in acanthus paterae from which hang a swag of acanthus husks. There is a shell centrepiece and other leaves. Further examples of this cresting may be seen in

2. *St. Andrews University Library, an Illustrated Guide*, 1948.

Colour Plate 10.
Miniature longcase
(only 5 ft. 6 ins. tall)
for a clock by Joseph
Knibb. It is veneered
with olivewood with
oyster pieces and small
panels of marquetry.
The mouldings on the
entablature to the hood
are not strictly architec-
tural. Circa 1680. The
skirting round the base
is a later addition.

Colour Plate 11. A
longcase for a striking
clock by Joseph Knibb.
It is veneered with
olivewood with oyster
pieces as background to
the marquetry panels
which have stained bone
leaves. Circa 1680.
(Also shown in Plate
356.)

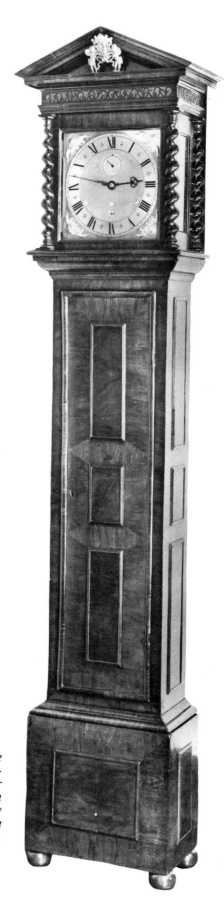

Plate 328. Longcase veneered with pearwood, stained and polished black, for a clock by Edward East. Circa 1670-75. The skirting is a later addition.

Plate 329. Longcase veneered with an unidentified hard brown wood, for a clock by John Fromanteel with an early fret in the frieze. Circa 1675.

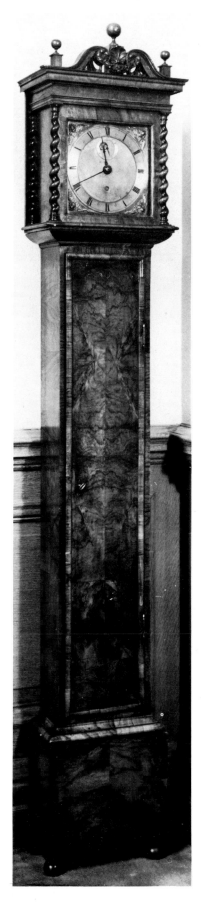

Plate 330. Longcase veneered with walnut for a timepiece movement by Joseph Knibb, with cross-banded mouldings and the earliest type of carved cresting. One of a pair with that in Plate 331. 1673. (The movement is shown in Plate 258.)
University of St. Andrews

Plate 331. Longcase veneered with walnut for a timepiece movement by Joseph Knibb, with cross-banded mouldings and the earliest type of carved cresting. One of a pair with that in Plate 330. 1672. (The movement is shown in Plate 259.)

Plate 332. The carved cresting of a longcase veneered with walnut. Circa 1675-80.

Plates 332 and 344. The better use of matched veneers is also seen in these cases.

During the early years of these somewhat larger cases, the cases were constructed very much as they had been for the earlier narrow cases. Oak was still the standard wood for most of the carcases. It is of interest to note however that the man who was making the longcases for Joseph Knibb, appears to have obtained a log of a different wood from which he made a number of cases. This has been identified as Coriniana or Jaquitiba Rosa.[3] It proved a very suitable wood but does not appear to have been used again.

The practice of constructing the fronts and sides of the hoods of half-lapped frames was continued by most makers and in Plate 335 will be seen the foundation construction of a hood of this period. This method of constructing the hood was continued by the best makers right into the next century but some of the lesser makers towards the end of the seventeenth century made the hood sides all in one piece and then usually the windows were much shorter. In these instances, the front was framed up on the sides with butt joints. The columns were usually slender twists, right-handed and not paired. Some of the columns had Corinthian capitals and bases in fire-gilt brass, but these were soon superseded by plain wood capitals and bases turned as an integral part of the column, with the addition of thin square tablets above and below. The fact that these tablets gradually ceased to be included by most makers as the century passed, is a sign, together with the simplified hood construction, of a slight lowering of standards. It is not possible to assign these capitals and bases to any of the classical orders.

The clock movements in these larger cases are not raised up on wood blocks as formerly for the sides of the cases are extended so that the seat board may be in the

---

3.   Ronald A. Lee, *The Knibb Family, Clockmakers,* Byfleet, 1963.

Plate 333. Longcase veneered with ebony for a clock by Joseph Knibb with raised panels on the door and sunk panels on the sides with small raised panels. Circa 1672-75. (The dial is described on p.208.)

Plate 334. Detail of the hood of the clock in Plate 333 showing the long side windows of the period and carved cresting on the sides.

249

Plate 335. The inside of the hood of the longcase clock described in Chapter XI showing the construction (the clock is illustrated in Plates 737-743).

correct position to take the clock. Original seat boards are always made the full depth of the case and are cut away for the lines and the pendulum. Both the sides of the case and the back board extend right to the bottom, thus providing a firm foundation upon which to construct the base. It is today fairly rare to find a longcase which has survived complete to the very bottom. Usually, at the very least, the bun feet have been destroyed and often the lower part of the carcase has either been cut away or has fallen to pieces. An illustration which shows the normal base construction is seen in Plate 338. It is the case of a Knibb clock shown in Plates 336-338 which has survived intact except for the feet, the holes for which are clearly visible. The soundness of the construction is well demonstrated here. The base itself is usually built up of pine, with the grain running horizontally.

The long doors are normally clamped at each end in order to keep them flat and it is quite surprising that one can find many of these clamps which have remained secure through three hundred years, in spite of the fact that they are merely glued on. However, unfortunately a great many of these glued joints have broken through the years, with the result that the veneered surface of the door has, at best, become uneven and in many cases suffered even worse damage. This is particularly so with regard to marquetry cases where pieces of the marquetry have often fallen out. Not all longcases have apertures cut in the long door through which to view the pendulum oscillating. When they do, in the early period the aperture is fairly large, often octagonal in shape (Plate 328), although a few are circular (Plates 344 and 358). The majority later in the century have an overlaid retaining moulding of convex section round them to match that round the door. A number of the earliest have

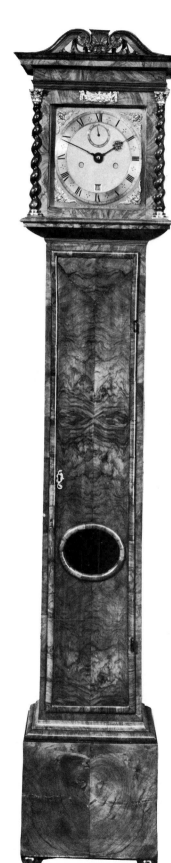

Plate 337. The upper part of the clock in Plate 336.

Plate 336. Longcase veneered with walnut for a clock by Joseph Knibb with bun feet replaced. Circa 1675. R.A. Lee

Plate 338. The underneath of the case shown in Plate 336, showing the method of constructing the base of longcases at this period and the holes for the pins of the bun feet.

251

Plate 339. The hood of a longcase veneered with olivewood, with olivewood and ebonised pearwood mouldings, the latter with painted decoration, with a three-train movement by John Knibb. Circa 1680.

a little quadrant moulding inserted which is similar to that which surrounds the glazed apertures in the hoods. Clear glass was used in the pendulum apertures, not the roundel glasses which are often seen. These were not introduced until much later.

In the earlier narrow longcases, it was just the thickness of the carcase sides which provided the framework around the long door. Now that the cases are being made larger, most features are being made proportionately larger and soon this framework is increased in width by the addition of a strip of oak about 2 ins. deep inside the trunk, which on most cases is chamfered along the back edge, but on some cases made for Tompion, there is a concave moulding worked on the edge.

Olivewood was probably the most popular wood to be used for the veneering of longcases in the period between 1675 and 1690 and during that time some of the most attractive cases were produced. It was almost always used in conjunction with some black mouldings. It was the finer mouldings in particular which were made black because of the unsuitability of olivewood for fine detail. This may not have been the only reason for using black however for the effect of these black mouldings against the rich colouring of the olive is sufficient. The broken ogee moulding above the base, for instance, which consists of both a convex and a concave member, is made with one member in olivewood and the other in ebonised pearwood. This juxta-position of the two woods occurs also in the cornice and elsewhere. In a few cases the severity of the black has been relieved by the addition of painted decoration, an example of which is seen in Plate 339, which is well preserved. It may well be that such decoration was more popular than we can tell today, since it would be easily rubbed off or obscured by successive layers of varnish.

The most distinctive feature of the olivewood cases is without doubt the use of 'olive oysters'. These are made by cutting the veneers across fairly small limbs of the wood so as to show the annular rings. When cut at a slight angle the rings produce figuring similar to that on oyster shells, hence the name given to these pieces. They are usually fitted together in geometric patterns within panels and framed with either straight grain or crossgrain olivewood or by ebony stringing. In a few cases there is no further decoration than just the oyster-pieces themselves as for example the clock in Plate 344.

Decorative woods were at no time used for clock cases to the exclusion of black and during the period we are discussing now there were a number of ebony and ebonised pearwood longcases made, the design of which differed very little from those made a decade earlier, except that the size was larger. In these cases it is quite normal for the long door to be relieved by the addition of raised veneer panels. Indeed this type of case was made right to the end of the century, although at that time they were usually made of pearwood and ebonised. Some of these later cases also had a small moulding mitred round the raised panels on the door (Plate 378) and they occasionally had raised panels also on the sides.

One of the black cases illustrated here in Plate 345 is a miniature longcase standing only just over five feet tall.

The gable-end pediment does not appear often on clocks made after about 1675 and if anything was added above the cornice in the following few years it was usually the carved pediment. The earliest type of these has already been described but some of the later ones varied quite considerably from that. One interesting one is to be seen in Plates 368-369, which has a crown as a centrepiece, suggesting that the clock had some Royal association. For brilliance of treatment, however, that seen on the

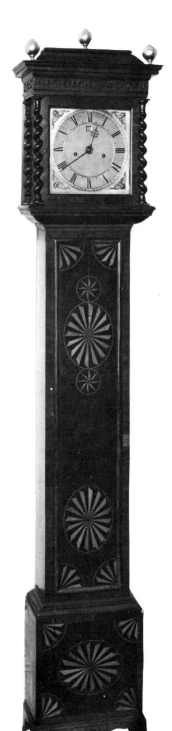

Plate 340. Longcase veneered with olivewood for a clock by Joseph Knibb. The long door and base has oyster pieces and star inlays in panels and the hood has a low dome. Circa 1680. The skirting is a later addition.

Plate 341. Longcase veneered with olivewood for a clock by Thomas Tompion, the long door and base with oyster pieces unrelieved by inlay. Circa 1675-80.

Plate 342. Detail of the clock in Plate 341 showing the unusual broken pediment.

254

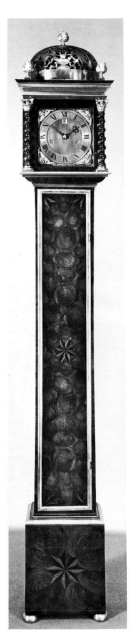

Plate 343. *Miniature longcase veneered with olivewood for a clock by Edward East, the long door and base with oyster pieces and star inlays, fire gilt metal mouldings and pierced metal dome. Height 5 ft. 8 ins. Circa 1675-80.* R.A. Lee

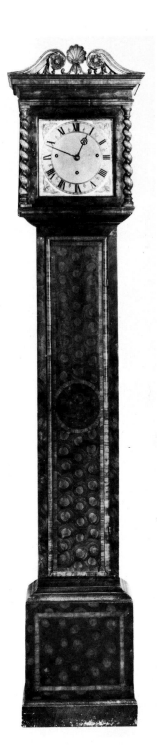

Plate 344. *Longcase veneered with olivewood for a clock by Joseph Knibb, the long door and base with oyster pieces and cross-grain olivewood banding. Circa 1675-80. The skirting is a later addition.*

Plate 345. *Miniature longcase veneered with ebony for a clock by Joseph Knibb, the long door with raised panels, and a low dome to the hood. Height 5 ft. ¾ in. to the cornice. Circa 1675-80.*

Plate 346. *Upper part of a longcase veneered with walnut for a clock by Joseph Knibb. Circa 1680.*

Tompion clock in Plate 363 cannot be excelled with its parcel gilding. This cresting was normally only placed on the front of the case but there are a number which have it also on the sides. Examples are given in Plates 333, 363 and 367. If the cresting found on the front of the clock is finished off at the ends with a mitre, the clock has at least been intended to have the cresting also on the ends. One such clock is shown in Plate 393. The Tompion clock in Plates 341-342 has a more unusual finish with a broken pediment of straight mouldings.

Another finish to the tops of cases which was introduced about 1680 is the low dome similar to that which was being used at the same time on the spring clock cases. When these domes were used it is quite common to find that there have been three or even five finials fitted although often they are missing. The finials are normally not spherical but a crushed ball either in wood or brass. Unlike most later domes, these are moulded on all four sides (Plates 340, 345, 352-353, 365, 370-371 and 373).

Frets within the friezes are not usual in the 1670s (Plate 346), although a number of these cases has unfortunately had them added subsequently. Some makers made provision for the outlet of the sound of the bell by cutting a large hole in the top of the hood which was then covered by a piece of fabric. Occasionally one will find a case which has a Bible-back moulding in the frieze and one such is illustrated in Plate 377. By the end of the decade, however, frets were being used more frequently and as

Plate 347. Longcase veneered with walnut for a clock by Greenhill, showing a provincial attempt to emulate the London design of 1680. (The movement is shown in Plates 283-286.)

Plate 348. The top part of the longcase shown in Plate 347.

Plate 349. Carved cresting on a longcase veneered with walnut for a clock by Daniel Quare. Circa 1680. The fret is not contemporary.

Plate 350. Carved cresting on a longcase veneered with walnut for a clock by Daniel Quare. Circa 1680.

Plate 351. Carved cresting on a longcase veneered with walnut for a clock by Henry Jones. Circa 1680. The fret is not contemporary.

258

Plate 352. *The upper part of a long-case veneered with walnut for a clock by Joseph Knibb, the hood with frets in the frieze and side windows of the design associated with this maker, and a low dome. Circa 1685.*

Plate 353. *Hood of a longcase for a clock by Joseph Knibb showing frets in the frieze and side windows. Circa 1680-85.*

a rule they were on both the front and the sides, and the carcase wood was cut away behind them. The designs were quite simple at first and fall into two main types. The most elaborate consisted of a very basic reciprocal scrolling design with stylised flowers or fruit at the termination of each scroll (Plate 329). Another very simple design, which was probably the work of only one man who was making the cases for the Knibbs, is usually only seen on their clocks. This, seen in Plate 339, is a formal arrangement of convolute scrolls and ovals or circles and is very much in keeping with the very earliest fret design discussed in Chapter V. Indeed, this same fret design is still used in the side windows at this period (Plate 352). A more elaborate side window fret was also used at this period and may be seen in Plates 353 and 354-355. It is found on clocks by both Knibb and Tompion (Plate 367) and would seem to be in keeping with the more elaborate frieze fret.

In every period special clocks and cases were made and one example of this can be seen in Plate 343. This is a very small olivewood case with a particularly interesting gilded metal dome which is pierced and engraved with tulips and daffodils. This is

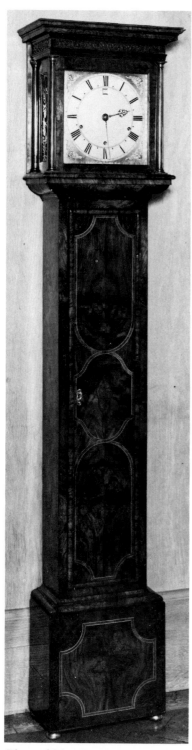

Plate 355. The upper part of the clock in Plate 354 showing the frets in the frieze and the side windows.

Plate 354. Longcase veneered with walnut for a clock by Joseph Knibb, the long door inlaid with crossbanding and stringing. Circa 1680-85.

Fitzwilliam Museum, Cambridge

probably a unique feature on a small longcase although a somewhat similar, but cast dome appears on the spring clock in Plate 240. This little longcase has also a number of metal mouldings. Metal mouldings are found on a small number of other seventeenth century clocks, the earliest probably being that described in Chapter XI (Plate 738).

It was during the 1670s that marquetry made its appearance on clock cases. To begin with, it was not often used on cases that were veneered with walnut but only on the olivewood cases. Some of these early cases merely have inlays of stars in the corners of the panels while others have small oval or quadrant panels with fan inlays made up of alternate pieces of ebony and holly or box. Instances of this type of decoration may be seen in Plates 340 and 343. When true marquetry was first used

Plate 356. The upper part of the clock in Colour Plate 11 (page 245) showing the frieze fret associated with Knibb clocks.

Plate 357. The upper part of the clock in Colour Plate 12 (page 264) showing the conventional frieze fret of the period.

on longcases it was usually contained within quite small panels either oval or circular in shape, outlined with stringing of ebony or holly and set in the olive oyster background of the long door and the base (Colour Plate 12, page 264, and Plate 357). Occasionally a little marquetry will be found in the front frieze of the hood. The design of the marquetry in these panels usually consisted of a spray of flowers springing from a vase or acanthus husk against a background of ebony. It would seem that it was the intention of the men who designed the marquetry to endeavour to copy the floral contemporary paintings by using woods of differing colours. The outline of the various flowers and leaves in this early period may seem to us to be very crude and basic when compared with the marquetry of later periods. There is no doubt that this is so and that this was due to the fact that marquetry was then a new art form and the cutters were lacking in experience. Chopped-in marquetry had been used for some time on oak furniture, but entirely new techniques had to be evolved for use with veneered surfaces and this took some time to perfect. The overall effect of this early work is however far superior and more artistically satisfying than the later work often is, in spite of the more technically perfect designs and superior cutting. The small and boldly coloured panels stand out well in contrast to the olive-wood background. They are more suitable as decoration on such a piece as a longcase than are the more intricate patterns of the early eighteenth century, which often cover almost all veneerable surfaces. This is particularly true with regard to many seaweed examples where the elaboration of detail merely applies a certain texture to the surface while the detail remains unseen. The flowers in the early marquetry are cut from woods of varying colours and the leaves from holly or pearwood. In some of the most attractive cases the leaves are cut from ivory or bone, in which case they have usually been stained green (Colour Plate 11, page 245, and Plate 356, and Colour Plate 12, page 264, and Plate 357). There are a few examples of small flowers also being cut in ivory and these are very conspicuous. In many cases the staining of the leaves has faded but where it remains it is very effective. It was not usual in the early period for the flowers to be stained although a little later they were. The husks from which the stems of the flowers grow, were sometimes shaded. This shading was achieved by dipping the individual pieces into very hot sand.

Stalker and Parker describe in their treatise the method used for staining wood for marquetry as follows:

"*To Dye or Stain Woods of any colour, for Inlaid or Flower'd work done by Cabinet Makers.*

"Use the moistest Horse-dung you can get, that has been made the night before, through a sieve or cloth squeeze out what moisture you judge sufficient for the purpose, convey it into several small vessels fit for the design; in each of these disolve of Roach-Allom and Gum-Arabik, the bigness of a nutmeg, and with them mix reds, blews, greens, or what colours best please you, suffering them to stand two or three days, yet not without stirring them. Then take your woods (of which I think Pear-tree is the best if't be white,) cut them as thick as an half-crown, which is in all reason thick enough for any Fineered or Inlaid work, and of what breadth you please; making your liquors or colours boiling hot, put the wood into it, for as long time as will sufficiently colour them; yet some must be taken out sooner than the rest, by which means you'l have different shades of the same colours; and such variety you may well imagine contributes much to the beauty and neatness of the work, and agrees with the nature of your parti-coloured flowers.

Plate 358. Longcase veneered with olivewood for a clock by Joseph Knibb, the long door and base with oyster pieces and small panels of floral marquetry. Circa 1680.

Plate 359. Longcase veneered with walnut for a clock by George Aries, the long door and base with floral marquetry. Dated 1683. The dome and skirting are later additions.

Plate 360. Longcase veneered with olivewood for a clock by John Knibb, Oxon, the long door and base with oyster pieces and panels of floral marquetry and with a marquetry frieze to the hood. Circa 1680-85. The skirting is a later addition.

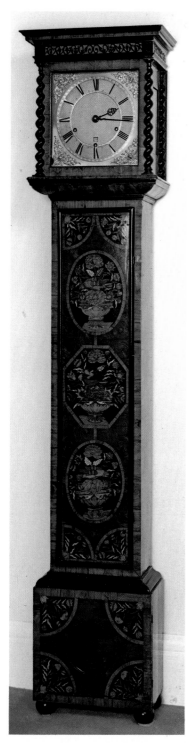

Colour Plate 12. *A longcase for a three train clock by Joseph Knibb with 1¼ second pendulum. It is veneered with olivewood with olive oyster background to the marquetry panels which have stained bone leaves. Circa 1680. (Also shown in Plate 357.)*

Colour Plate 13. *Miniature longcase veneered with walnut for a clock by Charles Goode, 7½ ins. dial, 5 ft. 9½ ins. tall. This case has floral marquetry with stringing on the framework round the long door. Circa 1695.*

Colour Plate 14. *A longcase veneered with walnut and with a dome and three finials for a clock by Thomas Tompion. Circa 1695-1700. (Also shown in Plate 397.)*
Petworth House

"To Stain a Green colour on Wood, Ivory, Horn, or Bone.

"First prepare either of them in Allom-water, by boiling them well in it, as you were first instructed. Afterwards grind of Spanish-green or thick common Verdegreas, a reasonable quantity, with half as much Sal-Amoniak; then put them into the strongest wine vinegar, together with the wood, keeping it hot over the fire till tis green enough: if the wood is too large, then wash it over scalding hot."

The flowers which are used in these marquetry panels include such varieties as peonies, carnations, tulips and daffodils. One of the most attractive features of almost all of the floral marquetry longcases throughout the century, is that somewhere in at least one of the panels and usually in a most prominent position, there is a colourful bird.

When the sides of the trunk are panelled, as they often were in olivewood cases, large oyster pieces were used for the panels, with a framework of crossgrain olive, sometimes outlined with stringing of black or white lines. It is less often that the sides of the base were panelled. The sides of walnut longcases were often panelled also, whether the front was veneered with marquetry or not, with more well figured wood in the panels and straighter crossgrain wood for the framework. It is most unusual to find floral marquetry on the sides of English longcases but a number were made towards the end of the century.

While marquetry was not commonly used on longcases veneered with walnut much before about 1685, when it was used it was usually set into a background of walnut and not ebony (Plate 361). When walnut became the more popular wood, which it did in the last decade of the century, the marquetry background was usually stained black. However on most cases this has now faded out. As the years pass we find that the makers gradually increased the size of the panels and added more panels with the result that less of the olive oyster work or other background wood is visible. The shaping of the panels varies, quadrant corner panels which were commonly used at first give place to panels with a serpentine outline. The ovals extend to the full width of the door and have break-arch ends. In the last decade of the century it became almost standard practice to have three large panels on the long door and one large rectangular panel on the base (Plates 388 and 389). By that time it was also usual to have marquetry on the front frame of the hood. An oval panel with four quadrant corners is seen on the base of the clock in Plate 360. That in Plate 359, however, is rectangular. It will be seen that on this latter case, a brass plate has been applied to the top of the long door with a contemporary engraved inscription which relates to its donation by the maker in 1683.

The standard of cutting rapidly improves and both flowers and leaves not only become more shapely but have added detail. The vase which had normally been the basis of early floral marquetry panels was less used on these cases, its place being taken by elaborate acanthus scrolling leafwork. It is not usual to find bone or ivory used towards the end of the century but it is then that the practice of staining the flowers was used. However very little of the colour is usually visible today.

Plate 387 shows a longcase which is veneered with burr elm and is decorated with a large variety of marquetry panels leaving little of the background wood visible. The marquetry is cut in pewter, which is unusual. However, pewter had been used for line inlays, and can be found in a number of fairly early cases.

The availability of a greater variety of woods during the later years of the century and the higher skill shown by the case makers in using them, is demonstrated in the

Plate 361. *Longcase veneered with walnut for a clock by Henry Jones, with panels of floral marquetry on a walnut ground and the hood with marquetry frame and frieze. Circa 1680-85.*

Plate 362. *Longcase veneered with olivewood for a clock with a second and a quarter pendulum by James Clowes, the long door and base with oyster pieces and panels of floral marquetry and with a hinged base having a pendulum aperture. Circa 1685.*

Plate 363. *Longcase veneered with olivewood for a clock by Thomas Tompion, with panels of floral marquetry, the hood having fine carved cresting on the front and sides, parcel gilt and with gilt metal frieze. Circa 1685. The skirting is a later addition.*

changing appearance of the cases made at that time. In the early seventies, for instance, the walnut cases were usually veneered with wood that was cut from the butt end of the trunk and it was used with economy, the plainer parts being used as well as the more figured, sometimes even on the long doors. Later in the century the makers were able to be more prodigal and to select only the best figured veneers for the more prominent parts and then usually properly quartered and matched. Occasionally one will find a case that has in addition some restrained inlaid bandings such as are seen in the case in Plate 354. It is at this period that burr walnut is being used and also other imported woods. Plates 379 and 380 are excellent examples of cases made later in the century using finer figured veneers.

While the vast majority of the clocks and cases made in the seventeenth century were pieces of fine craftsmanship, from about 1675 onwards there were also a great many less expensive examples made which usually had their cases made of pine. These were either painted or japanned, but the majority were made to almost identical standards of design and construction as the veneered examples and were obviously made by the same case makers but made for below stairs. Most of them housed quite good standard eight-day movements, many by famous makers. It is greatly to be regretted that many and indeed most of these movements have since been found what was considered to be more suitable cases. Some forty or so years ago many of these pine cases were fitted with second rate movements and restored as stripped pine cases, while others were veneered and as such may still be found. There were also a number of even cheaper cases made. These were usually for thirty-hour or lantern movements and were not necessarily made by the specialist clock case makers; this type is dealt with more fully in Chapter X.

During the last thirty years of the seventeenth century, there were a number of longcase clocks made which had pendulums which were longer than the normal seconds pendulum and which extended down to the very bottom of the case. In these instances the makers would frequently cut an aperture, similar to that often made in the long doors, for the insertion of a glass, in order to see the swinging pendulum. Examples may be seen in Colour Plate 12, page 264, and Plates 362, 376 and 395. In most cases they would also make the whole of the front of the base to open as a door to enable adjustments to be made to the pendulum. This was normally hinged as usual with the hinges on the right hand side and with a lock, similar to that used on the front doors of the spring clocks, on the left hand side (Plate 364). An example is

Plate 364. The base of a longcase having a second and a quarter pendulum, the base of which opens in the conventional manner.

Plate 365. Longcase veneered with walnut for a clock with a second and a quarter pendulum by William Cattell, the front of the base hinged to fall downwards, and the hood with a low dome. Circa 1680-85.

Plate 366. The base of the clock in Plate 365 showing the base door open.

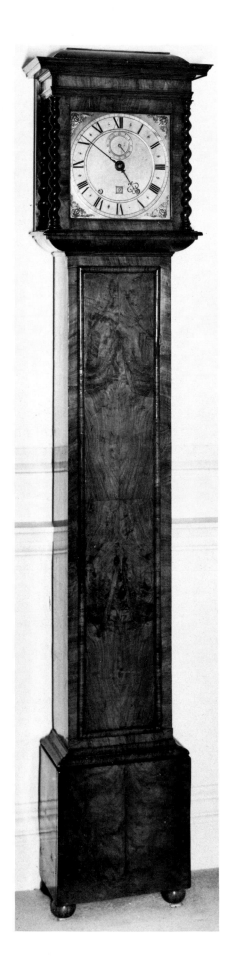

Plate 367. The hood of a longcase veneered with walnut for a clock by Thomas Tompion, the hood with cresting front and sides, and with frets in the side windows and the frieze. Circa 1685-90.

Apollo

however shown in Plates 365-366 of a clock by William Cattell where the base has been made to fall open. It is held in the closed position by an iron bolt on the inside of the bottom rail of the trunk, operated through the long door aperture.

Although for more than twenty years the 10 ins. square dial was almost standard for longcase clocks, throughout that time quite a number were made which had smaller dials only about 9 ins. square and a smaller number with much smaller ones of about 7 ins. As a rule these were miniature copies of the normal majority, and have become known as grandmother clocks. They usually stand from 5 ft. to 6 ft. tall and examples are shown here in Plates 327, 343, 345, 402 and 403 and Colour Plates 10 and 13 (pages 245 and 264). The earliest amongst them is probably that by Edward East in Plate 327. At least two are known that were made by Joseph Knibb and quite a number later in the century by Christopher Gould.

At the end of the century it would appear that the greater demand was for larger clocks, although 10 ins. clocks were made right into the eighteenth century. As with most evolutionary changes, it is impossible to say just when the 11 ins. dial was introduced, but certainly it was used in the 1790s. The case was then made proportionally larger and the increase in size brought problems which in turn brought about other changes. The hood of the longcase clock had from the beginning been made to

269

Plate 368. *The upper part of a longcase veneered with walnut for a clock by Thomas Tompion, with unusual carved cresting. Circa 1685-90.*

slide upwards for removal and for winding. Even with the 10 ins. dial this is sometimes a difficult operation, with the proportionally taller 11 ins. dial case, it is even more so. Nevertheless a number of such cases were made with sliding up hoods, just a few had no front door to the hood, but in most cases the entire front frame was made to swing open, in some instances with no interior frame round the dial. However, this dial frame soon became an essential part of longcase hood construction, and when the opening door was fitted, the brass lock commonly used on spring clocks was used (Plate 616). These hoods were also much heavier and consequently were soon made to slide off forwards.

Plate 369. The cornice and carved cresting of the clock in Plate 368.

It was at approximately the same time that the makers began to return to the earlier practice of using straight columns with brass capitals and bases. These latter were not as a rule of the Corinthian order but approximated more to the Doric and the capitals and bases on the right were drilled to take pivot pins for the front door. On many of the best cases the columns are veneered, which required considerable skill when one remembers that the veneer used was fairly thick, for, although we refer to the columns as straight, they are not in reality, as the diameter remains constant for only about the lower third of its length after which it tapers slightly to the top. The capitals and bases were always cast at this period and in most cases were very well finished. In the eighteenth century their design began to vary from the classic orders on many clocks.

The frets that were used at the end of the seventeenth century were more advanced in design and cutting than those used earlier. The basis of the design is similar but the treatment very different. Plate 393 is a very good example of the period. It will be seen that the stems are proportionately narrower and the scrolls more rounded than before, while the flowers are even less like real flowers. Side window frets have not often survived but were in all probability fitted to many cases.

On a number of the hoods of good longcases, repoussé mounts or frets have been applied to the friezes. Two excellent examples are given in Plates 371 and 378. In general design these follow that of the wood frets, being scrolling leafwork, but as it is worked in relief there is more detail. In the examples shown, the stems flow from acanthus husks in a very similar way to those found in floral marquetry at the same period. Where repoussé is applied on the side friezes of the hood, it is usual for the join between the front and side to be covered either by a repoussé leaf, as in the first example, or by a cast putto as in the second.

Plate 370. Longcase veneered with ebony for a clock by Thomas Tompion, the long door and the sides with raised panels on a sunken ground and with fire gilt mounts. Circa 1685-90. The movement is shown in Plate 270.

Plate 371. The upper part of the clock in Plate 370 showing the repoussé fret in the frieze with cast winged cherubs masking the corner joints and Doric capitals and bases.

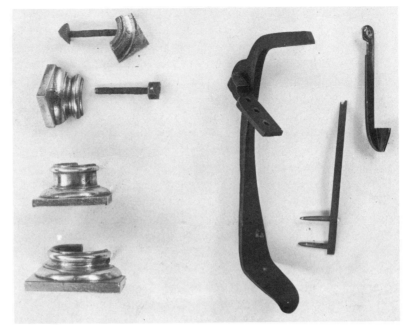

Plate 372. The capitals and bases from the clock in Plate 370 showing the fixing screws. Also a wrought iron lever catch for holding down the hood and a hook and spring for holding the hood up.

Plate 389 shows a walnut longcase veneered with floral marquetry and with a marquetry dome. Longcases had been made with little shallow rectangular domes for at least two decades but this taller dome is quite different in that it is flush at the back and it dates the clock as belonging to quite the end of the century. Once these taller domes became popular a number were added to earlier cases and considerable care is necessary before presuming that a dome which is obviously old was in fact originally made at the time when the case was made.

A case which has the long door completely covered with floral marquetry is shown in Plate 395. This was done on many cases at the turn of the century and it will be seen that the designer has returned to the use of a vase as a central feature which had not normally been done in the previous decade or so. In this instance the framework round the door and the base panel has marquetry in the form of a banding of repeated acanthus leaves, sometimes referred to as wheat-ear banding. It is similar to the engraved bandings found on dials and spring clock back plates at this period. In this instance it is particularly wide. The Quare clock in Plate 390 is also similarly veneered but the banding here is much narrower. This case is unique in that the hood has been made without an opening door in front but with a separate frame in front of the dial which slides upwards behind the cornice for the winding of the clock.

At the end of the seventeenth century and at the beginning of the eighteenth, the skill of the marquetry cutters was at its peak. The men who designed the marquetry panels could, therefore, give full rein to their ideas and they were not slow to do so. The result was that rapid changes took place in the years from about 1690 onwards. The use of naturalistic floral designs is no longer a necessary feature of the marquetry panels although floral marquetry continued to be used for some years. It must not be presumed that all floral marquetry cases pre-date those with one of the types which emerged at this time. Also, while many cases from this time had the entire long door completely covered with marquetry, many were still made with smaller panels.

The marquetry which is found on cases made about the turn of the century can be divided into two main types, one is usually referred to as 'seaweed' and the other as 'arabesque'. The Quare clock in Plate 390, although of floral marquetry, has above the lenticle features which seem to herald the change, with the association of strap-work with acanthus scrolls. It is the development of these features with the addition of other elements into the design such as grotesque figures of animals, birds, shells and fans, which produced the designs which we call arabesque. This marquetry is usually cut in two or three self-coloured woods which could be interchanged to make as many panels as there were different woods. Examples may be seen in Plates 400, 401, 420 and 421.

Seaweed marquetry is normally cut in just two colours and is usually a reciprocal design of delicately scrolling stems which makes little attempt to represent acanthus leaves or natural forms at all. Examples of the use of seaweed marquetry are in Plates 391, 396 and 425. It is not always possible to define some of the marquetry by either of these names for frequently the styles are interwoven as in the Gould clock in Plate 418; this case and that in Plate 420 show the skill of both the marquetry cutters and the case makers to good advantage. Even the columns are veneered with marquetry and also some of the smaller mouldings.

Daniel Quare made a number of clocks which had cases veneered with boulle work, that is, marquetry cut in tortoiseshell and metal. One of these is illustrated in Plate 417 where brass and pewter are used against a background of vermilion backed shell. The design is very much like that which we have called arabesque. Here again even the columns are veneered.

Inlaid stringing had been used in conjunction with decorative woods since quite early days on some longcases, most particularly for outlining the veneer panels on the sides of the trunk, although the sides of the base were not always panelled in the same way. Banding, that is parallel lines of stringing or strips of veneer of contrasting colour between stringing, was used more towards the end of the century but usually in a very restrained manner. One example of this may be seen in Plate 398. This clock is veneered with a wood which has for many years been called mulberry. It provides a very attractive finish and was used for many fine pieces of furniture and clock cases around 1700. It has caused restorers many problems because mulberry burrs are very difficult to find and if found they are close-grained without any of the contrasting grain needed for matching the veneers on these cases. As a result of his researches Edward Pinto wrote:[4] "Because a lot of mystery has been made about it, I decided to try to find out how the tortoiseshell mottle effect was produced or executed. Nothing could have been easier; all that is necessary is to take some dark brown pigment from the bottom of a tin of paint, rub it over the maple burr veneer and wipe off the surplus... The pigment sinks in the open grain and wipes off the close grain. Mulberry burr is close grained throughout and will not absorb pigment in this manner." So, Mr. Pinto argues, these clocks are in fact veneered with maple. This particular one has mouldings of cross-grain princes wood and this wood is also used in the bandings. A more elaborate, though tasteful use of banding is to be seen in the long duration clock in Colour Plate 15, page 283, and Plates 409-411. Here the bandings appear not only on the front but in shapely panels on the sides and base.

The most common size for longcase dials by the end of the century was 12 ins. and

---

4. Edward Pinto, "The Myth of Mulberry Veneer", *Country Life,* 2nd October, 1969.

Plate 373. Longcase veneered with ebony for a clock by Joseph Knibb with panelled door and sides and a low dome. Circa 1685-90.

Plate 374. Longcase veneered with olivewood for a clock by Nathaniel Barrow, the long door with oyster pieces and panels of floral marquetry, a full panel of marquetry on the base and a marquetry frieze to the hood. Circa 1685-90.

Plate 375. The upper part of a longcase veneered with olivewood for a clock by Richard Browne. Circa 1685-90.

the clock was no longer the small clock of a few decades earlier. The moulding round the base, which had for more than three decades been a broken ogee, had changed through the years to a much flatter profile than when first used and in the 1690s was replaced by many makers with a moulding similar to that used on spring clock cases consisting of a fillet, an ogee and a bead. This can be seen in a number of the illustrations but clearly in Plate 398. This is only one of the design changes which were taking place at that time. We have already referred to the dome which gradually became the normal finish to the longcase, but at the bottom end a single or double skirting was replacing the former bun feet, adding height to the clock which now is often seven and sometimes eight feet high. The earlier domes were simple but they developed until the simple dome was raised on to an attic storey above the cornice and there would be rectangular pedestals at the corners directly above the columns on which metal or carved and gilt finials were set. Between these pedestals or blocks a blind fret was often placed, matching that in the frieze. Plates 409, 418-419, 420 and 423 show such a dome. Occasionally a block and finial is placed on top of the dome. It is unusual for the domes at this period to be moulded at the back but an exception will be seen in that illustrated in Plate 410. Simpler domes than these are quite common, for instance Plates 385, 396, 416 and 422.

From the introduction of the longcase clock until almost the end of the century the mouldings on them have been predominantly convex. This may well have been

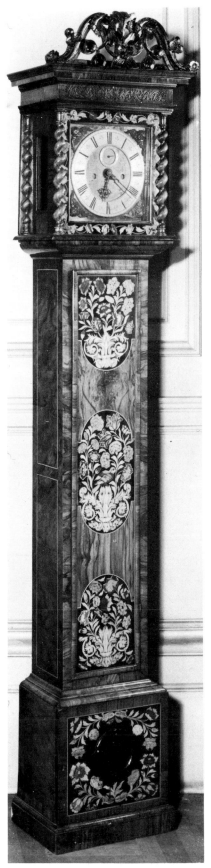

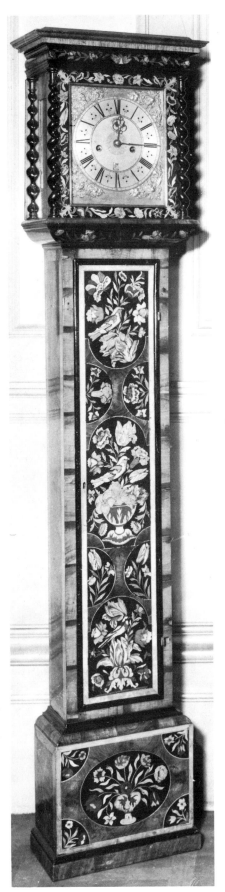

Plate 376. Longcase veneered with walnut for a clock by William Clement, with one and a quarter second pendulum, the long door with three panels of floral marquetry and the hinged base panel with floral marquetry and a pendulum aperture. Circa 1685-90. The skirting is a later addition.

Plate 377. Longcase veneered with olivewood for a clock by Thomas Harris, the long door and base with numerous panels of floral marquetry, the hood with elongated dial surrounded by marquetry and marquetry on a 'Bible-back' moulding in the frieze. Circa 1685-90. The skirting is a later addition.

Plate 378. The upper part of a longcase veneered with ebony for a clock by Edward Bird, the frieze to the hood with a gilt repoussé fret front and sides, the corner joints being masked by repoussé acanthus leaves. Brass bosses are placed by the hinges of the long door to prevent bruising of the moulding when the door is swung open. Circa 1690. R.A. Lee

because such mouldings were easier for the cabinetmakers to make. If this was the case, then it is another sign of their growing confidence in their ability, that in the last decade more concave features appear. This brought about a radical change in the appearance of the clock by giving it more elegant lines. The most noticeable change was in the mouldings above and below the trunk and the graceful sweep of these new mouldings was usually veneered with the choicest of veneers. The moulding round the long door, which had been a simple flat convex, was soon replaced by a broken ogee moulding, the concave part of which was the most noticeable. No longer are the mouldings used, copies of classic architectural mouldings and even in the component parts of the cornice the concave sections are the more pronounced. Domes frequently have a concave member making them similar to the inverted bell tops on spring clocks.

A great number of longcase clocks were being made at this time and it is understandable that not all were up to the high standard of the majority and one can frequently see signs in these later cases of labour being saved. The quarter columns which are placed at the back of the hoods of most longcases are made to fit against barge boards and these on most seventeenth century cases are about half an inch thick, are parallel and are veneered on two sides. They also extend from the lower moulding of the hood to the overhanging member of the cornice, thus going behind the architrave and frieze. This practice was continued on most of the best cases right into the eighteenth century but it was gradually discontinued and the barge boards

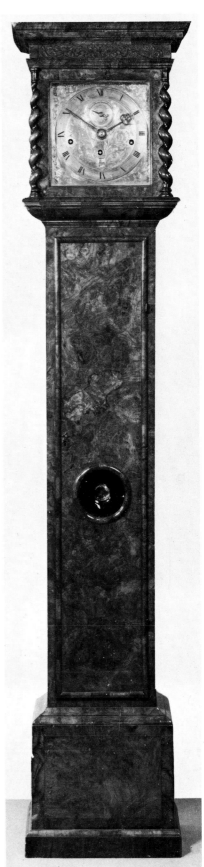

Plate 379. Longcase veneered with burr walnut for a clock by Thomas Tompion. Circa 1690. The skirting is a later addition.

Plate 380. Longcase veneered with walnut for a clock by Edward East. Circa 1690. The skirting is a later addition.
Christie, Manson and Woods Ltd.

Plate 381. Detail of repoussé frieze fret on the walnut marquetry longcase in Plate 382.

were frequently made to end under the architrave, to be thinner, unveneered and sometimes tapered.

Some of the finest and most elegant longcase clocks ever made were produced during the last years of the seventeenth century or the early years of the eighteenth. A number of these were made for William III and many more for the stately homes of the nobility. Many of these stood more than 8 ft. tall. It is more than likely that there was keen rivalry between the clockmakers' patrons for the possession of a clock of outstanding importance, for certainly the clock and case makers must have received every kind of encouragement to produce speciality pieces of the highest quality. Whilst these special clocks in general conformed to the fundamental designs of the period, they were nevertheless elaborated and ornamented in a variety of ways, but usually in the very best taste. Of simple elegance is the clock in Colour Plate 14, page 264, the upper part of which is shown in Plate 397. There are a number of clocks extant which stand on metal bases and others where the skirting is heavily metal mounted (Plates 412 and Colour Plates 15 and 16, page 283). Usually the domes have received special treatment with individually designed metal features such as finials and statuettes, often considerably increasing the height of the clock. Several of these are shown here, in particular those in Plates 405 and 412. The latter clock also has fine gilt metal trusses supporting the hood and gilt metal mouldings and frets. It will be seen that the veneers chosen for these cases are of the very finest. Fine wood frets are also to be seen in Plates 407-408 and 409-411.

No better example of the skill of the cabinetmakers of the time can be found than the longcase shown in Plates 426-429. Here the princes wood has been used in a similar fashion to the earlier olivewood oysters, by cutting the veneers from small limbs at a slight angle to get the best effect from the straight grain and then fitting the pieces together in a most artistic manner, not only on the flat surfaces but also on some mouldings.

Plate 383. Longcase veneered with walnut for a clock by Daniel Quare. Circa 1690-95. (Views of the movement are in Plates 278-279.)

Plate 382. Longcase veneered with walnut for a clock by William Snow, the long door with three panels of floral marquetry and a full panel on the base. The frieze to the hood has gilt repoussé fret. Circa 1690.

Plate 384. Longcase veneered with burr walnut for a clock by John Clowes, with flat pilasters to the hood and a 12ins. dial. Circa 1695.

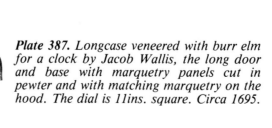

Plate 385. *Longcase veneered with walnut for a clock by Thomas Tompion, showing the frieze fret which was in vogue at the end of the century. Circa 1695.* Chatsworth House

Plate 386. *The upper part of a longcase veneered with walnut for a clock by Richard Lyons. Circa 1695.*

Plate 387. *Longcase veneered with burr elm for a clock by Jacob Wallis, the long door and base with marquetry panels cut in pewter and with matching marquetry on the hood. The dial is 11ins. square. Circa 1695.*

Colour Plate 15. Longcase for a year equation timepiece by Daniel Quare. It is veneered with walnut and inlaid bandings with gilt metal mouldings and fine frets. Circa 1700. (Other views are shown in Plates 292-293 and 409-411.)
Pelham Galleries

Colour Plate 16. Longcase for a year equation timepiece by Daniel Quare. It is veneered with walnut, with gilt metal mounts and mouldings. Circa 1700-10.
Trustees of the British Museum

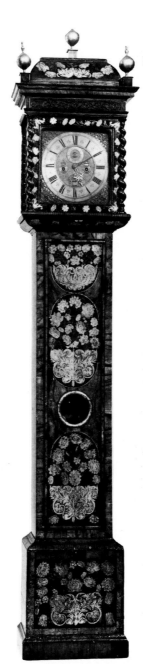

Plate 388. *Longcase veneered with walnut for a clock by Izaac Goddard, with three panels of floral marquetry on the long door, a full panel on the base, marquetry on the top moulding and the dial framing, and stringing on the framework round the long door. Circa 1695.*

Plate 389. *Longcase veneered with walnut for a clock by Edward Orton, with floral marquetry which is also on the dome. Circa 1695. The skirting is a later addition.*

Plate 390. *Longcase veneered with walnut for a six-month clock by Daniel Quare, with full panel floral marquetry and acanthus banding. The glass covering the dial is in a separate frame behind the marquetry front, which slides upwards for winding. Circa 1695. (The movement is shown in Plate 290.)*

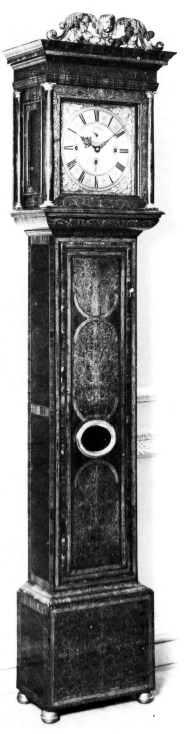

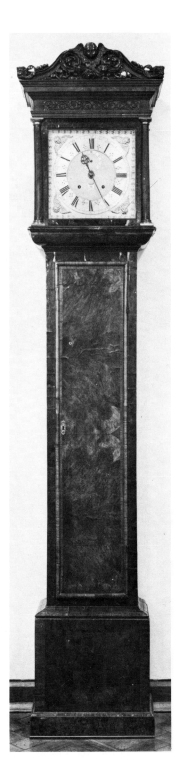

Plate 393. *The upper part of the clock in Plate 392 showing the frets in the frieze and side windows and the veneered columns with Doric capitals and bases.*

Plate 391. *Longcase veneered with princes wood for a clock by James Markwick, with panels of seaweed marquetry framed with acanthus banding, the sides and door with oyster princes wood. There are side doors to the hood. Circa 1695. The carved cresting may be a later addition.*

Algernon Asprey

Plate 392. *Longcase veneered with walnut for a clock by John Knibb, with 12ins. dial and carved cresting. Circa 1695-1700.*

Ashmolean Museum, Oxford

Plate 394. *The upper part of a longcase veneered with walnut for a clock by Christopher Gould, with floral marquetry on the moulding under the hood and the framing of the dial. Circa 1695-1700.*

Plate 395. *Longcase veneered with walnut for a clock with a second and a quarter pendulum by Benjamin Johnson, the long door and base with full panel floral marquetry, framed with a repetitive acanthus banding and a door in the base with a pendulum aperture. It has an 11ins. dial. Circa 1695-1700.*
Derek Roberts Antiques

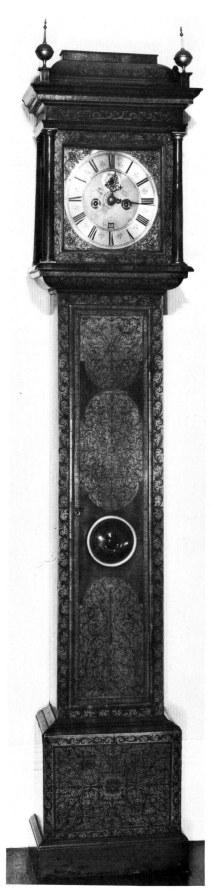

Plate 396. Longcase veneered with walnut for a clock by Edmund Day, with panels of seaweed marquetry. Circa 1695-1700. The skirting is a later addition.

Plate 397. The upper part of the clock in Colour Plate 14 (page 264) showing the taller dome.

Plate 398. Longcase veneered with stained maple and with mouldings of princes wood for a clock by Christopher Gould, the panels framed with cross-grain bandings and stringing. This veneer has often been described as mulberry wood. Circa 1695-1700. (The movement is shown in Plates 287-288.)

Plate 399. The upper part of the clock in Plate 398 showing the inlaid bandings and the veneered columns.

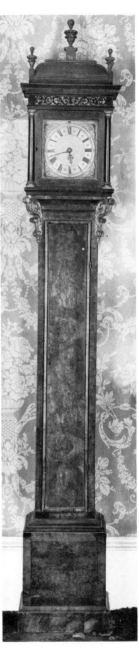

Plate 400. *Longcase veneered with marquetry of arabesque design for a clock by Robert Dingley. Circa 1700.* Sotheby Parke Bernet

Plate 401. *Longcase veneered with marquetry of arabesque design for a year timepiece by Edmund Wright. Circa 1700. (The dial is shown in Plate 294.)* Derek Roberts Antiques

Plate 402. *Miniature longcase veneered with walnut for a clock of thirty-hours duration by Christopher Gould with 7½ins. dial. Trusses to the hood, and finials carved and overlaid with silver leaf, standing 6ft. 3ins. to the top of the dome. Circa 1700. (The movement is shown in Plates 307-309.)* Godden of Worthing Ltd

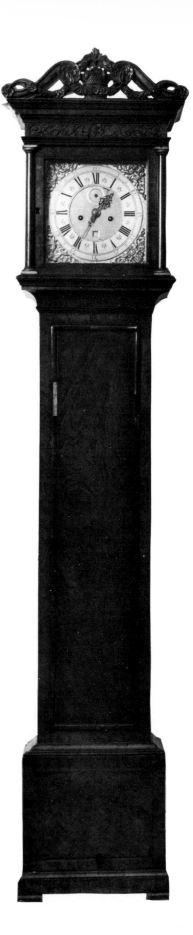

Plate 403. Miniature long-case veneered with walnut for a clock by Charles Goode. Circa 1695. (Also shown as Colour Plate 13, page 264.)

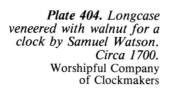

Plate 404. Longcase veneered with walnut for a clock by Samuel Watson. Circa 1700. Worshipful Company of Clockmakers

290

290

290

Plate 405. *Longcase veneered with walnut for a year equation clock by Thomas Tompion. Known as the 'Drayton' clock, it is one of Tompion's monumental productions. It has a unique pendulum aperture in the long door. Circa 1700. (The movement is shown in Plates 295-298.)* Fitzwilliam Museum, Cambridge

Plate 406. *The upper part of the longcase in Plate 405.*

Plate 407. Longcase veneered with walnut, with burr walnut panels for year timepiece by Daniel Quare. Circa 1700. (The movement is shown in Plate 291.)

Plate 408. Side view of the longcase in Plate 407 showing the panelled side.

Plate 410. Side view of the year time-piece in Plate 409 showing the decorative bandings.

Plate 411. Side view of the hood of the year timepiece in Plate 409 showing the fine frets in the frieze and side window and the gilt metal mounts in the frieze.

Plate 409. The upper part of the year timepiece in Colour Plate 15, page 283. (The movement is shown in Plate 292.)   The Pelham Galleries

Plate 414. *A side view of the upper part of the longcase clock in Plate 412.*

Plate 413. *The hood of the clock in Plate 412 showing the fine gilt metal mounts.*

Plate 415. *The gilt metal stand of the longcase in Plate 412.*

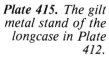

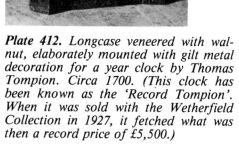

Plate 412. *Longcase veneered with walnut, elaborately mounted with gilt metal decoration for a year clock by Thomas Tompion. Circa 1700. (This clock has been known as the 'Record Tompion'. When it was sold with the Wetherfield Collection in 1927, it fetched what was then a record price of £5,500.)*

Plate 416. Longcase veneered with walnut for a clock by John Wise with full panel floral marquetry. Circa 1705.

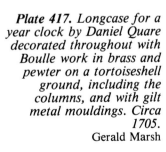

Plate 417. Longcase for a year clock by Daniel Quare decorated throughout with Boulle work in brass and pewter on a tortoiseshell ground, including the columns, and with gilt metal mouldings. Circa 1705.
Gerald Marsh

Plate 418. Longcase veneered with marquetry in arabesque designs for a clock by Christopher Gould. Circa 1705-10.

Plate 419. The hood of the clock in Plate 418 showing that the columns are also veneered with marquetry.

Plate 420 (left). A longcase veneered with arabesque marquetry for a striking clock with a 12 ins. dial by Christopher Gould. Circa 1705-10.

Plate 421 (above left). Arabesque marquetry on a longcase door of circa 1710.

Plate 422 (above right). Longcase veneered with walnut for a clock by Henry Massey. Circa 1710.

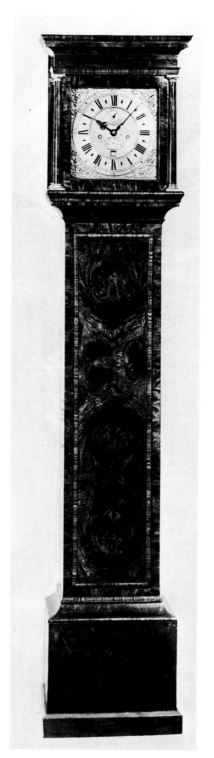

Plate 423. *Longcase veneered with pearwood and ebonised for a clock by Thomas Tompion. Circa 1710.*

Plate 424. *Longcase veneered with walnut for a clock by Tompion and Graham. Circa 1710.*

Castle Museum, York

Plate 425. *Seaweed marquetry on a longcase door of circa 1715.*

Plate 426. Long-case veneered with princes wood for a time-piece by George Graham. Circa 1715.

Plate 427. Detail of the veneering of the dome of the clock in Plate 426.

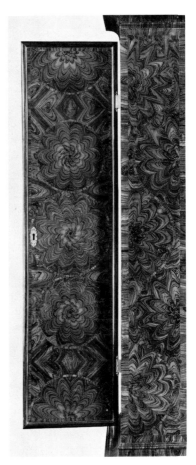

Plate 428. Detail of the hood of the clock in Plate 426 showing the type of capitals and bases used on many good clocks of the period.

Plate 429. The side and long door of the clock in Plate 426 showing the intricate arrangement of the princes wood veneers.

Chapter VIII
Later Spring-driven Clocks

The spring-driven clocks of the 1670s provide us with interesting evidence of the trade practices of the day and of the working relationship between individual makers. In spite of the fact that there must have been competition between them, one can find common features on clocks by a variety of makers which must indicate that they originate from the same source. This was not an entirely new situation, for earlier lantern clocks also had included such parts as finials, frets and pillars which were identical on the clocks of different makers and which almost certainly had been supplied by specialist workers. This specialisation must have developed considerably by the 1670s and it may well be that by then partly made movements were available to the trade which could then be finished to the individual degree of refinement practised by the purchasing maker.

The maker of a movement would first make a rough plan of the clock and then, having worked out the sizes and numbers of the wheels and pinions and also the sizes of the barrels and fusees, he would be in a position to assess the size and shape of the plates required. The pillars would then be turned to shape and length, and the wheels and pinions made and mounted. The inside faces of the plates would then be filed flat, after which they would be pinned together. The next stage would be to mark out the movement on the plates, to drill a pilot hole in the centre, mark off all depths and drill pilot holes. When all the parts to go between the plates have been marked out and their pilot holes drilled the plates can be parted. The pillars are then let in and the plates held together with a 'U' spring. Once the pinions are pivoted, the holes may be opened and the train assembled with the movement held together with the spring. It is now made but not finished, and could be sold for finishing, as it could indeed have been at any other stage.

There are extant numerous clocks which have been completely finished, including the engraving of the back plate but with space left for the addition of a maker's signature which has never been added (Plate 674). There are others which have a signature which, although contemporary, is by an entirely different hand from the rest of the engraving (Plate 588). Unfortunately unsigned clocks have often proved irresistible to unscrupulous dealers with the result that not many are to be found today.

It will be seen from the above that there was plenty of scope for specialising in the provision of the various parts for a clock. Pillars and plates could well have been bought either in the rough or finished. Wheel cutting certainly required a special skill as would the forging of fusee and barrel arbors. The making of spring barrels and fusees would almost certainly have been done by a specialist, as would pinions. Such

Plate 430. The dial and hands of a spring striking clock by Henry Jones with his typical heavy engraving and bold hands.

things might well have been bought much as they have in more recent years from material dealers.

A maker whose work is distinctive and recognisable is Henry Jones and the features of his work which are peculiar to him are in the main consistent, thus suggesting that he, at least, was the actual maker. Nevertheless, many of these features may be found in clocks bearing the names of other makers of the period, which suggests that he may have been willing to provide others with clock parts or even partly made movements. Take, for instance, the clock by him illustrated in Plates 430-432 and compare it with that attributed to Thomas Tompion in Plates

Plate 431. *The striking side of the clock in Plate 430, which has Dutch striking.*

Plate 432. *The back plate of the clock in Plate 430, showing the back plate pinning, the outside ratchets and the unusual positioning of the signature.*

Plate 433. The striking side of a Dutch striking clock by Thomas Tompion which differs from the previous clock only in detail. The case is shown in Plate 605-606.

Plate 434. The going side of the clock in Plate 433.

433-437. Both are half-hour striking clocks with the trains planted in the same positions in the plates. The crown wheel cocks on both are on the front plate instead of the back plate as was normal which, since the crown wheel would revolve the reverse way from usual, meant that a different cutter was required for the wheel teeth. Also the verge would be different.

Clocks constructed in this way are to be found which bear the names of other makers of the period but the way in which they are finished varies considerably from clock to clock. For instance the position and finish of the bell stands vary as does the degree of refinement in the turning of the wheel collets and the finishing of the stop-work and hammer-tail blocks, and the ornamentation of barrel ratchets and clicks. All such details reflect the character of the man who finished and signed the clock.

Another clock which bears the same stamp as the previous two is that signed

Plate 435. The movement of the clock in Plate 433 viewed from the top.

Plate 436. The unusual spandrel corner mount on the clock in Plate 433.

Plate 437. The back plate of the clock in Plate 433 showing greater refinement than that shown in Plate 432, helped by the fact that the barrel pinning and the barrel ratchets are on the front plate. (The front view of this clock is in Plate 605.)

Plate 438. *The back of a similar clock but with outside barrel ratchets, by William Cattell. (The case and dial are shown in Plate 608.)*

Plate 439. The back view of a clock by Henry Jones, very similar to that in Plate 432.

William Cattell and shown in Plate 438. This, however, is a plain striking clock but has the crown wheel cock on the front plate and like the other two, the striking train straddles the crown wheel pinion enabling the train to be distributed more evenly over the plates than was done in most clocks and making possible the use of larger wheels and pinions. Later in the century the name of Cattell appears on clocks of quite different character, more in line with the work of Quare and Windmills.

In many ways Henry Jones's practice was quite different from the normal run. He frequently used brass screws. He often made his stopwork 'irons' of brass with springs of steel, his hammer springs and counter springs of brass. The springs were squared into the plates and cross-pinned, as may be seen in Plate 432. His pendulum hold-fast is fixed in the same way, while smaller springs are just squared and driven into the holes. The barrel ratchets of his clocks are normally on the back plate, elaborately turned with decorative clicks and often click springs. His hour hands were not as a rule squared on to the hour socket as was normal practice, but fitted with greater security into a Maltese cross, as may be seen in Plate 448.

The decorative features associated with Henry Jones's work are very pronounced, heavy without being clumsy; his engraving often includes strong black lines and large circular dots and the shaping of such components as hands and clicks is bold and confident.

Back plates of clocks by Henry Jones and other makers are illustrated in Plates 439-443.

There is another group of movements that was made in the 1670s which, although

Plate 440. *The back of another Henry Jones clock with outside barrel ratchets, back winding and hold-fast clips.*

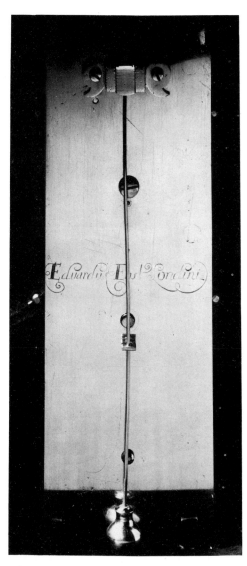

Plate 441 *(above). The back plate of a timepiece by Edward East which can be seen in its case in Plate 593.*

Plate 442 *(above right). The back of a striking clock by Joseph Knibb of the first phase. It has maintaining power, a small count wheel high up, a new type of pendulum hold-fast and floral engraving with grotesque figures.*

Plate 443. *A clock of the same phase as in Plate 442 with Dutch striking and similar hold-fast. The count wheel is lower and there are screwed on spigots at the corners for holding the movement in the case.*

they bear the names of a variety of makers, have common characteristics suggesting that they also have a common origin. The illustrated examples, which are attributed to both Joseph Knibb (Plates 447-453) and Thomas Tompion (Plates 458-463), are not of the high standard associated with these makers and found on their longcase clocks at this period. The movements belonging to this group frequently have plates almost identical in size and shape and have a peculiar back cock with one large foot and one small. This can be clearly seen in Plates 446 and 450. The Tompion clock in Plate 458 probably had the same type of cock originally, which was thought to be inappropriate for a Tompion, but it has been replaced by one which would be appropriate on a Tompion of a decade later.

The clock by James Clowes in Plates 444-445 may well have had the other type of back cock also. All of these clocks are finished in a very different way however. Some in the group are plain striking clocks while others are half-hour strikers. Some are two train clocks striking the hours with ting-tang quarters on the same train, while others are simple timepieces. One common feature of the group is the work-

Plate 444. The dial of a clock by James Clowes, the hour hand of which is too short.

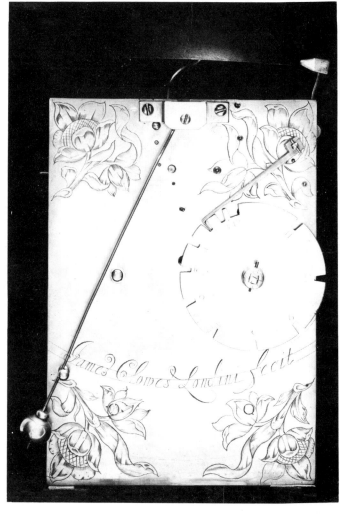

Plate 445. The rear view of the clock in Plate 444 with engraving in the corners of the back plate only. (The case is shown in Plate 607.)

Plate 446. *A striking clock by Joseph Knibb of the first phase engraved in a similar fashion to the previous clock. It has an odd footed back cock and the style of the pendulum hold-fast has again changed.*

manship of the barrels and fusees, all of which must have been by the same hand. The Knibb clocks which have the grotesque fish engraved on the back plate are in the group (Plates 450 and 455). The hammer and counter springs are of steel, brazed or silver soldered into brass feet which are often quite large and decoratively filed.

The Knibb clock, illustrated in Plates 447-453, is most interesting, with a typically Knibb style of dial complete with its original gilding and with a beautiful skeleton chapter ring. There are however four stopped holes in the dial plate, made for a normal chapter ring, and the dial feet which would normally have been sited under the chapters of a skeleton ring are here visible since the rivets have 'started'. This suggests that the clock was supplied to Knibb in almost completed condition.

Plate 447. *The dial of a striking clock by Joseph Knibb, the chapter ring of which was not originally a skeleton. The hands are in the style of Henry Jones. (The case is shown in Plate 601.)*

Plate 448. The front plate of the clock in Plate 447 showing the hand fitting in the style of Henry Jones.

Plate 449. The going side of the clock in Plate 447 showing the big fusees and the thick rings on the pillars.

Plate 450. The back plate of the clock in Plate 447 with an odd footed back cock and original apron. It has a small amount of primitive engraving.

Plate 451. The escapement of the clock in Plate 447, with swan neck cock for the verge pivot.

Plate 452 (right). The striking side of the clock in Plate 447.

Plate 453 (far right). Another view of the striking side of the clock in Plate 447.

Knibb skeleton rings are usually held by six or eight pegs of only about ³/₃₂ in. diameter, riveted into the ring in the places where the metal is thickest. In the case of eight pegs, this would be in the minute and quarter rings at the cardinal points. This is particularly the case when the chapter ring is made of silver. There are instances, however, particularly amongst the group of clocks that we are now discussing, where the skeleton ring has been made of quite thick brass and only has four ordinary pegs placed in the centre of the cardinal chapters. The pegs on ordinary chapter rings are not so disposed but are usually placed where there is no engraving.

It must be a matter for conjecture why such makers as Knibb and Tompion at this early period, should find it necessary to use movements made by other men for their spring clocks. Knibb, it is true, was making many fine longcase clocks at the time and may have found them occupying all his time and Tompion may have been more involved with instrument making, for there are few clocks by him of any kind that date from the 1670s.

The Tompion clock illustrated in Plates 458-463 must have been supplied to him in unfinished state, for it is much more refined. For instance, it has maintaining power, the pillars are much better finished and the stopwork springs are separate items, whereas it was normal for them to be fixed to the irons in this group of clocks.

Plate 454. A time-piece movement by Joseph Knibb with the same style of primitive engraving as that shown in Plate 450.
R.A. Lee

Plate 455. *The under dial work of the clock in Plate 454.*

Plate 456. *The dial and hands of the timepiece in Plate 454.*

Plate 457. *The dial plate of the timepiece in Plate 454 showing the precise area of the gilding and the roller matting done in the up and down directions only.*

316

Colour Plate 17. *Spring clock case veneered with ebony for a grande sonnerie striking clock by Joseph Knibb, with a velvet dial and silver mounts. Circa 1675-80.*

Nevertheless, it will be seen from the illustrations that the wheel bosses conform to others of the group and that the hammer and counter springs are of steel with brass feet.

The hammer stems also conform, being made of steel wire, tapered at the arbor end and driven into a tapered hole in the arbor and riveted over. They are filed to a gradual taper at the head. Thus made, the hammer gives a smart, clean blow to the bell. Although the counter spring gives a little, it produces a stop which is an improvement on the solid stop made on a stout pin or the edge of the plate. This is not the way that they were made on the clocks which Tompion himself made. It will

Plate 458. *An early spring clock by Thomas Tompion emanating from the same source as some of those by the Knibbs and Henry Jones but with Dutch striking and maintaining power. (The case is shown in Plate 602.)*

Plate 459. The going side of the clock in Plate 458, with the verge and pendulum removed, showing work similar to previous clocks.

Plate 460. The going side of the clock in Plate 459 showing the under dial work, and the hammers which are linked to their tails.

Plate 461. The under dial work of the clock in Plate 458. The hand fitting is again in the style of Henry Jones.

Plate 463. The going side of the clock in Plate 458 showing the striking work springs. (The case is shown in Plate 602.)

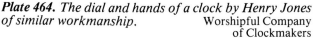

Plate 464. *The dial and hands of a clock by Henry Jones of similar workmanship.* Worshipful Company of Clockmakers

Plate 465. *The back of the clock in Plate 464 showing the small amount of primitive engraving. (The case is shown in Plate 592.)*

be seen in the illustration that the large hammer stem on this clock is not tapered. It is a replacement.

Further clocks in this group are to be found which are signed by Henry Jones. One of these is in the Clockmakers' Company's Collection in Guildhall, London (Plates 464-465). In that instance the hands are more suggestive of the work of Tompion, the hour hand being squared on.

Although most of the clocks which we find today are of eight-days' duration, clocks of shorter duration were being made at this time. It is probable that many more were made than have survived since it is quite an inconvenience to have to wind daily. An example of one which fits well into this group and made by Henry Jones, is shown in Plates 466-468. It has a duration of thirty hours but its quality leaves nothing to be desired. The hour hand has the familiar Maltese cross fitting, there is a brass cannon for the square of the lifting piece and the crown wheel cock is on the front plate. The clock has a fine dial with a well matted centre and beautifully engraved corners (Plate 466). The gilding is original and in good condition and as will be seen has been economically kept outside the scribing lines of the chapter ring. Incidentally, chapter rings are made to just cover the scribing lines. Unfortunately

Plate 467. *The side view of the clock in Plate 466 showing the typical Henry Jones hand fitting.*

Plate 468. *The back view of the clock in Plate 466 with minimal engraving similar to that in Plate 465.*

322

the original ring has been replaced on this clock by one which is wider with the result that the hands, which appear to be the originals, have been shortened. The scribed lines on dial plates are not intended to indicate the width of the chapter ring but are merely a guide to the man matting the centre and finishing the area outside the ring. The chapter ring is always larger than the scribed lines indicate and it is quite common to find that some letters of a signature or part of the engraving are slightly covered by it.

It is on the group of clocks which we are discussing that the back cock apron first makes its appearance. Many of these aprons are quite small, just sufficiently large to cover the 'V' slot in the cock and they are screwed on to function as a back stop for the verge. It is important for good timekeeping that the knife-edge of the verge should be finished off at an angle at the back so that it is the point only that touches the back stop, giving minimal interference with the swing. Some aprons found on clocks today are merely decorative additions made during the present century. That on the Knibb clock in Plate 451 does however have an air of authenticity, in spite of the fact that the back plate engraving takes no account of it.

These clocks seem to be the last spring clocks to retain any significant visible signs of the clockmaking practices of the 1660s. Clocks made from this time onwards have hour sockets and date wheels of higher numbers. Whereas they had been 12 and 24, the later movements have 18 or 24 teeth in the hour socket. The motionwork seen in Plate 455 shows how the hour wheel had been held on to the socket up to this time, by a key and the date wheel held on the socket by two screws between the teeth, one of which is just visible in this view, at three o'clock.

A clock which clearly demonstrates the fact that one cannot define exactly when one style or practice began or ceased, is shown in Plates 469-472. Here one might imagine that the hour hand was made in 1665 while the chapter ring has the quarters marked in the manner of a quarter of a century earlier and yet the chapters themselves are correct for about 1675. The dial and back plate engraving would also suggest the former date. When one comes to the movement the same mixture applies. The striking train is similar to that of Edward East of the mid-'60s with floating motionwork but the pillars are bossed and fixed to the back plate. The movement is over 2ins. deep with wide plates, a plain back plate and large count wheel squared to the main wheel arbor. The chains are modern but the barrel caps are pinned.

A somewhat similar clock is to be seen in Plates 473-474 where the dial is matted all over in the style of the '60s but with a roller instead of a punch and where the border has been scraped it can be seen that all the matting marks have not been removed. The hands, chapter ring and signature, however, could well have been made in the '80s. The movement displays the plainness of the '60s with the signature more in the style of the '80s and the big count wheel on the fusee arbor and the outside lever would fit the mid-'70s. It could well be that the clock was finished in the late '70s.

Joseph Knibb would appear to have been the most prolific of the clockmakers at this time, using both bought-in movements, which he completed himself, and also those which he made in their entirety. Those which he made himself are easily distinguished by their superior quality. Much of the workmanship of the others will offend the eye of the craftsman, whereas Knibb's own work displays an artistry and refinement beyond compare. Probably the best example of his work from this period is that illustrated in Plates 475-477.

Plate 469. *The dial and hands of a clock by Francis Strelley with the quarters engraved in the minute ring.*
Gerald Marsh

Plate 470. *The movement of the clock in Plate 469 showing an odd mixture of styles, some as early as 1665. The chains are modern.*

Plate 471. The back plate of the clock in Plate 469 showing the wide plate, the count wheel on the fusee arbor and an early style of engraving.

Plate 472. Another view of the rear of the clock in Plate 469.

Plate 473. *The dial and hands of a clock by Joseph Knibb with an oblong matted dial plate. The clock in its case is shown in Plates 236-237.*

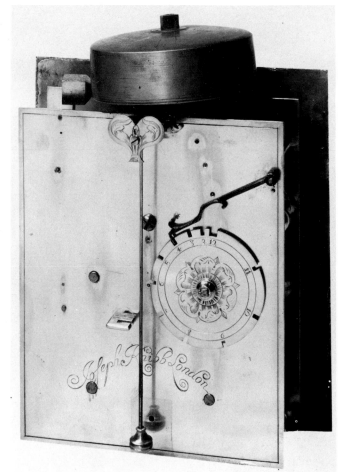

Plate 474. *The back plate of the clock in Plate 473 with minimal engraving, a single line border and signature in the style of the mid '70s.*

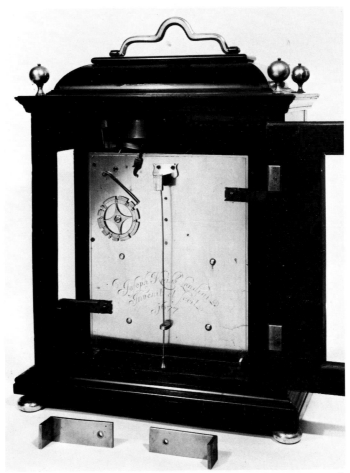

Plate 475. The back plate of a superb spring clock by Joseph Knibb of a month's duration with Roman striking and engraved with "Joseph Knibb Londini Invenit et fecit 1677". (This clock is shown in its case in Plate 599.)

This is a month clock and may indeed be the first English spring clock of that duration and the invention claimed in the inscription on the back plate may well be his method of economising in power for the striking train, to enable it to run for this period. This clock has what has become known as Roman striking. That is, the use of one bell to strike each I of the Roman numerals on the chapter ring and another to strike each V. The X is struck as two Vs and a further economy of power is made by engraving the four as IV instead of IIII, thus saving two blows. 78 blows of the hammer are required to strike the hours in the conventional manner in each twelve hours. The Knibb Roman strike, using two bells, the larger for the V and the smaller for the I, requires only 30, thus making a significant saving of power. 30 is also a convenient number of pins to place round a rather large pin wheel. The pins for the 'I' hammer are placed on one side of the wheel and those for the 'V' hammer on the other. This wheel, which makes one revolution each twelve hours, has 90 teeth, with double locking on the hoop wheel and a locking pinion of six leaves which proves a very satisfactory arrangement. An extension of the arbor carries the count wheel. Both the lifting piece and the counting lever on this clock are of steel and the warning is between the plates.

The dial is most attractive with a silver skeleton chapter ring. The whole clock is of

Plate 476. *The striking side of the clock in Plate 475, showing some of the superb workmanship and the skeleton dial.*

Plate 477. *The going side of the clock in Plate 475, showing the tick-tack escapement and wheels mounted on the pinion heads.*

the finest quality, the wheels are quite thin, finely crossed and with shallow collets. The pinion arbors are of a pleasing shape and all of the working parts, such as pinion leaves and wheel teeth, are formed in such a way that they not only perform perfectly but also satisfy aesthetically. The large steel pinion of the pin wheel is brazed on to the arbor, which is simpler than turning it from the solid. The hammer stems are also brazed to the arbors instead of being driven into holes in them. The hammer springs and counters are all of steel.

To obtain the duration of one month, it was necessary to introduce an intermediate wheel and pinion into the going train, the consequence of which was that the clock needed to be wound anticlockwise and this, in turn, made it necessary for the fusees to be grooved in the reverse way. The barrels, however, still turn in the usual direction with the result that the lines do not cross over the train as is customary. Knibb also considered it to be desirable for both fusees to be wound in the same direction, although, since there is no intermediate wheel and pinion in the striking train, that train could be wound clockwise. The trains were therefore changed over so that the hammers could still be drawn outwards.

This clock is in superb original condition, including its tick-tack escapement. All the parts have been made to such perfection that friction has been reduced to a minimum with consequent minimum wear during its three centuries of use. A clock of this excellence required no additional decoration in the way of engraving on the back plate to distract from the inscription ''Joseph Knibb Londini Invenit et Fecit 1677''. When first made the clock was held in the case by two pegs in the seat board and damage done to the back plate by the faulty hammering in of these pegs, is clearly visible. The present decorative steel brackets are a more recent addition.

Joseph Knibb made another clock which he engraved in the same way as that just described and which is illustrated in Colour Plates 18-20, pages 336-337, and Plates 478-479. It is very different in appearance, having a dial plate faced with dark blue velvet and the dial and case mounted in silver. Velvet covered dials were not an entirely new idea for the first clocks made in Holland had them with gilded chapter rings and hands. It was however a new idea at this time for English clocks. The effect of the silver mounts against the ebony and dark velvet is most attractive and another example is shown in Colour Plate 17, page 317. In addition to the chapter ring and corner mounts on the dial there is a pierced and engraved silver mount in the centre which includes a signature and ornamental surrounds to the winding holes. Since a silver hand would not show up well against the silver of the chapter ring, the minute hand has a blued steel end to provide a contrasting colour.

There are a number of other clocks extant with velvet dials, but this is a small example of the second phase of spring clocks made by Knibb with a number of interesting features. Like the clock illustrated as 475-477, which belongs to Knibb's first phase in design, the clock in Colour Plates 18-20 and Plates 478-479 has Roman strike and a tick-tack escapement but this is an eight-day clock and the back plate is beautifully engraved with a floral design similar to earlier Knibb clocks (Plate 450), but in this instance has the addition of a wide border. It has its original gilding in almost untouched condition. The back cock has a single screw and is fretted, an unusual feature at this period, as are the screws on the back plate which have Dutch-type heads. All the steelwork in the clock, with the exception of pallets and pinions, is blued.

The movement is held in the case by spigot plates screwed into the bottom of the back plate and inserted in the seat board. Although they are the original plates, like

Plate 478. *The going side of the clock in Colour Plates 18-20, pages 336-337, showing the tick-tack escapement and single footed screw back cock.*
George Daniels

Plate 479. *The striking side of the clock in Plate 478 with blued steelwork.*

the pendulum rod and bob, they are not gilded. The clock has suffered somewhat through the years from repairers but has recently been properly reinstated. It has brass hammer heads and is the earliest clock we illustrate to have them.

Since in a Roman striking clock the normal pin wheel and pinion are omitted, the train would run too fast unless, as in this case, the warning wheel was increased in size and number and the fly increased in size. When this is done, however, the locking piece often jumps out. This is usually subsequently corrected by a wire spring bearing on the locking lever, which has been done in this clock.

The illustrations in Plates 480-483 are of another clock of the same period as the last. It is a half-hour striking clock belonging to the intermediate stage between the earlier clocks (referred to as belonging to phase one) and the later, smaller clocks of the third phase. It has characteristics of all the phases. It had had its verge escapement converted to one with a detached pendulum but has more recently been correctly restored.

Plate 480. The dial and hands of another eight-day clock of the second phase by Joseph Knibb with excellent gilding. (The clock in its case is shown in Plate 604.)

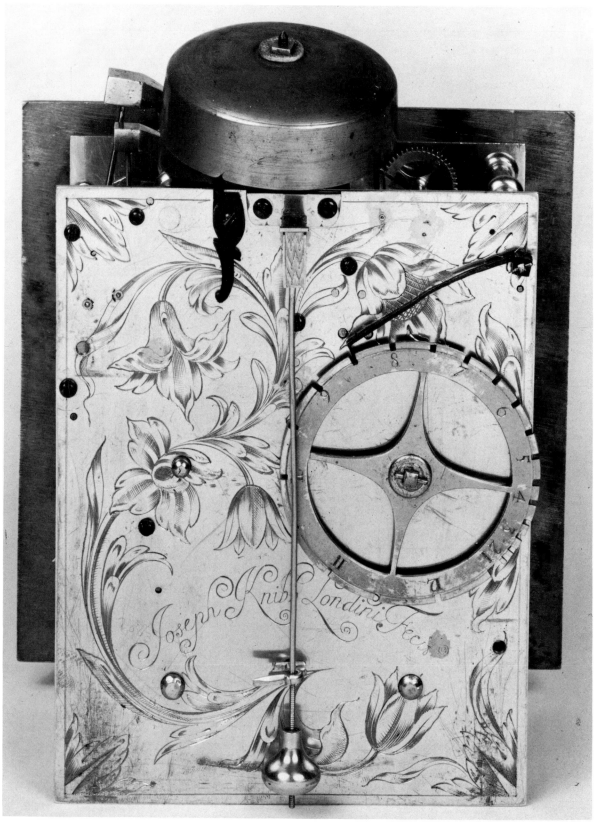

Plate 481. *The back view of the clock in Plate 480 showing the chafing where the retaining pegs have been, the increased amount of engraving and the count wheel covering some of the signature.*

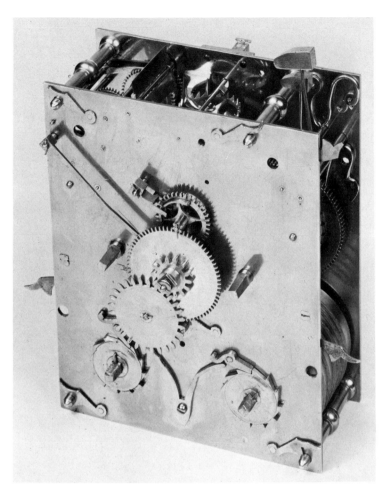

Plate 482. The under dial work of the clock in Plate 480. It has brass hammer springs and face cams on the minute wheel for Dutch striking.

Plate 483. The movement of the clock in Plate 480 partly dismantled.

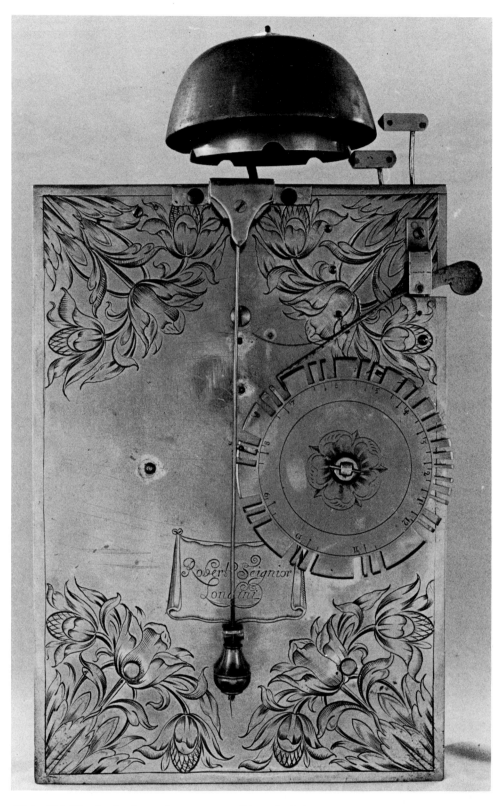

Plate 484. *The back plate of a quarter striking clock by Robert Seignior, the cartouche partly covered by the count wheel. The going train has a fourth wheel.*

In Plate 481 one may see the fairly plain overhanging type of back cock secured by two screws and with no engraving on the foot. The engraving on the back plate is more characteristic of the later clocks and does not extend beneath the count wheel although it has been crossed out and engraving would have been visible. Much of the gilding on the back plate remains, some on the back cock but hardly any on the count wheel. The bad scoring seen at the bottom of the plate indicates that the clock was originally held in the case by two pegs driven into the seat board. It is now held by two small brackets. As there were signs of original blueing the steelwork has been reblued.

Plate 482 shows the movement of this clock and it is very much like the earlier clocks which came from Knibb's own workshop and one gets the impression from it that he is beginning to cheapen his work at this time. There is no motionwork bridge here. In the illustration of the partly dismantled clock in Plate 483 the various component parts may be seen. The hour hammer spring and counter are made of steel but those for the half-hour are of brass. The nice shaping of the lower crown wheel cock can be seen and the squareness of the upper one, while the swan neck part may be seen in Plate 482.

While a little swan-neck cock was sometimes used for the front pivot of the verge, to give some scope for adjustment, it is not used in this clock which has no provision for adjusting the escapement depth. The bottom bearing of the crown wheel arbor is a wedge shaped piece of hardened steel. Bending, as a means of adjustment is not approved of in modern times but is a very ancient method and was used in many crafts, particularly organ tuning. The clock has a fly pinion of five, leaves and is quite deep, being 2⅛ ins. between the plates.

The dial (Plate 480) is in fine condition with only a small mark where the gilding has gone and the corner mounts, peculiar to Knibb, are also gilded. It is very probable that any clock which has original corners of this pattern, has had some association with Joseph Knibb. The hands also admirably demonstrate the broad and flat bevelling which characterises all Knibb hands. Replacement hands can usually be detected when the bevels are not flat.

The quarter striking clock shown in Plates 484-489 is an interesting piece dating to the middle '70s although its size might suggest that it is the work of one of the traditional makers of a decade earlier. The count wheel is now on the end of the fusee arbor which is its normal position at this period. The larger amount of engraving on the back plate is also in keeping with the period (see also Plate 490). Although it is by Seignior, the design and workmanship of the movement differs greatly from a number of his clocks which were made later in the century (Plate 512 for example). These latter are so similar to each other as to identify them as his own work whereas this movement so closely resembles others bearing the names of a variety of makers as to suggest that it may not have been entirely his own work. There are also others bearing his name which are of quite different character which tend to confirm that he was one who was selling clocks which were at least partly made by others. Apart from the fact that the fusee chains were probably added in fairly recent times and that the minute hand has been broken, this clock is in good original condition. It is of interest on two particular counts. Firstly on account of the quarter striking work but also with regard to the extra wheel in the going train.

In the previous chapter we saw how one school of makers achieved half-hour striking on a separate bell. The more usual method adopted when a second bell was

Colour Plate 18. Spring clock case veneered with ebony and with silver mounts for a small Roman striking clock of the second phase by Joseph Knibb, 1677. The finials are recent replacements. (Other views of the clock are shown in Colour Plates 19-20 and Plates 478-479.)

Colour Plate 19. The silver mounted velvet dial of the clock in Colour Plate 18. Note the blued steel end to the silver minute hand.

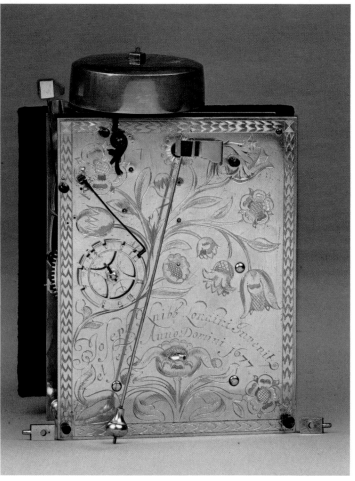

Colour Plate 20. The back plate of the clock in Colour Plate 18 showing the engraving and the date.

Plate 485. The clock in Plate 484 viewed from the top, showing the crown and contrate wheels.

Plate 486 (right). The striking side of the clock in Plate 484, showing the arrangement of the hammers.

Plate 487 (far right). The going side of the clock in Plate 484 showing the extra wheel and pinion and the short pendulum.

Plate 488. The under dial work of the clock in Plate 484.

Plate 489. The dial and hands of the clock in Plate 484.

Plate 490. *The back plate of another striking clock by Robert Seignior with full engraving. It strikes the half-hour on a smaller bell with one blow.*

Plate 491. *An almost identical dial as that shown in Plate 489 by the same maker.*

required was to use a hammer-tail block which could be moved back and forth or 'pumped' by leverage from a cam on the minute wheel. This will bring one of the hammer tails into contact with the pins on one side of the pin wheel and at the same time clear the other hammer tail from the pins on the other side. The reverse movement will bring the second hammer tail into contact with these pins and thus the appropriate bell will be struck. The count wheel is appropriately divided.

Whereas in most clocks with quarter or half-hour striking that were made at this period the hammer tails are connected to the hammers by links, in this instance the hammers and their springs are on the pumping block. Although this might appear to be an improvement, since the whole of this work had to be pumped from the face cam on the minute wheel, it was necessary for it all to be much lighter; the brass footed springs are quite slim, the hammer heads are small and made of brass and this lightness evidently results in the blow being too gentle for there are lead filled holes in the hammer heads.

The extra wheel in the going train is a feature which is also found in clocks signed William Knottesford, one of which is shown in Plates 492-493. This clock has a seconds hand. The dial is well proportioned with the seconds circle placed midway between the hand centre and the chapter ring, whereas in the long pendulum weight clocks of the period it is normally placed higher and touching the chapter ring. The lower placing of this seconds circle is necessitated by the fact that an additional wheel and pinion is required to provide for the seconds arbor to turn in a clockwise direction, thus making the contrate wheel the fourth wheel. This arrangement usually results in the pendulum swinging short of the full height of the plates. It may well be that the Seignior clock in Plates 484-489 was constructed to carry a seconds hand, for there is a large stopping in the front plate contrate pivot hole where the extension of the pivot for a seconds hand could have been. As finished by Seignior, however, there is a date aperture in the dial instead. The hour wheel in this movement has not been keyed to the socket but secured by two pins or screws and there is a mark between two of the teeth to enable the hands to be lined up. It will be noted that these movements are made with the striking detents pivoted in cocks, a fact which greatly facilitates the assembly of the movement and makes the provision of split front plates less important. These cocks are not engraved. Such plain cocks have not been appreciated by some restorers who have added engraved decoration to them and also to the feet of the back cocks.

Quite early in the second half of the 1670s, a further innovation was introduced into the spring clock by some makers which greatly influenced the spreading of their reputation overseas. This, known as quarter repeating work, was a device to enable the time to be struck to the immediate last quarter of the hour, usually by the pulling of a cord. When first introduced, the quarters were struck on a single bell, smaller and of higher pitch than the hour bell. Later, when the quarters were struck on more than one bell, these were always smaller than the hour bell. The convention was also established from the first that during the first quarter past the hour it was the past hour only that was struck on the hour bell, that during the second quarter one blow would be struck on the small bell and the past hour on the larger, during the third quarter, two blows on the small bell and three during the last quarter. Some variations from this are to be found, for instance, some strike one bell during the first quarter, two during the second and so on.

Apart from some three-train clocks such as those illustrated later in Plates 580-583

Plate 492. *The back view of a striking clock by William Knottesford with a four wheel going train similar to that of the clock in Plates 484-489.*

Plate 493. *The dial and hands of the clock in Plate 492. This dial has a seconds hand which is the reason for the fourth wheel.*

which repeat the quarters by the pull-string unlocking the hour and quarter trains, most repeating work is done by a separate mechanism with the spring pull-string wound for each action.

It is not known who was first to devise a repeating mechanism but Derham says that it was Edward Barlow in 1676.[1] The earliest instance of its use known to the writers is in a clock by Joseph Knibb, which has a tick-tack escapement and 'Roman' striking. The repeating mechanism is crowded into the top right hand corner of the plates and is of the type which continued to be used in timepiece movements where all the blows are provided by the separate mechanism. These clocks had count wheel striking at this time, and the number of blows struck by the repeating train is controlled by a snail and the quarter blows are determined by a face cam on the minute wheel and a pumping piece.

The mechanism is powered by a small coil spring housed in a spring box permanently fixed on to the front plate and to which the outside end of the spring is locked. The winding pulley, which is squared on to the main arbor passing through the spring box, is so constructed that, while it fits freely over the spring box, to carry the winding cord about a quarter of the depth of the box extends into it. It is to this that the inner end of the spring is locked.

The main repeat arbor is usually of $\frac{3}{16}$ in. or $\frac{1}{4}$ in. diameter and has permanently fixed to it the ratchet and pin wheel. The pin wheel is similar to a recoil escape wheel of 20 or 21 teeth, with all but 12 teeth cut off to the tooth root. These teeth draw the hour hammer tail. It is the radial face of the teeth which does the drawing. After the last tooth and at the same pitch as the cut away teeth, the three quarter hammer pins are placed as near to the edge as is practical. They are of graduated height so that the quarter hammer-tail, which is spring-loaded and pumped from the front by a lever from the face cam on the minute wheel, will make contact with the requisite number of pins.

Keyed against the ratchet on the main arbor is the first wheel of the train and on to it is mounted the click and spring. There are usually two wheels and pinions to the train and a fly, the wheels being of 54 and 48 teeth and the pinions of six leaves. The main wheel is normally of 72 and the ratchet most often of 48.

The hammers are remotely controlled and are positioned above the hammer tails. The links between them are heavy and hooked, with long shanks to the hooks. When the cord is pulled, the pin wheel is rotated anticlockwise, pushing the hammer tails down and pulling the lever side up to enable the hooks to ride up their connecting pieces. As soon as the mechanism is fully wound, the weight of the hooks returns the hammer tails to the drawing position and the hammers will be pulled. At the same time the pinion squared on to the main arbor, which engages a toothed quadrant, moves it until it is arrested by its arm resting on the snail (Plate 494). This determines the number of hour blows to be struck. Here then is the basic principle for rack striking mechanism. The snail is there but there is a pinion and toothed quadrant instead of a gathering pallet and rack.

The snail is rotated by a pin in the minute wheel and is retained in position by a spring at the top of a very sturdy brass stud providing sufficient friction to maintain it in place and yet to allow for movement. This is precisely the same device as is used with the friction held hands of a clock with a minute spring where they are held

---

1. William Derham, *The Artificial Clockmaker,* 1696.

together under tension by a hand collet and pin. This stud is always sturdy, for violent pulling of the pull-string could easily bend a slender stud with consequent failure of the mechanism. Occasionally the star wheel is positioned by a spring jumper instead of a friction spring.

During the running of a timepiece the snail moves very slowly and it could happen, if the repeating mechanism is operated just before the hour, that the quadrant lever makes contact with the next position on the snail, causing the following hour to be struck. To avoid this happening, some timepieces are fitted with a small lever operated by a pin in one of the minute wheels, the other end of which contacts a notch in the pulley or hooks over a pin and thus prevents the pulley from turning. This device usually operates for about four minutes before the hour and is released at the hour. The timepiece illustrated in Plate 494 does not have this addition.

Plate 494. *The front plate of a timepiece with the earliest type of quarter repeating mechanism.*

344

Plate 495. *A pre-numbered striking clock by Thomas Tompion with alarm, a count wheel and quarter repeating work repeating the hours up to six blows. It is shown with its case as it is inserted through the bottom. (The clock in its case is shown in Plate 620.)*

Plate 496. *The back plate and base plate of the clock in Plate 495 showing the bolts which hold the movement in its case.*

345

One of the earliest clocks which appears to have been actually made by Tompion, is shown in Plates 495-496. It is also a striking clock with a count wheel which makes it necessary that all the quarter and hour blows of its repeating must be obtained from the pull-string mechanism. It has both hour and quarter snails with followers in continual contact and their up and down motion is cleverly converted into an in and out movement of the hammer tails. The levers of this work are so linked together that whichever of them is activated first automatically activates the other. For purposes of economy, the repeating mechanism does not strike more than six hours; consequently the hours from seven to twelve are indicated by one blow for seven, two for eight and so on.

Tompion must have started numbering his clocks shortly after he made this clock for, although it is unnumbered, there are two very small timepieces numbered 21

Plate 497. A small metal cased timepiece alarm by Thomas Tompion with the same type of repeating mechanism as the clock in Plate 495 but improved to strike the hours fully. (The clock in its case is shown in Plates 623-625.)

346

(Plate 497) and 23 which must have been made not long after it. Both are exceedingly small and have blued steel cases with gilded basket tops and mouldings. One of these, No. 23, was altered at the beginning of the eighteenth century, but the other is in mint condition and has the same type of repeating mechanism as we have been discussing except that it has been further developed to strike all the twelve hours. The work is however much smaller and more precise.

There is no better demonstration of the rapid development which had taken place in the art and craft of clockmaking during the 1670s and early 1680s than the clocks shown in illustrations 498-502, 503-508 and 509-511. These are highly complicated and extremely beautiful mechanisms with repeating work which is almost grande sonnerie. They were certainly made at about the same time as the clock in Plate 497, and that known as the 'Tulip' Tompion in Plates 503-508 has stamped in the top left hand corner of the back plate the figure 16. Since the timepiece shown in Plate 497 is stamped 21, it would be reasonable to presume that it was intended to stamp this clock 12 but that the number punch for the 2 was held upside-down when struck. None of the other clocks of this type, such as that in Plates 509-511, are numbered, which suggests that the group was made at the time when Tompion began to number his clocks, usually thought to be about 1680. Further evidence for this is given in Colour Plate 27 (page 472) which shows a painting, dated 1682. The clock depicted in it is very similar to both the Tulip Tompion, Plates 503-508 and Plate 634, and the Sussex Tompion, Plates 509-511 and Plate 635.

These clocks employ racks in their striking mechanism and it appears to be the earliest use of this device in a striking train. Two racks are required, one of which is gathered and the other fixed. The gathered rack is held in suspension by the fixed one until all the gathering is completed, when it drops by gravity and locking takes place. This happens at each quarter hour, at which time one more tooth is gathered than the hour required. The hour hammer tail is held out during the first gather while a system of levers enables the required quarter blows to be delivered, whereupon the quarter hammer tail is pulled out and the hour hammer tail released to strike the hour. A somewhat similar mechanism is to be found in the Tompion longcase clock, No. 3, which is described in Chapter VI and illustrated in Plates 268-269. In that instance the hammer tail is moved from an edge-cam attached to the count wheel. This suggests that the rack was introduced between the making of that clock and those shown in Plates 503-508 and 509-511.

Four of these clocks are known and there is in existence the dial of one other. It could be therefore that six were made and that another is yet to be discovered, unless it has been destroyed.

Three of these clocks have the striking train on the left and they all have control pointers on the dial and no back doors to their cases. The first one illustrated in Plates 498-502, which has a silver-mounted velvet dial, has the striking train on the right. The control pointers in this instance are on an engraved and gilded dial mounted on the back plate, and so the case has a back door which is glazed and not the elaborate metal fret as found on the others.

All the signs are that this silver mounted clock was the first of the group to be completed. That the striking train is on the right is of no particular significance or consequence apart from being the reverse of customary practice in an eight-day clock. Some of the other details of mechanism make it fairly obvious that it was the first.

Plate 498. *The front view of the silver mounted semi grande sonnerie clock by Thomas Tompion showing that the movement is mounted on the metal bottom of the case which has the feet attached. (The case is shown in Colour Plates 23 and 24, pages 444-445.)*

Plate 499. *The right hand side of the movement in Plate 498, showing the quarter bells and the pendulous hammers.*

It has previously been mentioned that in the Tompion longcase No. 3, the hour and quarter hammer tails are moved by an edge cam; in these clocks it is by means of a pumping piece at the top and bottom of the gathered rack, with the exception of the silver-mounted clock where there is only one pumping piece which works on the top end of the gathered rack. This holds the hammer tail out for the first gather, then lets it in while holding the quarter tail out for the remainder of the gathers. This may be seen in Plates 498 and 499 pivoted rather oddly at an angle between the side of the top striking train plate and a bent up cock. The hook which holds the hour hammer tail in operation can be seen in Plate 499, it must be spring-loaded in the 'out' position. In Plate 499 can also be seen the three quarter bells, the pendulous hammers for bells two and three and their hammer heads. Also to be seen are the pivoted pieces on the hammer arbors which are spring-loaded in the 'in' position to be drawn by the double hook on the arbor of number one quarter hammer, the head of which cannot be seen. The position of these pieces, which have extensions outside the front plate, is decided by the piece working upon these extensions. This is a spring-loaded 'L' shaped lever, the lower end of which rests upon the quarter snail; thus, the striking or non-striking of bells two and three is simple but not that of bell one, which is not struck at the hour. This is effected by a rod which is pivoted in the vertical arm of the lever, which operates on the pivoted bell stand for the number one bell so that when the lever is riding on the bottom step of the quarter snail, the bell is turned free of the hammer. In the other three clocks in this group the equivalent rod strikes an additional small piece upon the quarter hammer tail to hold it out so that the blow is not delivered.

The subsidiary dial shown in Plate 502 has the control hands as follows. The large hand in the centre with the ring numbered 1 to 60 is for the pendulum rise and fall. The pinion behind the dial upon which the hand is mounted and the rack with which it engages, may be seen in Plate 500, although the exact method of its operation is not obvious. The fixed cock at the top of the suspension spring would appear to be redundant. In the other clocks this cock is below the rise and fall suspension with the spring sliding through, thus effecting regulation. The pointer at the top right is for strike and non-strike, there being two pins in the dial to restrict its movement; its arbor can be followed through in Plate 500. The two bottom pointers are to operate the pendulum hold-fast. It is difficult to understand why it was necessary to lower them about $3/16$ in. but there are holes which show that this was done and also in the back plate, as can be seen in Plates 499 and 502. The pointer at the top left has no purpose except to provide symmetry and the locking disc to hold it in place may be seen in Plate 499.

The dial itself is beautifully engraved and gilded and the central motif of a vase with the lilies and their stamens are very reminiscent of other clocks. It is mounted on the back plate by three dial feet which are retained by pins and not the nicely shaped latches which retain the main dial, the plate pillars and the striking train plate pillars. One has the feeling that this back dial was an afterthought since it is not latched on, it has a pointer with no purpose, the pendulum hold-fast pointers have been moved — as indeed have those on the clock in Plate 507 — and it has been gilded where everything else is black and silver.

In Plates 499 and 500 it will be seen that there are steel vertical pieces up each side with two holes for the insertion of pull-strings, the first of these having a double 'set'. The side frets have been so designed in the other clocks that there is a hole suitably placed to take this pull-string but not in this clock which consequently has none.

Plate 500. *The left hand side of the movement in Plate 498, showing the rack for pendulum adjustment.*

Plate 501. *The velvet covered, silver mounted dial of the clock in Plate 498, showing the minute hand with the blued steel tip. The bushes for the winding holes are missing.*

Plate 502. *The rear view of the movement in Plate 498, showing the subsidiary dial. The holes just above the pendulum hold-fast indicate that they have been moved.*

All in the group are so constructed that, should the string be pulled for the clock to repeat just before the clock's normal let-off, this is precipitated and the next quarter is sounded. In other words, if the string is pulled a quarter of a minute before 12.30, it is 12.30 that will be sounded then but not again at the half-hour.

The movement is inserted in the case through the bottom and is fixed to a brass plate which forms the bottom of the case and has the case feet attached to it. The feet are fixed to the case on the other clocks.

A snail is required for these spring clocks. Previously we have described how this was used in connection with repeating work, where a toothed quadrant was used. Now, however, it is used with a rack and gathering pallet. The rack hook for arresting had not been introduced when this clock was made. It seems to be widely thought that the rack, when first used, was an inside rack and that it was mounted on an arbor pivoted between the plates. If we are right, however, in thinking that the earliest use of it is to be found in the clock in Plates 592-594, where two racks are used, one to gather and one to hold, it would seem to be a logical development to have both racks on the same quadrant. We can see that this has been done in the Seignior clock in Plate 512. This clock (Plates 512-517) may well have been made before 1680 and to be contemporary with the Henry Jones clocks which have count wheels. The hammer marks at the bottom of the plate indicate that the movement

Plate 503. *The dial of the clock known as the 'Tulip Tompion'. The clock in its case is shown in Plate 634.* Christie, Manson and Woods Ltd.

352

Plate 504. The under dial work of the 'Tulip Tompion'.

Plate 505. A view of the 'Tulip Tompion' with the hour bell removed showing the original chains.

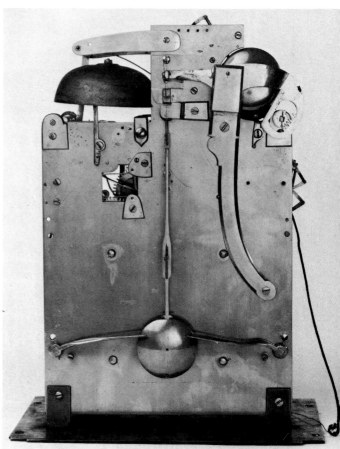

Plate 506. An angled view of the 'Tulip Tompion' showing the rise and fall work and the pivoted hammer tails.

Plate 507. The back of the 'Tulip Tompion' showing the pendulum hold-fast.

Plate 508. Part of the back plate of the 'Tulip Tompion' showing the figure 2 punched upside-down. The nib has been cut from the verge cock and a new cock fitted, thus modifying the length of the pendulum.

354

Plate 509. *A similar clock to the last known as the 'Sussex Tompion'. (The clock in its case is shown in Plate 635.)*
Christie, Manson and Woods Ltd.

Colour Plate 21. *A superbly fine gilt metal case for a grande sonnerie spring clock by Thomas Tompion, with engraving and finely finished silver mounts. Circa 1680-85. (Other views of the case are shown in Plates 627-628.)*

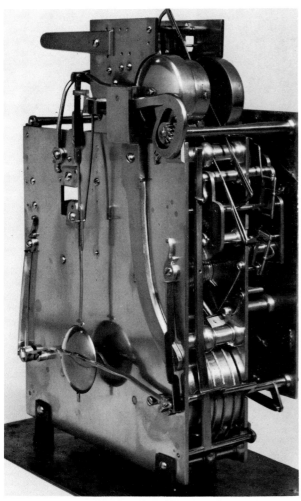

Plate 510. An angled view of the clock in Plate 509.

Plate 511. A view of the top of the clock in Plate 509
with the bell removed.

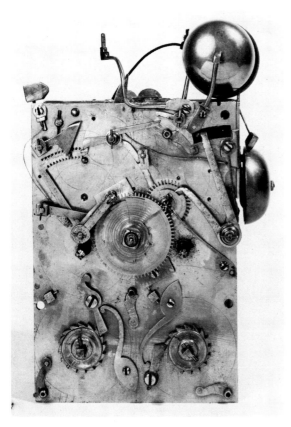

Plate 512. *The under dial work of a quarter repeating clock by Robert Seignior. (The clock in its case is shown in Plate 639.)*

Plate 513 *(below left). The striking side of the clock in Plate 512.*

Plate 514 *(below right). The quarter repeating side of the clock in Plate 513.*

358

was originally held in the case by the early method of two pegs knocked into the seat board. The present brackets are almost certainly a later addition.

Normally a rack will fall away from the snail with a pin in the end of the rack arm being arrested by the snail. The rack on this Seignior clock falls on to the snail and is gathered away from it. Thus the gathering pallet must work on the underside teeth and the rack hook on the outside teeth. Its position is such that it cannot fall by gravity and it is therefore spring-loaded. Presuming that this is the way in which rack mechanism evolved, it is interesting that it is placed in approximately the same position in which it became standard.

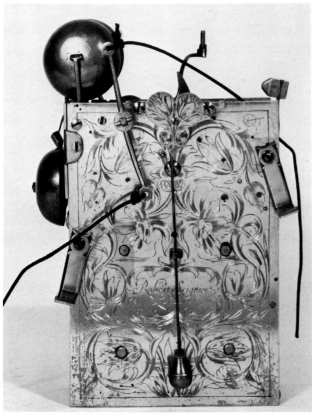

Plate 515. The back of the clock in Plate 512.

Plate 516. The top view of the clock in Plate 512 showing the quarter hammers in their block, the moving hammer block with the pendulous tails which either miss or draw the hammers.

Plate 517. The pendulous hammer tails of the clock in Plate 512. They are positioned by the lever riding on the quarter snail. The arced lever is to arrest the warning pin of the strike train.

These early rack striking mechanisms included a separate locking device for the train. In this Seignior clock it is the lever with the triangular end, squared on to an arbor, raised by a pin in the rack and it lifts the locking lever between the plates into the path of a pin in the locking wheel to arrest the train. It is an indication that this is an early use of rack striking in that there are two lifting pieces, one for unlocking and one for warning. The former is an extension of the rack hook and is lifted by a pin in the minute wheel whilst the other is lifted by the minute wheel on the minute pipe. This complete rack assembly consists of a cannon riding on a stud in the front plate on which are mounted the quadrant rack at the bottom, and the rack arm at the top.

The strike/silent mechanism on this clock is unusual and worthy of note. The second minute wheel, to which the quarter snail is attached, is extra thick and retained on its stud by the pressure of a light spring on the snail. Above it, on the left, can be seen in Plate 512 an arbor to which is pinned a piece bevelled on the under side to enable it to be pumped back and forth from the dial. Behind the front plate is a piece attached to this arbor with a pin, which, passing through the plate near the minute wheel stud, will exert pressure on the minute wheel when pumped and cause the lifting pin on the wheel to miss the unlocking lifting piece and so effectively silence the clock. The maker of this clock still followed traditional practice by keying the hour wheel. Since the hour socket carries the snail, any movement of the hour hand without regard to its correct relationship to that of the minute hand will cause the wrong hour to be struck.

The Robert Seignior clock in Plates 512-517 has repeating mechanism. The part of this mechanism which is planted on the front plate is clearly visible in Plate 512. That which is between the plates needs some explaining. There is a large hammer block, shown detached from the movement in Plate 517, which has pendulous hammer-tails. The long double-ended lever seen on the front plate with one arm bent through the plate, is so constructed that, according to on which of the steps of the quarter snail the shorter arm is resting, it holds out of contact either one, two or three hammer tails. Thus, when the repeat cord is pulled during the first quarter after the hour, the repeat train will make a complete run but only release the hour train to strike the hour. During the second quarter, one blow would be struck, two during the third and so on. This repeating mechanism appears to be peculiar to Seignior, although one other example is known which bears another maker's name. The arrangement of the bells is unusual. The top crown wheel cock is not cast, but made from bent sheet metal.

Plates 518-522 are of a clock by Thomas Tompion which is in the National Gallery of South Australia. It is a sturdy, straightforward clock of the late 1670s or early 1680s and a good example of quality workmanship. Unfortunately, it has been converted to anchor escapement but has not otherwise been mutilated. The count wheel is screwed to the strike side main wheel which makes one revolution in twelve hours and there is an attractive refinement of an aperture in the back plate having a pointer indicating the last hour on the count wheel. This aperture has a deeply bevelled plate screwed behind it which greatly enhances its appearance. Here we see Tompion's typically sturdy pillars. Half of the lower ones have been filed away in order to clear the barrel lines. This is fairly common practice. What is unusual, however, is that the cutting away of the pillar on the strike side is almost two thirds of its diameter.

The springing of this clock is worth noting. A single strip of metal bent around the retaining screw operates both barrel clicks, a steady pin being formed in the under-side of the strip (Plate 522). A similar practice was adopted at a later time in clocks

Plate 518. The dial and hands of a striking clock by Thomas Tompion. (The clock in its case is shown in Colour Plate 26, page 469, and Plate 641.)

The Art Gallery of South Australia

Plate 519. The clock in Plate 518 dismantled showing each individual part.

Plate 520. The inside of the back plate of the clock in Plate 518.

Plate 521 (below). The back plate of the clock in Plate 518.

Plate 522 (above). The under dial work of the clock in Plate 518.

Tho: Tompion Londini Fecit

of the Colston school. The hammer spring is of the customary Tompion shape, but the counter spring is purely functional and devoid of decoration. A place where typical Tompion decoration may be seen is on the bell-stand foot, it is a simple shape but has a little ridge at the point where the stem joins the foot. It is one of the unfortunate mistakes which many restorers make when replacing missing parts, that they over decorate; original makers rarely did. Such pieces as bell stand feet are rarely decorated, they are normally just pointed with the end bent over to form a steady pin. The stopwork springs here are of flat steel with bevelled disc ends for the screw and the springs are flat on the underside but rounded on top.

This clock is not numbered, from which fact we may presume it to have been made about 1680. There are other clocks like it and one of these (not illustrated) was evidently returned to Tompion after a few years for modernisation including the removal of the count wheel and the addition of quarter repeating mechanism with rack. The original holes are still visible and it can be seen that the count wheel aperture has been filled in and engraved over. Some idea of when this took place may be assumed from the fact that Tompion has stamped his number 100 over the engraving, using large numbering punches.

It was during the 1670s that the back plates of the spring clocks received more attention from the engravers. In the earlier period, these had been either entirely plain or merely engraved with the maker's name. It was possibly because the cases were being made with glazed back doors that back plates began to receive more attention. The treatment varied quite considerably according to the skill or preference of the engraver or wish of the maker. Some of the most interesting treatments are to be found on Joseph Knibb's clocks. Reference has already been made to some which have a fish as a centrepiece (Plates 450 and 454). These usually have a rather crude floral branch sprawled across the plate. Other of his clocks have better designs and finer engraving with more realistic flowers, often the figure of Death or Time will form the centrepiece.

The man who engraved the back plates for Henry Jones succeeded in capturing the essential characteristics of that maker's work, for the engraving is boldly executed with heavily blacked in features totally in keeping with Jones's treatment of his ratchet wheels, clicks and springs (Plates 432 and 439). Probably the best engraving of the period is to be found on the plates which have almost symmetrical corner decoration (Plates 442 and 446). Almost all include a Tudor rose, particularly on the count wheel.

There is no doubt that the introduction of the rack was a technical advance but not all of the makers took immediate advantage of it. Joseph Knibb, for instance, seems to have preferred to continue to use the count wheel except on those clocks which incorporated quarter repeating mechanism, in which case the rack was always placed between the plates.

After the end of the 1670s, Knibb ceased to make such large movements but made smaller clocks in great variety and all of very attractive appearance. It is quite erroneous however to consider them all to be of the same high quality for some have pinions which have not been hardened, in some the depths are bad and some cannons are ill fitting on their studs. Frequently the strike/silent work is faulty and no provision has been made for preventing malfunctioning of repeating work during the warning period before the hour. The plates of Knibb spring clock movements are always thin and he seldom fitted them with a bridge. This is a disadvantage in his quarter repeating clocks incorporating a rack, for the rack arm needs to drop on to the correct step of the snail at all times and the change from one step to another must be done during the period between the warning piece being positioned to arrest the train and the unlocking of the train. This is particularly critical at the approach to one o'clock.

Joseph Knibb made a great variety of clocks. Timepieces with or without repeating mechanism, hour striking clocks, three-train quarter striking clocks and clocks striking the hours and the quarters by the double-six method as well as those with Roman striking. His dials also were not standardised. Some have chapter rings wider than others, while a few have skeleton chapter rings and just a few have dial plates covered with velvet. No Knibb clocks are known which have pendulums on spring suspensions and none have rise and fall work. All have knife-edge suspension. In spite of the great variety of his clocks and the differing quality of the workmanship found in them, all from this period bear his own undoubted stamp and must have been made in his workshop or at least under his supervision. Some made in these circumstances do not bear his name, one such being a three-train quarter clock which is signed Thomas Taylor.

A Knibb clock which is quarter striking or grande sonnerie and which uses the double-six method of striking, is shown in Plates 523-524. Early Italian clocks frequently used this method of striking and in some cases have six hour dials. The purpose is presumably to economise in power since 78 blows are required for a normal striking clock in any twelve hours. This did not trouble English makers until they approached the making of a clock to strike the hour at each quarter, when it would be necessary to strike 312 blows every twelve hours. In this clock Knibb overcame the problem by adopting the double-six system, thus reducing the number of blows required to 168. This can be achieved within the normal train construction, by a main wheel of 84, doubling the number of pins to 16 in a 48 tooth pin wheel with double locking or with 96 teeth and single locking.

The striking of the quarters is regulated by a count wheel on an extension of the pin pinion, as will be seen in Plate 523, with slots for striking one bell during the first quarter, two during the second, three during the third and four during the last quarter. There are four pins, so placed on the count wheel as to release the hour train on completion by the lifting of the pivoted lever. No warning is needed.

The back plate of a month, Roman striking clock is shown in Plate 525 and that of an ordinary striking clock is shown in Plate 526. In this instance the count wheel has been given a little extra finish by the bevelling of the edge. It is not unusual to find the count wheel covering some of the signature. The back cock here has only one foot, otherwise it is similar to that seen on the clock in Plate 531. The delicate acanthus engraving on the back cock would appear to be by a different hand from that of the rest of the engraving on the back plate. Another back plate of a Knibb clock is shown in Plate 527.

Count wheels from this period are crossed out and exposed. It is not easy to distinguish the work of John Knibb from that of his brother and there is no doubt that there was close cooperation between them and also with Peter Knibb, but Joseph was the main producer. Brass is mostly used for hammer, counter and repeat springs on clocks signed by Joseph, while steel is mostly used on those signed by John, but this is not always the case and sometimes both types are used in the same clock. Plate 528 shows a clock which demonstrates the close cooperation between the

Plate 523. The fully engraved back plate of a 'double-six' grande sonnerie clock by Joseph Knibb.

Plate 524. The under dial work of the clock in Plate 523 showing the split plates and replacement bell stands which are too elaborate.

366

Plate 525. *The fully engraved back plate of a month, Roman striking clock by Joseph Knibb.*

Plate 526. *The fully engraved back plate of an eight-day clock by Joseph Knibb. The count wheel covers the engraving.*

Plate 527. Engraved back plate of a striking clock by Joseph Knibb with no engraving behind the count wheel which normally indicates an earlier clock. There are many stopped holes visible showing that it has been altered about three times.

Plate 528. An amply engraved back plate of a striking clock by Joseph Knibb with a covering plate bearing John Knibb's signature.

two brothers. It was evidently made by Joseph and sold by John. The hammer spring visible above the back plate is brass.

Plate 529 is of the front plate of another clock by Joseph Knibb which has push-bar repeating mechanism. This is in original condition including the gilding at the ends of the bar. It is one of very few such clocks which remain today, for push-bars do not enhance the appearance of a clock and they are very difficult to assemble. The result has been that many have been converted to pull-string, with the slots in the case for the push-bar fitted with pulleys, sometimes set in brass sleeves. The motive power for this repeat train is provided by the long brass spring which is of round section, bearing on the lower arm of the double-ended lever pivoted on an arbor close to the minute wheel. This is brought into operation when the lever is turned in a clockwise direction and it will be seen that this can be done whether its lower arm is moved to the left or its upper arm to the right by the push-bar lever. The

Plate 529. The under dial work of a clock by Joseph Knibb with pull/push lever.

arbor on which this double-ended lever is pivoted, carries a piece, the end of which may be seen protruding through the plate to the right of the minute wheel, which contacts the quarter snail behind the minute wheel. On the same arbor is a quadrant which drives the quarter train by engaging a pinion with a three-toothed ratchet, to permit its passing as the train is set up, and then to drive. The normal method was to have three lifting pins around the ratchet and a spring-loaded hammer tail on the quarter hammer arbor which was passed on the set-up, but when the train was running, the hammer was drawn.

Another method was to have a fixed hammer tail with pins in the first wheel and a stop piece in the quadrant arbor which moved into position to arrest the train on the lifting pins. The lifting piece in that instance (Plate 529) was the steel piece running across the plate, on the underside of which three saw-cuts were made to produce three arms when bent down. The arm on the left is lifted by a pin in the cannon wheel. The other two arms leave the main arm beneath the left arm of the push-bar lever. One of them is bent towards the centre and is lifted by a pin in the minute wheel while the third, which is hardly visible, contacts a bent back pad on the upper end of the double-ended lever, thus setting off the strike when the bar is pushed. It will be seen that a spring bears lightly upon the surface of this piece near to its cannon, making the pin in the end of the stud unnecessary. The top right hand end of the lifting piece is bevelled at the back. The strike/silent lever is pivoted on a stout stud in the back of the dial plate and is wedge shaped so that, when it moves over the bevelled end of the lifting piece, it raises the bent down arms out of the way of the lifting pins. The warning piece on the lifting piece rests on the edge of the aperture in the front plate through which it passes; an arrangement which is unsatisfactory and frequently, modifications which have been attempted have made no improvement.

Plates 530-531 are of the only known spring clock by Peter Knibb. This also has the push-bar repeating mechanism, which is original excepting for the pear-drop ends. It is however different from the last mentioned in that much more of the work is done between the plates. It is one of the better made Knibb clocks although it has some less commendable features such as the lifting piece which is cocked on the front plate. This is unevenly balanced, with the longer arm on the left lifting both the lever on the rack hook arbor for unlocking and also doing warning through the aperture in the plate, while the shorter arm provides this motion from the lifting pin in the minute wheel. It is true that this inequality is somewhat mollified by the sliding action of the curved lifting arm. Perhaps it is some evidence that difficulties were encountered by the engraving of an 'F' on this push-bar to indicate the front. There is an ingenious arrangement of levers between the plates which enables the repeat to be operated whether the bar is pushed from either direction. The long brass leaf spring on the right of the front plate provides the motive power for the repeat, it is round in section, squaring off where it bends through the plate. Another ingenious arrangement of levers with spring-loaded passing pieces, unlocks the hour train at the end of the quarter train run, obviating warning when pushing the bar.

One of the best known of the seventeenth century clockmakers is Daniel Quare, who was trading from 1671 for nearly fifty years and whose name appears on a great many clocks. It appears quite legitimately on movements of very different types, some of which have a close affinity with the work of Henry Jones, some with Knibb or Tompion and others with a variety of different makers. The quality of the workmanship also varies as widely. This poses problems when trying to identify which

Plate 530. *The under dial of a quarter repeating clock by Peter Knibb with the original pull/push bar. (The clock in its case is shown in Plate 636.)*

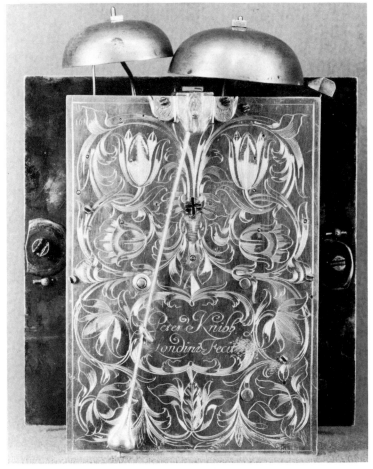

Plate 531. *The back of the clock in Plate 530 with turn buttons on the dial for securing the movement in the case.*

clocks were actually made by him, for it must be fairly obvious that he used the productions of other makers in order to satisfy the requirements of his clients. there is also little doubt that he was able to let other makers use movements which he had made. The fact that there is such wide variety in the clocks which bear his name is probably one reason why his signature has been used, as it has by the unscrupulous in more recent years, to add to unsigned clocks.

A clock which legitimately bears Quare's name is shown in Plates 532-536. It is a clock with a four-bell pull repeating mechanism and is one of his better productions, stoutly made of good materials and almost certainly originally made with fusee chains. In a number of ways Quare's clocks were different from the majority. For instance the crown wheel cocks were mounted on the front plate and about half of them have the centre wheel mounted in the front. This has not been done in the case of the clock illustrated and consequently the crown wheel rotates anticlockwise. It was also usual for him to cock the front verge pivot making the mounting of the mock pendulum more convenient, and cocks were used elsewhere on the front plate, where studs were more commonly used by other makers. The back cock here is quite plain, which is most often the case, but unfortunately many of these have since been engraved or have had decorative aprons added during the last half century.

In the illustration in Plate 532 it will be seen that the rack teeth have been cut like

Plate 532. *The under dial work of a clock by Daniel Quare with quarter repeating work. (The clock in its case is shown in Plate 710.)*

Plate 533. *The dial and hands of the Quare clock in Plate 532.*

Plate 534. The back plate of the clock in Plate 532.

Plate 535. *View of the movement of the clock in Plate 532 taken from the top.*

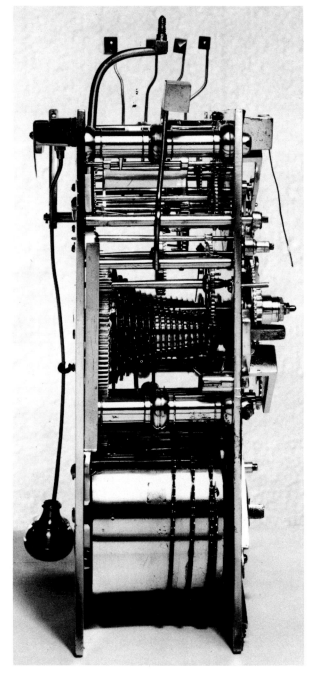

Plate 536. *The strike side of the movement in Plate 532.*

374

wheel teeth; this is not always the case. The rack is well finished, the shank being bevelled and a heart-shaped pattern has been made where the quadrant joins the shank. The gathering pallet does not lock but there is a pin in the rack which during its last gather lifts the lever which partially covers it, and a locking piece on the same arbor, bringing it in contact with a pin on the locking wheel and thus arresting it. The rack hook is beneath the locking lever on the front plate, in this instance mounted on a stud, but sometimes found without a brass cannon pivoted on a double-shouldered screw which usually has a decorated head. There are other points worth mentioning which are visible on the front plate of clocks constructed like this; for instance, there are deep circular lines on the snail and the star wheel with its click, and the well-made leaf springs are of steel and each is numbered.

The quarter snail is under the minute wheel, an unusual feature as is the strike/silent mechanism pumping the minute wheel instead of the lifting piece. This means that both the minute wheel and the quarter snail must be twice the normal thickness to enable them to function when pumped forward into the silent position by the spring which is mounted inside the front plate. The wire spring along the horizontal part of the lifting piece, spring loads the vertical part to permit the hands to be set backwards past the hour when in the strike position.

The fundamental basis of the repeating mechanism in this clock is of the simplest kind. It is operated by a pull-cord on the extremity of the lever on the back plate (Plate 534) which is squared on to the main arbor. When pulled, this winds a cord on to a snail-shaped pulley squared on to the other end of the arbor and seen in the front plate (Plate 532), held in tension by a hardened and tempered leaf spring with a very high 'set'. Thus, when fully wound the spring is exerting its maximum power on the smallest diameter of the pulley and on an increasing diameter as the power decreases enabling the speed of the train to remain fairly constant. Motive power provided by such a leaf spring is distinctly a Quare feature.

Pivoted below the main arbor on the front plate is a 'V' shaped lever. When the train is wound by the pull-string, the left-hand arm of this lever contacts the quarter snail and a piece pivoted and spring-loaded on the end of the other arm is contacted by the appropriate part of the stepped cam on the main arbor, pushing it down and rotating the right-hand arm of another lever pivoted on the main arbor, causing its left-hand end to lift the lifting piece. The striking train is thus unlocked and the rack drops. The double-ended lever pivoted above the rack, which has the quarter train warning piece at its bent upper end, also drops. The movement of the double-ended lever on the main arbor also pushes out with its bent right hand arm, a spring-loaded piece holding the right hand arm of a further double-armed locking lever which is squared on to an arbor situated above the main arbor, thus releasing it. On this arbor, between the plates, is a piece for locking the quarter train which is spring-loaded for unlocking. When the pull-string is released and the tension taken off the stepped cam, the strike train is allowed to run and, upon its last gather, the quarter train will run until a pin in the stepped cam rotates a piece behind it to move the locking lever into the locking position.

This clock is in fine original condition. It is a little disappointing to find it with such a heavy pendulum bob. The theoretical ideal pendulum is a mass concentrated at one point upon a weightless rod, something which cannot be obtained. With a heavy bob and a knife-edge, the knife-edge will wear into the 'V' cut in the back cock causing the arc of swing to be reduced as the side of the knife-edge is restricted by its own cutting. It will be seen that this has happened in this instance as there are two

Plate 537. The rear of a quarter repeating clock signed "J. Windmills" but of Quare workmanship.

sets of steady pins in the cock feet. The wear in the V-cut has been filed out and the cock raised to compensate. The deeper V has also made it necessary to file down the top of the cock and lower the apron. A lighter pendulum would have lessened this wear.

Tompion's workmanship may be seen in a number of clocks signed by Quare and at least one Tompion clock — No. 315 — would appear to have been made by Quare. Clocks signed by Samuel Watson are also to be found which could have been made by Quare, also some by Windmills (Plate 537). The engraving of repeating work shown in Plate 541 suggests that Massey also used his movements. A clock by Joshua Wilson is illustrated (Plates 538-540) in which Quare features may be seen. The cocked rack, the identically shaped springs and the same method of locking. There are however differences such as the suspension spring on the pendulum.

It would seem reasonable to presume that Tompion introduced in about 1680, the repeating mechanism which became standard on both his timepieces and his striking clocks. This can be seen in Plate 542, and in Plate 543 can be seen the heavy leaf spring which is screwed inside the back plate to provide the motive power. A good diagram of the working of this mechanism is given in Figure 1 on the engraving reproduced in Plate 541.[2] It may be helpful to run through the method of working since all the parts are shown and lettered although not all that are shown are sited on the front plate. The layout is also over simplified and many parts are normally in different positions. It shows the position of the parts half way through the run.

2.   Antoine Thiout, *Traité d'Horlogerie*, 1741.

Plate 538. The front view of a three-train chiming clock signed Joshua Wilson but made by Quare.

Plate 539. The under dial work of the clock in Plate 538.

Plate 540. *The back plate of the clock in Plate 538.*

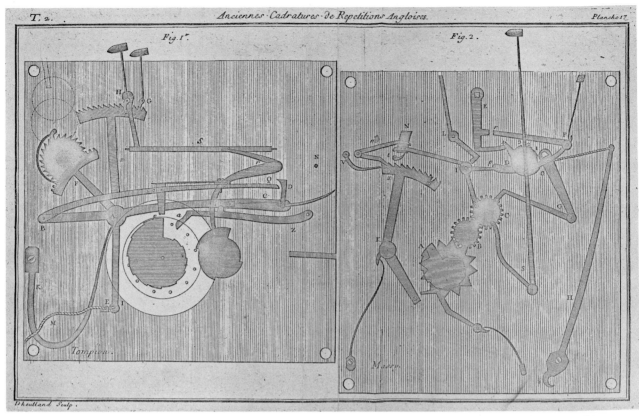

Plate 541. Quarter repeating mechanisms reproduced from the Treatise on Horology *by Antoine Thiout.*

Plate 542. *The under dial work of a timepiece by Thomas Tompion with pull-cord quarter repeating work. (The clock in its case is shown in Plates 658-659.)*

Plate 543. *An angled front view of the timepiece in Plate 542.*

The quarter hammer is operated by pins in the rack on the vertical arm of the piece B-Q. When the mechanism is not operating, this piece rests on the piece B-C to which it is pivoted, thus lowering the rack out of contact with the hammer tails. Pivoted on the right hand end of B-C is a small spring-loaded piece, D, with a horizontal arm. Attached to B-Q at the end of a spring is a piece extending downwards which, when the pull-cord on the arm, E, is pulled, rotating the arbor, A, clockwise, will rest on the appropriate step of the hour snail. In the illustration this is in the 1 o'clock position. The effect is the lifting of Q over the spring-loaded D to rest on top of it and at the same time to bring the rack in line with the hammer tails. When the pull-string is released, the spring, K, drives the repeat train and the appropriate blows are struck. The quarter blows are provided by the three pins in the rack which are of graduated height. The quarter hammer arbor is pumped so that the hammer-tail will either be free of the pins or in line with one, two or three of them. The pumping is done by a forked lever working in an annular groove in the hammer arbor which is connected to another arbor, S, pivoted on cocks on the inside of the back plate. (One end is visible in Plate 543.) This arbor is rotated by the double-armed lever 'r', the lower arm of which rests on the quarter snail and the upper presses on a pin in the arbor protruding through the plate. Thus, the four steps of the snail will produce the four positions of the pumping quarter hammer. The horizontal arm of the piece D, contacts a pin marked N as the train runs down, causing its vertical arm to move to the right and piece B-Q to be freed to return to rest on B-C and to take the rack away from the hammer tails.

This engraving also shows the hour snail, 'p', riding on a disc which has twelve projecting pins and a lever, Z, contacting them at 'a'. This is a device providing positive contact with the correct step of the snail when approaching the hour. The most primitive method of achieving this was to employ minute wheels and an hour wheel with low numbers of teeth providing the hour wheel and therefore the snail, with a large amount of backlash. At the hour, when the lever Z passed from one side of a pin to the other, a positive snail step was assured. This idea was improved during Tompion's lifetime and became very sophisticated, with the snail being free to rotate about 2° on the hour socket, spring-loaded backwards and driven forwards against its spring just before the hour rack dropped. In the diagram the quarter hammer is placed at the top of the plate, but in practice it is placed elsewhere with the pumping hammer tail connected with it by a link. In the clock in Plate 542 the hammer may just be seen protruding on the right of the plate at the top. The engraving also shows three pins, graduating in height, for drawing the quarter hammer tails. This work was more frequently done however by a wedge-shaped thickening of the last three teeth of the rack so that the hammer could be drawn by the rack tooth at the thickest part of the wedge to give one blow corresponding with the longest pin in the engraving. The reason for making the hammer remote from the hammer tail is that the hammer arbor with springs acting upon it cannot be pumped satisfactorily. If a clock is found which is so constructed it is probably an incorrect restoration.

The quadrant, 'F', has not been mentioned. It is on the main arbor, A, and can be seen in Plate 543 between the plates where it engages the repeating train. It is shown as engaging a pinion of twelve, but all known Tompion clocks which are in original state have a pinion of eight.

In Plate 542 it will be seen that the double-armed lever cocked at the top right of the plate (equivalent to 'r' in the engraving) has a heavy spring loading and the lower arm has its end bent forwards. Also that the main arm has an angled arm at its end which lies alongside it. In order to prevent a malfunctioning of the movement should

Plate 544. *The back plate of the timepiece in Plate 542 showing that it may have either balance or pendulum control.*

the pull-string be operated during the warning period before the hour, Tompion introduced a slight rise at the end of the highest step of the quarter snail which caused the lever resting upon it to rise higher and consequently to carry the bent portion of its other arm beneath the lower arm of the main arm, thus effectively preventing its movement for approximately five minutes before the hour. The spring loading of working parts is done throughout Tompion's clocks with the intention of preventing stopping from a minor failure of some part.

Plate 544 is of the back plate of this clock. It is of particular interest since it is a clock which may be controlled either by a pendulum or a balance wheel. It may well have been intended for use at sea. That Tompion did not always use shapely cocks is demonstrated in this movement. Some here are straight-edged, some are curved and some have larger bevels than others. It is not uncommon to find on a Tompion clock a bridge with one rectangular foot and one that is shaped. One cock on the back plate of this clock is not even engraved.

We have described the repeating mechanism as used by Tompion in a timepiece. The next illustration (Plate 545) shows it when applied to a striking clock. It will be seen that the repeat arm works from the other side of the clock. The main arm, as before, of brass, now has a large circular right hand end in which the hammer drawing piece lever is pivoted; the upper arm has only three teeth and the whole

Plate 545. The under dial work of a spring clock by Thomas Tompion with pull-cord quarter repeating mechanism. Known as the 'Barnard Tompion', it is shown in its case in Plates 630-632.

works upon the quarter snail. Neither the rack nor the rack hook can be seen since they are between the plates but the cock for the front pivot of the rack is that on the right of the winding square. The rack arm with its spring-loaded end piece extends from it almost horizontally across the centre of the plate. The pull-string levers are similar to those seen in Plate 549, one of which is fixed to the arbor of the toothed quadrant driving the train. It operates in the same way as the timepiece except that it is rotated in an anticlockwise direction. The stop piece is the rise and fall arbor. When the mechanism is operated the hammer drawing piece with the three teeth on it is lifted to produce the appropriate quarter blows and the left hand end of the piece lifts the lever on the rack hook arbor unlocking the strike train, whereupon it is released and drops to the rest position.

Cocked on the left of the clock is an assembly of three levers upon one arbor, the horizontal lever is the lifting lever, lifted by a pin in the cannon wheel, its end is spring-loaded to permit the setting back of the hands. The left of the upright levers comes into the way of a spring-loaded piece on the end of the repeat arm to prevent the string being pulled during the warning period. The right hand upright lever is in its turn pivoted to move in and out, or backwards and forwards. The top end rides in a forked piece, a double-sided lever by means of which striking or silence is effected. When the upright lever is close to the plate, it lifts the rack hook through its lever and it is also the warning piece. When the clock is silenced the forked end keeps the lever away from the plate, in which position, in lifting, it misses the rack hook lever. The arbor of the strike/silent mechanism may be seen at the top right of the front plate and the small steel arc against the plate has an angled face which will lift the strike/silent lever when turned in an anticlockwise direction through ninety degrees from the dial.

This clock has a device for regulating the pendulum length from the dial. This was made possible by replacing the knife-edge suspension with a flexible suspension. Primitive pendulums were suspended from a silk thread but the new method was by a thin strip of steel usually referred to as a suspension spring. The suspension spring had been used on longcase clocks since the inception of the long pendulum but it is not known who it was who introduced it into spring clocks. Certainly Daniel Quare used it as early as any maker, while still using the knife-edge on some of his clocks. It may be that it was introduced, as in the clock in Plate 549 as a device to enable the clock to be regulated without the necessity of turning it round. It is more often found on striking clocks and less on timepieces. As usual, when Tompion used this device, it was used with refinements.

Tompion's method was to suspend the pendulum from an arm pivoted on the left hand side of the back plate, with a quadrant at its right end having teeth formed on the inside of the arc. (This mechanism as seen in Plate 549 is the reverse way round as it is applied to a month clock.) These teeth engage a pinion of six pivoted in a low cock on a long arbor extending through to the front of the dial, where it is squared to take a stout hand. Thus, by rotating this hand, one may raise or lower the pendulum suspension; consequently the device is generally known as rise and fall mechanism. There is no play in the engagement of the pinion and the quadrant teeth so that the slightest movement of the hand has effect on the quadrant. The suspension arm, usually known as the rise and fall rack, is pivoted on a stout pin in a flat cock and held tightly in place by a large washer and cross pin. It is important that it be firmly held. The suspension spring is usually screwed to a small cock about a quarter of the way along the arm. The suspension then passes through the nib of a fixed cock on

Plate 546. The under dial work of a spring clock No. 287 by Thomas Tompion with quarter repeating worked from the strike train employing two racks.

the back plate permitting movement up or down but no involuntary movement. The pendulum usually has a lenticular bob and it swings in an almost cycloidal arc without cycloidal cheeks because the centre of its arc lowers as the bend of the suspension lengthens with the width of swing. There is no advantage in this and the good timekeeping of Tompion's clocks is due to the correct depthing of his wheels and pinions, the tooth and wheel formation and the shaping of his fusees to match the spring output and not the cycloidal arc of the pendulum.

A further development in quarter repeating was introduced by the London clockmakers by very ingeniously making the striking train do all of the work involved. To do this it was important that the hour rack should not gather until the appropriate quarter blows had been delivered. At least two different ways of doing this were used. The most common was for the pin wheel to have pins on both sides and to have a pumping hammer-tail block. The problem with this is however for the quarter hammer tail to be pumped free of the pins and the hour hammer tail into their path in the very brief period when gathering occurs. This very critical difficulty is quite a drawback to this system.

Tompion nevertheless used the system in some of his clocks and that illustrated in Plates 546-547 is one. This has the normal Tompion striking mechanism, the lifting

Plate 547. The striking side of the clock in Plate 546.

piece, rack, rack hook and strike/silent work as in the clock in Plate 545 but it has a pumped hammer-tail block, pivoted in the flat cock which is by the quarter snail. It is spring-loaded backwards by the long spring running parallel with the strike/silent piece. The links for the hammer tails to the hour and quarter hammers may be seen in the cut-outs in the sides of the plate. There are two racks on the one train situated beside each other, pivoted between the back plate and two similar cocks on the front plate on the right. The quarter rack gathers first and the last tooth, being cut deeper than the rest, enables the rack hook, which has been holding back the hour rack hook, to drop deeper and to release the hour rack hook to drop in and work in the usual manner.

The back end of the hammer-tail block consists of two pegs to prevent it turning and they slide in a very large cock screwed inside the back plate. This may be seen at top left in Plate 546. It extends down over the wheels and racks, the hour rack being behind the locking wheel and the quarter rack over it. On the quarter rack arbor is a lever extending in roughly the same direction as the rack, which pumps the hammer-tail block forward on the last gather of the quarter rack. The discharge of the

Plate 548. The going side of a clock by Thomas Tompion of a month's duration with pull-cord repeating work and reversed trains and going fusee with original chains. (The clock in its case is shown in Plate 713.)

repeating work is done in the usual manner with two pull-string arms on the back plate as in Plate 549. The strong leaf spring screwed inside the back plate, which in an independent repeating train would drive the quarter train, now only returns the repeat levers to the rest position.

The long arm diagonally across the upper part of the plate, is the repeat arm, with at its end a spring-loaded piece to prevent pull-off during the warning period. The screw to the right of this projects at the rear to move a holding piece away from the warning pin while the arm is at rest against the stop pin, as in the illustration. The spring-loaded piece to the right of this screw, when lifted, discharges the train and racks by lifting the rack hook. It is spring-loaded in order to pass the quarter rack hook arbor as it falls. The train will not run until the repeat arm is in the rest position.

Stopped holes in the top left hand corner of the plate and a screw in the pillar there, indicate that alterations were made there by the maker.

Plates 548-549 are of another Tompion spring clock but one which has one month's duration and it demonstrates Tompion's ingenuity. It will be seen that in

Plate 549. The back of the clock in Plate 548 with the rise and fall bar pivoted on the reverse side from normal.

this instance the trains have been reversed. The striking train is on the right and the going on the left. The going train fusee is also reversed, probably to save space. The train has to be wound in the reverse way from normal because an intermediate wheel and pinion had to be introduced for the clock to run for one month. The provision for the required number of blows from the striking train is economically made by the use of a large pin wheel with a large number of pins and double locking. Since by this means an intermediate wheel and pinion is avoided and in order to make the striking train wind in the same direction as the going train, the train must run in the reverse direction from normal. It is more convenient, therefore, to site it on the right hand side so that the hammer can be drawn outwards. This clock has fusee chains with double and treble linkage, an almost infallible sign of their originality. Not all original chains were so constructed and one can only decide on originality by the workmanship. The fusee hook tends to be heavier and more rounded to go over a pin which is of larger size than that found in more modern clocks. Also the finish is flatter and the links of better shape.

Plate 550. The back of a miniature timepiece by Thomas Tompion with pull-cord quarter repeating mechanism. The back plate is made larger than the front in order to fill the case. There are strips of wood down the sides which effectively stop any interference with the movement from the back.

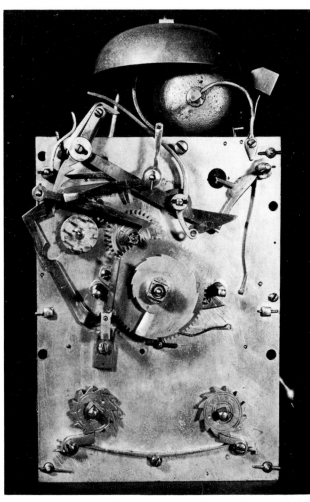

Plate 551. The under dial work of a spring clock by John Wise with pull-string repeating worked from the striking train.

Plate 552. An enlarged view of the rack in Plate 551 with inside and outside teeth. The strike/non-strike lever has been rotated out of the way to give a clearer view.

There were other methods devised for taking the power for quarter repeating from the striking train. Plates 551-552 illustrate one of these methods used by such makers as members of the Massy and Loundes families as well as some other makers including Robert Dingley. It will be seen that teeth are cut on both the inside and the outside of the rack which drops inwards and is gathered outwards. It is the inside teeth which are gathered and the rack is arrested on the outside teeth. An arbor between the plates carries the locking lever and has squared on its end the rack hook and a shaped lever extending upwards. Thus, when the rack hook drops over the end of the rack at the last gather, the locking lever also drops and locks on a stop pin. The gathering pinion extends through the front plate and is pivoted in a small cock. The gathering pallet is an integral part of the arbor and usually an extension of one pinion leaf. The pin wheel seen on the front plate is on an extension of the pin pinion which carries an identical pin wheel between the plates.

The quarter blows are struck on two bells of different pitch referred to as ting-tang quarters and both the hour and quarter hammers are situated in the top right hand corner of the movement. The hammer-tail arbor is in its normal position. There is a long push rod from the hammer-tail arbor up to the hammers, connected at its lower end only. Both of the quarter hammers are drawn by this rod. There is a spring-loaded piece on the hammer for the higher pitched bell and a hook on that for the lower which draws the other hammer until it slides off to deliver its blow and the lower pitched bell is struck when the drawing has been completed. This is not an uncommon arrangement and it appears to have been first used by Thomas Tompion in the group of clocks which is illustrated in Plates 498-511.

The top end of the push rod passes through the end of the lever which is pivoted on a stud on the front plate and which is bent through the large circular hole in the plate and the position of this spring-loaded lever determines the contact of the push-rod with either the hour or quarter hammers. The lower arm of this lever is in contact with another lever pivoted on an arbor, slightly to the right above the hand centre, which has an 'L' shaped left hand end upon which is pivoted a piece with three internal rack teeth. This piece is spring-loaded inwards and its movement is restricted by the slot in the retaining disc at its centre. This lever is free on its arbor and spring-loaded in a clockwise direction. Squared on to the end of this arbor is the pull-off lever which is also spring-loaded clockwise and provides the warning between the plates. The shaped lever on the extreme left, squared on to the locking arbor, will lift the rack hook free when the string is pulled. The very sturdy piece covering the rack is the lifting piece, it is spring-loaded forwards into the no-strike position and moved back into the strike position by the strike/non-strike lever.

The sequence of operation is as follows. The string, which is attached to the lower arm of the pull-off lever, is pulled to the right bringing the upper arm down and with it the lever carrying the three-toothed quarter rack to the point where it is stopped on the appropriate step of the quarter snail and also releasing the rack hook and holding the hour train on warn. The quarter rack has ridden over the pin wheel and either one, two or three of the teeth have been taken up by it according to the step of the quarter snail. The right hand end of this lever has at the same time moved the lever which is bent through the plate to position the hammer push-rod to contact the quarter hammer. On the release of the pull-string, the pull-off lever flies up to the stop screw, the train runs to deliver the appropriate quarter blows, the quarter rack lever returns to its stop position, the rack hook makes contact with the hour rack, the hammer push-rod is moved on to the hour hammer and normal gathering takes place.

A spring clock signed by Charles Gretton is shown in the next four illustrations (Plates 553-556). It also obtains all the required blows for the quarter repeat from the striking train, as with the Tompion system working with two racks on the same train. There is only one rack hook which is made wide enough to engage both of the racks and it is stepped so that the shorter part will engage the hour rack (which is close to the front plate) and the longer part, the quarter rack in front. Thus, when the rack hook is lifted for normal striking, the quarter rack cannot drop. The rack hook has an arm extending downwards behind the minute wheel, serving as a lifting piece. It is squared on to the extension of an arbor between the plates which operates the warning. An arbor between the plates on the left of the movement carries a lever to provide locking. Squared on to a front extension of this arbor is a lever working on the rack hook. Thus, when the rack hook drops over the end of the hour rack at the last gather, the locking lever drops into place. These pieces are visible in Plate 389.

There are three bells for the quarters in this clock and an hour bell, the hammers being contained in a pumping hammer block which also carries the hammer springs.

Plate 553. *The dial and hands of a spring clock by Charles Gretton with pull-cord quarter repeating worked from the striking train.*

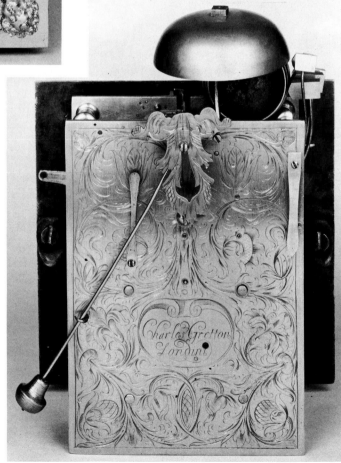

Plate 554. *The back of the clock in Plate 553.*

Plate 555. *The under dial work of the clock in Plate 553. There are two racks under one cock and one rack hook.*

Plate 556. *The striking side of the clock in Plate 553 showing the hammer block with springs for pumping.*

This makes for a heavy hammer block which is difficult to pump, a difficulty which is not lessened by the fact that the pumping is done by the end of a long extension of the quarter rack with only the rack spring to power it. The maker has, however, overcome the difficulty by providing an additional piece on the rack hook which, when the pull-off lever lifts, gives an initial impulse to the rack overcoming the inertia, after which the rack spring is sufficiently powerful.

The quarter rack arm cannot be seen in the illustration as it is under the hour wheel and hour snail. The quarter snail is on the minute pipe minute wheel. The pin barrel is uncapped as will be seen in Plate 556 and there is no reason why it should be. This illustration and that in Plate 554 also show the turn buttons on the back of the dial, which, when turned, slide into slots in the dial frame of the case and hold the clock in the case. This was a common method of fixing during the last quarter of the seventeenth century and in the early part of the eighteenth. An unusually heavy cock has been provided here for the gathering pinion. It is built up in three pieces with substantial pins and silver soldered.

Plates 557-563 are of a clock by Edward Burgis, the mechanism of which is typical of a number made during the 1690s by several makers including Richard Colston

Plate 557. The back plate of a spring clock by Edward Burgis with much of the original gilding. (The clock in its case is shown in Plate 662.)

Plate 558. The under dial work of the clock in Plate 557. It has quarter repeating work from the strike train and alarm.

Plate 560. The back of the dial of the clock in Plate 557 showing the levers for silence and the alarm stop.

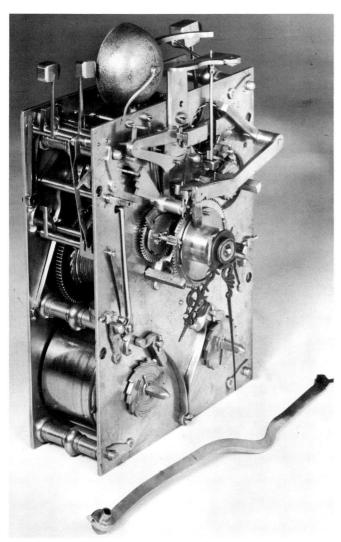

Plate 559. An angled view of the clock in Plate 557 with the repeat pull arm detached.

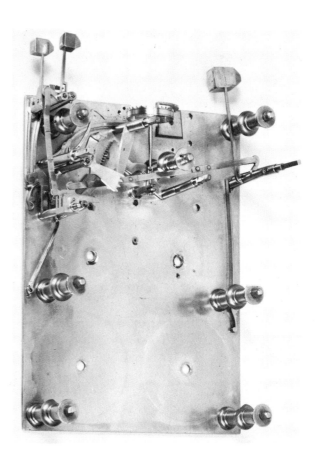

Plate 561. The inside of the back plate of the clock in Plate 557 showing all the repeat steelwork between the plates.

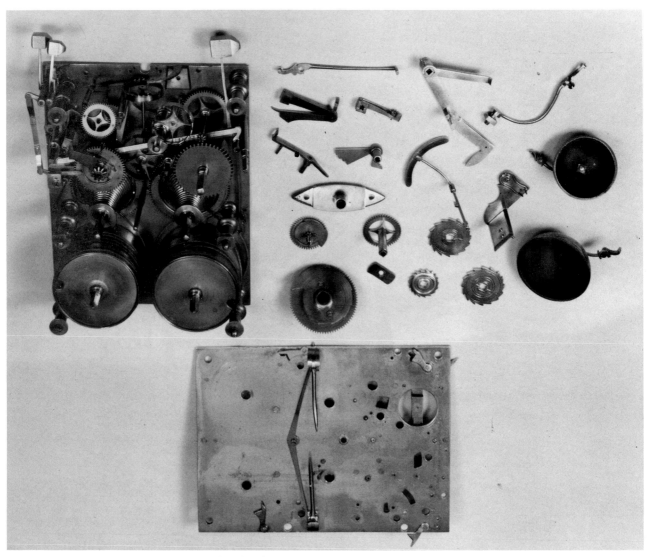

Plate 562. The clock in Plate 557 partially dismantled.

(Plate 564), William Herbert and Fromanteel (Plate 566). The repeat in each case is taken from the striking train. All of the clocks in this group are attractive pieces and very well made. One of the distinctive features of most of them is that there is a long pull-off arm for the repeat which is operated through the bottom of the case. Most of these clocks have the alarm work integral with the movement although Fromanteel appears to have preferred to have this mechanism screwed to the side. There are a few clocks which have no alarm work. The overall quality of this Burgis clock may be judged from the fine and almost symmetrical engraving on the back plate which retains much of the original gilding. The alarm work will run for at least a week with one winding and the release mechanism, which is very similar to that on the East movement illustrated on page 86, made about thirty years earlier. It is visible on Plate 558. There is a silencing lever pivoted on the back of the dial (Plate 560) which checks the alarm crown wheel.

The long pull-off arm is squared on to an arbor which protrudes through the front plate below the top left hand pillar latch (Plates 558-559). When pulled, this arbor is

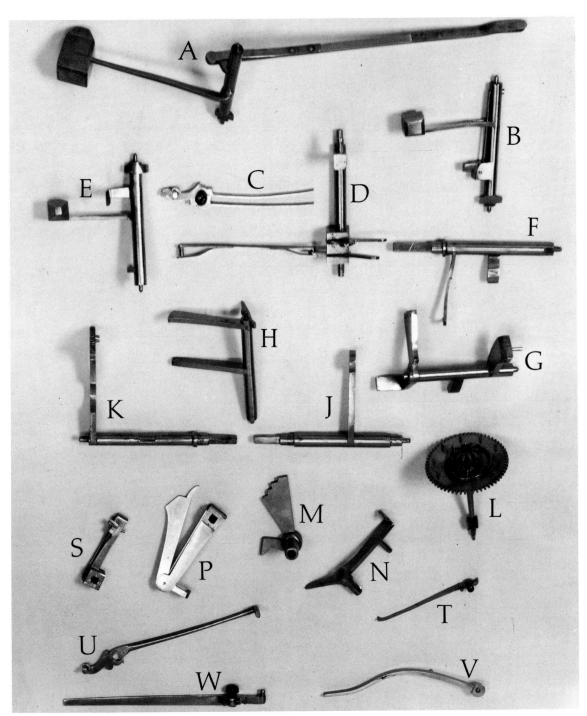

Plate 563. *The working parts of the clock in Plate 557. A. Hour hammer and its link. B. The hammer for the higher pitch of the two quarter bells. C. Double spring for the quarter hammers. D. Hammer-tail block with quarter hammer link. E. Hammer for the lower of the quarter bells with hook piece to draw 'B'. F. The pull-off arbor. The pull-off lever fits the square. G. The 4 toothed quadrant and stop piece, the hammer block pumping piece with canted corner and the pin for holding out the rack hook. H. The rack hook. In its place is the piece for the pin in 'G' to work upon and the tail for the spring 'T' to work upon. The lever in the centre of the arbor is lifted by the lever on 'J'. J. This lever lifts the rack hook and 'P' fits the square. K. The hour rack. 'S' fits the square. L. The pin pinion and solid pin wheel. There are pins on each side, click and click spring on the wheel for working on the 10 toothed ratchet which is fixed to the 10 toothed pinion free on the arbor. M. The piece which rides on the quarter snail. N. The warning piece. The pin works on 'P'. P. This fits upon 'J' and is moved sideways by the pin in 'N' and effects the no-strike. S. The rack arm. T. The rack hook spring. U. Spring for returning 'G' to the neutral position after its operation. V. Return spring for 'F'. It works upon a flat on the arbor. W. Hour hammer spring.*

Plate 564. The dial of a clock similar to that in Plate 557 by Richard Colston. (The clock in its case is shown in Plate 663.)

rotated clockwise depressing a piece on an adjacent arbor which has on it a four-toothed quadrant which will turn a pinion riding on the pin pinion arbor with a ratchet and click. This pinion has the same number of teeth as the solid pin wheel has pins. The amount that this pinion is turned is determined by an arm attached to the quadrant, protruding through the plate, being stopped on one of the steps of the four-stepped piece pivoted on a stud just above the minute wheel. It will be seen from Plates 558 and 559 that the appropriate step is determined by the quarter snail on the minute wheel. Attached to the quadrant arbor is a piece which at the same time pumps the hammer block backwards to strike the quarters and holds out the rack hook. The long spring with the fancy foot situated to the left of the minute wheel, just supplies sufficient power for the return of the four-toothed quadrant to the rest position. The spring beside it is the pumping spring. The pumping piece carries a pin which holds out the rack hook and can be seen in Plate 563. It is essential that the pumping spring be lightly loaded for otherwise the mechanism will not work, nor will it unless the angles on the two pieces effecting the pump are very acute since the action must be swift. Immediately the pull-off lever is released, the quarter blows will be delivered whilst the rack hook is held out. The rack hook drops when the quarter blows are completed and the hour blows begin.

This clock also has ting-tang quarters. The hook in the hammer for the lower pitched bell and the spring-loaded tail of the higher, may be seen in Plates 558-559. The connecting links between the hammers and their tails in the block are formed by strips of steel, the ends being bent over and formed into pins. Pieces of steel are pinned to these strips to cover the ends of the pins. These links must be very free in the holes in which they work for any tightness will prevent the return to neutral of all the parts after the draw.

The clocks in this group have a weakness in the planting of the rack, the rack hook and the gathering pallet, for the latter should be at the corner of the square of the other two. Because it is not, the rack hook needs to be spring-loaded. Many things have been done in this movement to reduce friction. For instance, the pieces on the hammer arbors upon which the springs act are made quite short. It will be seen that both the stopwork springs (Plate 562) and the barrel ratchet click springs (Plate 559) are made in one piece, the latter being formed by bending a strip of brass around the securing screw and making steady pins in the metal immediately above it. A similar method is adopted for the light springs bearing on the warning piece and the quarter snail riding piece (Plate 558).

The warning piece is studded just above the minute wheel and is moved by a pin in the minute wheel. A stout pin in it works upon an elbow piece squared on to an arbor just above it. This piece is required for silencing the strike, done by a lever pivoted on the back of the dial, pushing the forearm piece out of the way of the pin in the warning piece by acting on a projection at the elbow point. The snail is behind the hour wheel and the hour rack between the plates. The rack arm has a spring-loaded pin which will slip past the snail without stopping the clock should the striking train jam.

The long pull-off lever shown in Plate 559 is a replacement. The original was probably made in two pieces as is that shown in Plate 565. This is a piece discarded many years ago at a time when it was not regarded as a sin to modify a difficult mechanism. Other discarded parts are also shown in Plate 565 which come from

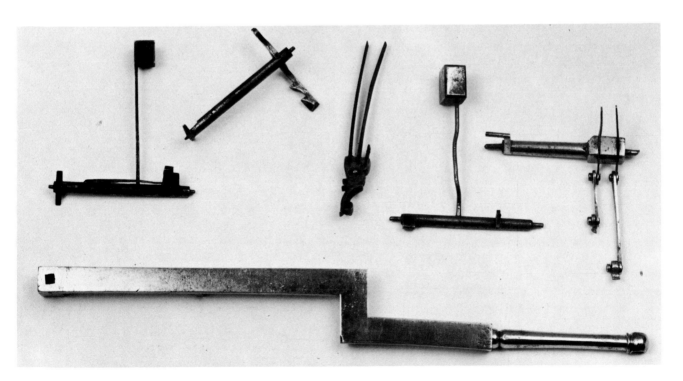

Plate 565. Parts taken from clocks of similar design to that in Plate 557.

Plate 566. The back plate of a clock similar to that in Plate 557 by Fromanteel, with alarm at the side.

Plate 567. The back of another clock by Fromanteel with the alarm at the side. (The clock in its case is shown in Plates 649-650.)

clocks of the type being discussed. Those on the left are quarter hammers and in the centre are three hammer springs from a three-bell repeating clock, brazed into a brass foot (one spring is broken). On the right is a hammer-tail block, the front part of which is canted to enable it to be pumped from the front. The other piece is probably an hour hammer.

Plate 566 is of a clock signed Fromanteel, probably Abraham, which has a large apron. It is constructed as described above but has alarm work attached to the side. Part of its pull-off lever may be seen low on the right. The other Fromanteel illustrated also has the side alarm but is of different construction (Plate 567).

The motive power for repeating mechanisms at the end of the century is normally supplied by a coil spring housed in a spring box fixed to one of the plates. One is seen on the back plate in Plate 579 behind the pulley. The two feet are visible at 5 and 11 o'clock.

398

Plate 568. A spring clock signed Samuel Watson showing the quarter repeating cam mechanism.

Plate 568 shows the front plate of a clock signed Samuel Watson, but the cocked hour rack and lifting piece, the rack hook pivoted on a double shouldered screw, the locking between the plates, the position of the snail, star wheel and click and also the springs, are all characteristic of the work of Daniel Quare. This clock is in very good original condition and illustrates the most commonly used method of obtaining the quarter blows in repeating work. The pull-cord runs round a pulley on the back plate which is squared on to the main arbor; on the front of the arbor there is squared a cam having four graduated steps on a semi-circle of it. A further pulley is fitted on to this for the power and then a quadrant cam. Between the plates is a ratchet of twelve teeth on the same arbor with the first wheel of the quarter train keyed to it, which has the twelve lifting pins for the hammer. There is a spring-loaded double-armed lever pivoted on a stud to the right, beside the driving spring, the left arm of which rides on the quarter snail mounted on the minute wheel as in the last clocks described. This rotates anticlockwise and thus rises a step each quarter and falls at the hour. The main arbor will also have a lever for locking the quarter train by arresting a pin in the second wheel. As there are twelve pins there would be a main wheel of 72 teeth and a first pinion of 6, thus making one turn for each blow. There would be a further wheel and pinion and the fly, making a slow running train.

The pull-cord will rotate the main arbor clockwise until it is stopped on the appropriate step of the cam by the lever on the right taking up one, two or three teeth on the ratchet. The quadrant will by the same motion raise the lifting piece, thus releasing the hour rack and holding it on warn. When the cord is released, normal running will ensure. The illustration shows the train during the first quarter after the hour. If the cord is pulled when in this position, no teeth in the ratchet will be taken up but the lifting will be knocked out and the hour train will be put on warn. The lifting piece is held forwards by a spring for normal striking and pumped back for non striking.

There are many variations of this type of repeating mechanism. Indeed, it is more common for there to be less pins in the first wheel and for there to be a greater number of degrees of arc on the cam and a faster running train. It will be seen that if the rest position were to be a little further round on the cam, the double-armed lever would be lifted clear of the quarter snail and this is more commonly the case. Some clocks have warning position on the quarter snail and a stop on the cam does not even permit interference with the lifting piece as it is lifting for the hour, it is done by having an even lower step on the quarter and a lower step on the cam. There are other clocks which have a further lever to work the lifting piece.

One example of this is shown in Plate 569. It has many signs of provincial manufacture but is quite legitimately signed Henry Jones. In this we see on the front plate, a pulley on the main arbor which is double-grooved to enable the repeat train to be wound from either left or right. This pulley is hollow turned to accommodate the spring box with the spring hook attached to the integral pipe of the pulley. The double-armed lever is held clear of the quarter snail. The repeat on this clock has several hammers each on its own arbor and each bell on a stand. There are four lifting pins to the wheel. A pinion on the first arbor engages a quadrant which, when activated, causes the piece on the quadrant arbor to lift the lifting piece and hold the strike on warn. The minute pinion, which has considerable end-shake, has a key-way in which a forked spring runs to allow the strike/silent mechanism to pump the lifting pin out of contact with the lifting piece.

By the end of the century many spring clocks had pull quarter repeating on a

Plate 569. A spring clock by Henry Jones showing the cam and pullies for the pull-string repeating mechanism.

400

number of bells. When this was first introduced, each hammer was separately pivoted together with its own spring and each bell was on a separate stand. Later a pin-barrel was used on the first arbor and a hammer block and hammers and the bells were mounted on one stand. Otherwise the mechanism was unchanged. Some of the less refined pieces even at that period, continued to be made on the earlier plan and are found bearing such names as Henry Jones, Thomas Taylor and Nathaniel Hodges. These are often quite crude and artless, bearing no comparison with fellow members of the Clockmakers' Company like Colston and Herbert.

One of these, which is signed John Clowes, is shown in Plates 570-576. Who the actual maker of these clocks was will probably never be known. It is unlikely that it was the Henry Jones whose work has been described earlier, since he died in 1695 at the age of sixty-three. However, it may well have been someone who had close association with him in his formative years for these movements have many features reminiscent of his work and artistry.

This particular clock was retrieved from the ruins of a house demolished by a flying bomb during the last war but, while its case was smashed, the movement survived almost unscathed and is in remarkably original condition. The hands are replacements but on the original bosses. Both the crown wheel and the verge were badly worn and have been replaced. The mock-pendulum is new and as the pull-off lever is of the wrong shape, it also may be a replacement. Much of the original lacquer remains on the back plate, apron and dial, and even the silvering, although in bad condition, appears to be original.

The impression which one gets of this dial is coarseness, from the wide chapter ring, the large winding holes which are not symmetrical and have wide rings, one of which is partly covered by the chapter ring. Also at certain times the tops of the date ring teeth are visible through the strike side hole. While it was commonly necessary to have to file off one of the chapter ring pegs to clear some part of the mechanism, in this instance three of the four pegs have been filed off, leaving only that at twelve o'clock, which has, however, proved sufficient. There is a very large aperture for the mock pendulum. The strike/silent piece is on the left.

It will be seen that the spring barrels project below the plates, making it necessary for the movement to stand on blocks as did the earlier movements. On the right side of the dial plate in Plate 571 one can see the retaining spring and cross pin of the strike/silent piece which will pull forward the spring-loaded lifting piece out of the path of the lifting pin in the cannon wheel.

One of the better features of this clock is the symmetrically engraved back plate. It has been said that where large aprons are used, the space underneath them was not engraved but this is not the case of the clock in Plate 571. The apron on this clock is quite correct but a glance at the illustration in Plate 573 will show that the engraver has not even taken into account the back cock nor left a space for the signature, hence its appearance on the apron. It will be seen that the back cock has been bent down. This was no doubt in order to deepen the escapement. Note also the odd-sided feet to the cock. This type of cock has been referred to earlier when discussing the early clocks of Knibb, Tompion and Jones. It has one high and one low screw and one frequently comes upon clocks with a neater cock with an unexplained stopped hole below the left hand screw. It may in those cases be reasonably assumed that the clock originally had a cock such as this.

The back cock is not the only feature found in this group of clocks which recalls the earlier group. One is that the centres of the rack, rack hook and gathering pinion

Plate 570. *The dial of an eight-day clock by John Clowes with repeating work.*

Plate 571. *The back of the clock in Plate 570 showing the name on the apron.*

Plate 572. *An angled view of the clock in Plate 570 showing the very clumsy work.*

Plate 573. *The back plate of the clock in Plate 570 with the apron removed. It will be seen that the back cock is just the same as we have illustrated on clocks made twenty years earlier.*

Plate 574. The under dial work of the clock in Plate 570 showing the hour hand fitting of twenty years earlier.

Plate 575. The going side of the clock in Plate 570 with the repeat spring in its own little barrel.

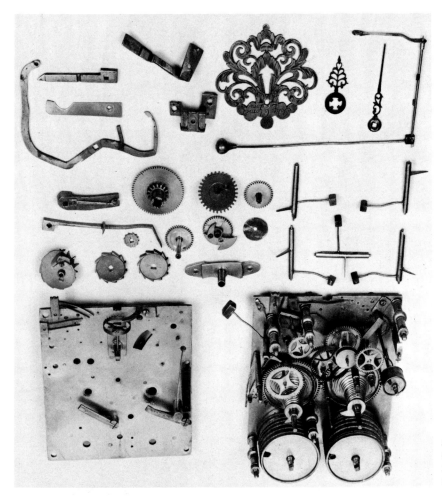

Plate 576. The clock in Plate 570 partly dismantled.

are planted almost at right angles to each other. However, the rack hook which in this case is on a screw, is sprung. This spring is just a strip of brass, an angled piece at the foot passing through a slot in the top right of the back plate and is cross pinned (Plate 573). Another crude feature seen in Plate 576 in the solid locking wheel and the steel hammer spring which is brazed into a piece of brass rod squared through the front plate (Plate 572). The other hammer springs are made up in a similar way but the brass feet are screwed to the plates. The star wheel click spring is a piece of steel wire brazed into a brass foot. The spring loading for the strike/silent work was formerly on the front of the arbor and its square hole may be seen between the hammer spring foot and the stopwork brass. The pendulum hold-fast is also squared into the back plate and cross pinned. This extensive use of squared-on fittings is fully in line with the practice of the earlier Henry Jones. The steelwork is far heavier than is necessary for its function.

Two levers are squared on to the lifting arbor, the lower one is the lifting piece, the upper is long and extends between the star wheel and snail to beneath the front verge cock and has the warning piece on it. The upper arm of the pull-off lever slides under this when the cord is pulled, providing the lifting and warning.

An almost unique feature of this particular clock is the provision of a spring-barrel for the pull quarter work instead of a spring box secured to one of the plates. The barrel is wound by a cord round a pulley on the first pinion upon which is keyed the first wheel of the train with its click and spring and five lifting pins disposed on both sides of the wheel. The pinion is engaged by a quadrant on the arbor of the pull-off lever so geared that it will pick up the required number of ratchet teeth when the cord is pulled, stopping when the projection on the pull-off lever engages the appropriate step on the quarter snail. This snail rides on an extra minute wheel. Everything on this movement is big and heavy. For instance, it was found necessary to cock the back pivot of the second pinion of this train to accommodate the quadrant (Plates 575 and 576). The empty holes seen by the barrel ratchets in Plate 574 are for ratchet springs which are missing. They would have been strips of brass with integral pins. The clicks are quite crude and have surprisingly slim rivets. Another feature of this clock which is reminiscent of the work of Jones is that the crown wheel and pinion are cocked to the front plate.

Another clock which might have come from the same workshop and is equally crude, is shown in Plates 577-578. It is, perhaps, more typical of this general group and has pillar latches. It is simpler and repeats the quarters on only one bell. Unfortunately it has been photographed with the pumping spring for the strike/silent work 90° from its true position, which should be on the lifting piece arbor. The motive power for the quarter repeat is provided by the massive spring squared on to its

Plate 577. *A clock similar to that in Plate 570 by Henry Jones with leaf spring drive for the repeating work.*

Plate 578. *The side view of the clock shown in Plate 577 signed Henry Jones.*

Plate 579. The back of an elegant clock by George Etherington with rise and fall and pull-cord quarter repeating mechanism. The back plate is much larger than the front to fill the case and prevent interference from the back. (The clock in its case is shown in Plate 697.)

equally massive foot at the bottom of the plate. This spring is $^7/_{32}$ in. square at its base. The pull-off lever has its own arbor and pulls to the right. Between the plates, a short lever engages another on the main arbor carrying the quadrant. Another massive steel lever, bent to contact the quarter snail, is squared on to the main arbor with a piece of brass pinned to it which will unlock the striking train. The pull-off lever on the Clowes clock is quite unlike that on this clock and must therefore be by another hand. In Plate 578 it will be seen that it is the hammer that is cocked instead of the second pinion. There is a spring pinned along the quarter hammer arbor, and it must have a push-past hammer tail with the lifting pins in the ratchet instead of the first wheel. This clock has the barrel ratchet and clicks on the back plate and they needed to be artistically turned and shaped to give some character to an otherwise very roughly made movement.

Plate 579 is of the back plate of a clock by George Etherington, a maker whose products display a uniformly high degree of quality. Here the rise and fall mechanism is of interest. Earlier, we have described this function performed by raising or lowering the pendulum suspension by means of a pinion working in a rack which has inside teeth. In this instance the same function is done by a pin at the end of the suspension arm working in a slot parallel with the edge of a snail. The arbor of the snail extends through to the front of the dial where there is a semi-circular ring (Plate 697) and a squared-on pointer by which the snail is operated. Consequently it will only rotate through 180°.

This clock is another example which has a back plate made wider than the front plate in order to almost fill the back door aperture. It is also another instance of the back plate engraving being done without any reference to any fittings which were to be added with the consequence that the very late placing of barrel ratchets and clicks on this plate does not enhance its appearance. It will be seen that the crutch pin has been given a spread-out end to prevent the pendulum from slipping free.

A rack and pinion rise and fall mechanism, slightly different from that used by Tompion and of lighter proportions, is seen in Plate 582. In this instance, situated on the front plate and with the rack teeth on the outside. The consequence of this is that the arbor must be rotated the reverse way and the dial ring also numbered backwards.

This is a three-train, six bell, quarter chiming clock of about 1700 (Plates 580-583),

Plate 580. The dial and hands of a three train quarter repeating clock by Charles Goode.   John Redfern

Plate 581. The back of the clock in Plate 580 with lenticular pendulum bob.

and by the time that it was made, striking was fairly generally governed by a rack in spring clocks although it was not in weight-driven clocks. In consequence racks were also used in the quarter trains. The result was that it was possible by adding a spring operated lever and simple discharging device to make this train repeat. In Plate 581 such a lever may be seen just below the quarter bells. This lever is on an arbor, the front end of which has a small pivot. Between the plates and fixed to the arbor are two levers with pins in their ends which act through apertures in the front plate to lift both the hour and the quarter lifting pieces. Separate lifting pieces are necessary if the clock is to provide for the choice of striking the hours without the quarters as this clock does. Here also the hour lifting and warning piece is spring-loaded at its upper end to bring it into the operating position. The lower end will bear on one end of a rocking lever pivoted in a small block squared into the front plate. (The square may be seen just above the upper bridge foot.) The other end bears on the pivot of the quarter lifting and warning piece. The front pivot of this latter piece may be depressed into three positions by means of a rocking lever working upon one of the steps of the circular cam situated at the top of the plate. The strike/silent hand is

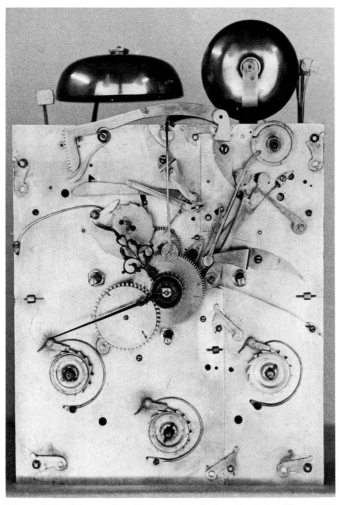

Plate 582. The under dial work of the clock in Plate 580, showing the split plates and the rise and fall rack.

Plate 583. The quarter repeating side of the movement in Plates 580.

squared to the arbor of this cam and when rotated will cause the clock to be silent, to strike the hours only or to strike the hours and the quarters by the varying length of the lifting pins.

The quarter snail is on the cannon wheel and is so remote from the rack that it has been necessary to employ the four-step lever previously described (Plate 562). One arm of this lever is spring-loaded to ride upon the snail so that the quarter rack arm will drop on the correct step at the other end. At the approach to the hour, the hour train is released and held on its warn, and then the quarter train is released and held on its warn. The hour train is then released and runs until arrested on the quarter warn. The quarter train is then released and strikes the appropriate quarter, releasing the hour train as it locks. The racks and the warn which the quarter train applies to the hour train must be between the plates. The finishing of the barrel ratchets, the shape of the click springs and the method of fixing the clicks in this clock are all reminiscent of the early work of Joseph Knibb.

Plate 584. The back of a clock by Jonathan Pullar with similar features to those in the previous clock. (This clock in its case is shown in Colour Plate 28, page 486, and Plates 683-684.)

410

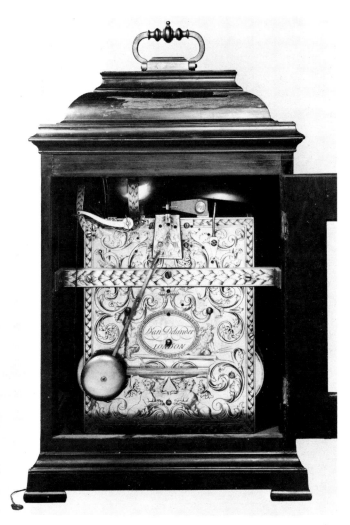

Plate 585. *The back of a three-train clock by Daniel Delander also similar to that in Plate 580.*

Plate 586. *The dial and hands of the clock in Plate 585 which has silver mounts of the highest quality. (Another view of the case is shown in Plate 720.)*

The quarter hammers are housed in a hammer block which is a block of brass into which the hammers are slotted and pivoted on a pin through the length of the block. At the time when this clock was made, these blocks were usually about ⅜ in. square but later they were made larger. It is essential for the hammers to have springs. In Tompion's three-train clocks they were of steel and worked on the external flats of the hammers and thus also acted as counter springs. They were individually screwed to a downward extension of the hammer block. While in the case of a Tompion this extension was an integral part of the block, in some others it was a piece screwed under the bell stand platform. This bell stand platform has its back end bent downwards to take a screw into the back plate and the front end is formed into two pins to fit into appropriate holes in the front plate or fitted into a dovetail in the plate. The individual bell stands are mounted on top and beneath are fixed the hammer springs which act then on the solid block of the hammer. Thus the whole assembly may be extracted by the removal of just one screw.

The hammers are operated by pins in the pin barrel which must have sufficient pins to lift each hammer once for every quarter. Thus, at each hour, with a six bell chime, four quarters are struck involving 24 bell strokes. The barrel on this clock is divided for the striking of ten quarters (Plate 583), which, allowing for a pause between the run of bells equal to that between each hammer blow, would mean seventy divisions, that is six hammer blows plus a pause, ten times.

The clock by Jonathan Pullar illustrated in Plate 584 may have originated from the same source as did the last clock. The rise and fall mechanism operates in a similar fashion, the hammers and bells are also mounted on a hammer block like the Goode. It has evidently had some replacement of parts such as the back-cock and the repeat pulley. One would expect an original pulley to have been engraved. It is, indeed, quite likely that this clock originally had a pull-cord lever as does the Goode.

Another three-train chiming clock is shown in Plates 585-586 which also may have a common origin with the previous two clocks. The rise and fall and the quarter bell stands are similar. One difference is that the hammer springs are screwed to a frame behind the hammers which is mounted on a fitting from the back plate. The bracket holding the movement in the case being made in one piece is unusual and peculiar to Delander. The dial mounts on this clock are of silver and extremely well finished.

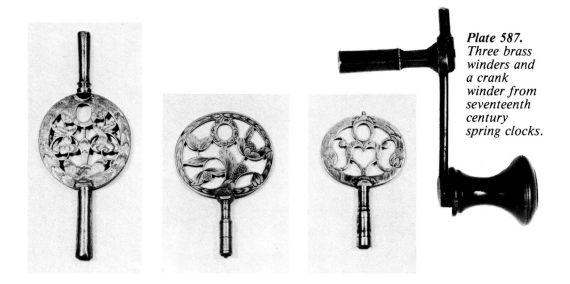

Plate 587.
Three brass
winders and
a crank
winder from
seventeenth
century
spring clocks.

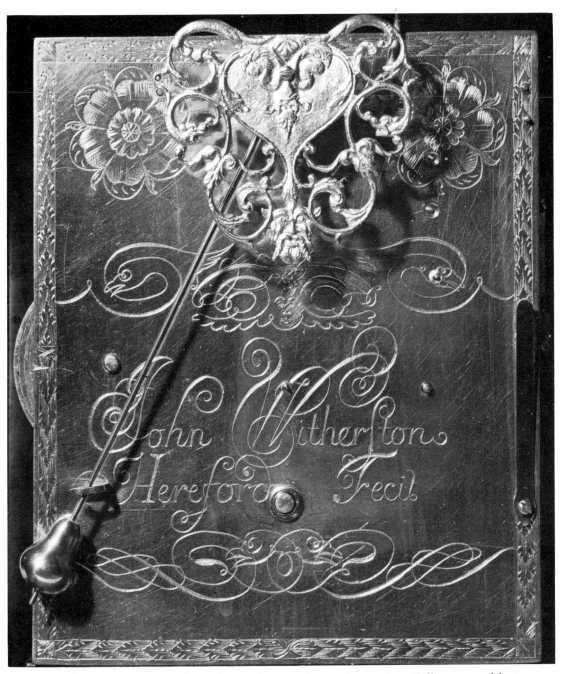

Plate 588. *The back plate of a clock made in London and partially engraved but finished and signed "John Witherston Hereford Fecit".*

Chapter IX
Later Spring Clock Cases

Turning our attention to the design of spring clock cases after the end of the architectural period, we find that the break with that period is more complete than it is with regard to longcases. Although the transition from the earlier type to the little portable case which is associated in the minds of most of us with the seventeenth century, began soon after 1670, it was not until the end of that decade that the transition was really complete. At the beginning of this transitional period — that is before about 1675 — a number of clocks were made with cases which, while they paid some attention to the principles of architectural design, ignored a great many of the details. One such case can be seen in Plates 589-590. Here it will be seen that the architectural cornice has been entirely discarded in favour of a moulding of convex section.

A much more significant step away from the tradition however, will be seen in Plates 591-592, where none of the mouldings are truly architectural although the retention of the frieze feature has some relation to past design. At the time when these cases were being made, the number of men who were making cases was growing but it was probably not until after 1680 that cases were in any sense mass-produced. It is almost certain that all cases made before 1675 were individual productions.

There is not the slightest doubt that one of the main reasons for some of the changes which took place, was the need to make a clock that was portable, as few houses at that time would have had more than one clock. In order to transport a clock from one room to another with any ease and safety, the clock had to be reduced in size and throughout the seventies this reduction was taking place, although very few really small clocks were made during that decade. In addition to reduction in size, a carrying handle was desirable, thus we find that most clocks made during the second half of the decade had one.

The early handles are very simple and the pivot pins enter the pommels from the inside, in a similar way to the bow handles which were used on contemporary furniture. Indeed, the handles on the majority of cases resemble furniture handles very closely. Knibb used very distinctive handles at this period (Plates 596, 597, etc.). In most cases the pommels of the very early handles are merely strips of brass bent round the pivot pins, laced through metal rosettes and through the case where they are bent over to secure. Such pommels are seen in the plates mentioned and one of the rosettes used is shown in Plates 614 and 645. The rosettes are always simple and when a ring of petals is used as those illustrated, the petals are sometimes bent upwards as in Plate 637. Quite plain circular plates are also found. One can sometimes

Plate 589. *Spring clock case, veneered with olivewood and with mouldings of olivewood and ebony, for a striking clock by Robert Williamson. The dial is 7ins. square. Circa 1675.*

Plate 590. *The rear view of the case in Plate 589 showing the mouldings on the back and the large glazed aperture in the door.*

Plate 591. *Spring clock case, veneered with olivewood with a flat top and olivewood mouldings, for a striking clock by Henry Jones. Circa 1675.*

Plate 592. *Spring clock case, veneered with olivewood, with a flat top and olivewood mouldings, for a striking clock by Henry Jones. Circa 1675. The frieze has fret apertures. (The movement is shown in Plates 464-465.)*
Worshipful Company of Clockmakers

Plate 593. *Spring clock case, only 11ins. high, veneered with olivewood with a flat top and olivewood mouldings, for a timepiece by Edward East. Circa 1675-80. (The movement is shown in Plate 441.)*
Camerer Cuss

Plate 594. *Spring clock case, veneered with olivewood, with dome top and mouldings of olivewood and ebony, for a striking clock by Henry Jones. Circa 1675-80.*

Plate 595. *A view of the top of the case shown in Plate 594 showing the repoussé end mounts to the dome.*

see on early flat-topped cases that the maker has protected the veneer of the top from any damage which might be caused by the handle as it falls, by adding brass bosses, as in the clocks in Plates 591 and 592. This kind of protection was not usually practical on cases with domes, however, with the result that some of these have become bruised. This is particularly the case with the heavier handles which were often used in later times, although the addition of mounts on the back and front of the domes usually prevented this bruising. One clock which has bosses on the dome is illustrated in Plate 607.

By 1680 it was the normal practice for a spring clock to have a dome. The earliest domes are usually fairly shallow, with a flattish profile and a capping which is thicker than on later cases, with a bold convex moulded edge. When finials are added, and this was by no means the rule, they were usually ball finials, occasionally more nearly spherical than previously and often with a small knob on top. The early brass turned feet were fairly large and bulbous with a very slender neck (Plate 600). Dome mounts are rare on early cases but one of the early designs to be used consisted of a cast brass winged head which is seen in a number of illustrations, for instance on page 419. Repoussé mounts were, however, also used and the designs like that seen on the silver mounted Knibb clock in Plate 603 were extensively used for many years.

Plate 596. Spring clock case, veneered with walnut with straight-grain walnut mouldings, for a striking clock by Joseph Knibb. Circa 1675-80. (The glazing beads are missing from the front door.)

Plate 597. Spring clock case, veneered with olivewood with cross-grain olivewood mouldings and unusual inlaid decoration on the door stiles and dome, for a striking clock by Joseph Knibb. Circa 1675-80.
Sotheby Parke Bernet

Plate 598. *Spring clock case, veneered with ebony with cast gilt metal mounts, for a striking clock by John Knibb. Circa 1675-80.*

Plate 599. *Spring clock case, veneered with ebony with ebony mouldings and cast gilt metal mounts, for a striking clock by Joseph Knibb. 1677. (The movement is shown in Plates 475-477.)*

Plate 600. *Spring clock case, veneered with ebony and very similar to that in Plate 599, for a striking clock by Joseph Knibb. Circa 1675-80.*

Plate 601. Spring clock case, veneered with ebony and very similar to the last three illustrated, but for a striking clock by Thomas Tompion. Circa 1675-80. (The movement is shown in Plates 447-453.)

Plate 602. Spring clock case, veneered with ebony and also very similar to the previous four illustrated, for a striking clock by Joseph Knibb. Circa 1675-80. (The movement is shown in Plates 458-463.)

Plate 603. Spring clock case, veneered with ebony with silver mounts, that on the dome being repoussé, made for a striking clock by Joseph Knibb. Circa 1675-80. It may be seen that the left hand escutcheon has been lowered to expose the keyhole which it would have covered originally.

Plate 604. Spring clock case, veneered with ebony, for a striking clock by Joseph Knibb. Circa 1680. The left hand escutcheon has been pierced and fixed. (The movement is shown in Plates 480-483.)

Plate 605. Spring clock case, veneered with ebony, for a striking clock by Thomas Tompion. Circa 1680. The moulding below the plinth is a later addition. (The movement is shown in Plates 433-437.)

Plate 606. The rear view of the case in Plate 605.

Plate 607. *Spring clock case, veneered with ebony of similar design to those made for Knibb, for a spring clock by James Clowes. The heavy handle is prevented from bruising the dome by brass bosses. Circa 1680. (The movement is shown in Plates 444-445.)*

Sotheby Parke Bernet

Plate 608. *Spring clock case, veneered with ebony and with repoussé metal dome, for a striking clock by William Cattell. Circa 1680. The keyhole mounts are later additions. (The back plate is shown in Plate 438.)*

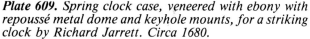

Plate 609. Spring clock case, veneered with ebony with repoussé metal dome and keyhole mounts, for a striking clock by Richard Jarrett. Circa 1680.

Plate 610. The rear view of the case in Plate 609.

Plate 595 shows the early use of repoussé mounts on the ends of the dome to cover apertures made to let out the sound of the bell. Almost identical mounts are seen on another Jones clock in Plate 611. Repoussé mounts used quite early were of much better quality than those used on the majority of cases towards the end of the century. Plates 612-613 and 614 show examples. The cases veneered with olivewood or walnut usually had no decorative mounts and the feet were normally of wood, heavier than the early brass foot and with no neck. Cases veneered with any wood other than ebony at this period are rare, but of those that are, olivewood cases are the more numerous. Ebony and other black cases normally have the inside of the case and the back of the back door coloured black. Cases veneered with other woods do not.

Throughout the last quarter of the seventeenth century, the most commonly used moulding for spring clock cases consisted of a fillet, an ogee and a bead. This moulding will be seen on many of the illustrations here and quite clearly on that in Plate 598. On the lower moulding the fillet is against the carcase and the bead outwards. On the top moulding the bead is halved and against the carcase with the fillet uppermost, giving a flat top to the case. This type of moulding appears again in

Plate 611. Miniature spring clock case, veneered with olivewood with cross-grain olivewood mouldings and repoussé end mounts to the dome, for a striking clock by Henry Jones. Circa 1680.

minute form round the base of the dome. When used on most of Tompion's later cases the bead is made larger in proportion, the top moulding is the same way up as that at the bottom and supported by a similar moulding with the fillet uppermost (Plate 643). Towards the end of the century it was often much modified and elaborated, but still in use.

It is in the years between 1670 and 1680 that one sees the most rapid changes in spring clock case design. It is not possible during this period to relate the design of any individual clock case to any particular clockmaker. It would appear, for instance, that Thomas Tompion, who is thought to have come to London in 1671, at first employed the same case maker as Joseph Knibb. There are a number of his clocks at this period which have cases identical to those of Knibb and the cases seen in Plates 602 and 605 are examples. It would seem that it was not until the output of both men was such that it was impossible for one case maker to supply the needs of both men, that Tompion employed another man and so established the particular style of case which we today recognise as a Tompion case. Henry Jones may not have been affected in the same way. In his early days he seems to have used the same case maker as did his former master Edward East (Plates 591, 592 and 593). Simple convex mouldings are a feature of his cases and are seen round the tops of two of these cases. These mouldings remained a feature of Jones' cases for some time, as did the simple moulding round the bottom of the case. This seems to suggest that he was able to use the same case maker continuously.

The change in the size of the average clock case in this decade is significant for at the beginning of the period the dial was often about 10 ins. square while at the end it was sometimes 6 ins. or even less. The early square Knibb clocks (Plates 599 and 600) had dials of about 8 ins. square. Some of the smallest clocks that were made in the early days were made at the end of this decade. Henry Jones, in particular, made a number of very interesting clocks with dials of only 4 ins. square. Two are illustrated here. That in Plates 612-613 is veneered in ebony as most were and this design of case is very typical of Jones cases at this period. That in Plate 611 is in olivewood and it will be noted that it has on that account to have modified mouldings to enable cross-grain olivewood to be used.

As the number of men making the clocks increased, so naturally did the number making the cases and there may well have been some competition amongst them in the introduction of new features. Nevertheless, they seem to have conformed, in the main, to a common, if evolving, basis of design. The basis remained the rectangular box carcase, dovetailed together, with a square dial frame, a front door, a glazed back door, side windows and a dome top.

Nevertheless, as the century progressed there was a growing diversity of detail in the cases and amongst new features which were introduced was the basket top. This

Plate 612. Miniature spring clock case, veneered with ebony with repoussé dome mounts and cast keyhole mounts, for a striking clock by Henry Jones. Circa 1680.

Plate 613. The rear view of the case in Plate 612.

Plate 614. Silver mounts removed from a miniature spring clock case similar to that in Plate 612-613.

Plate 615. The lock from the back door of a late 17th century spring clock case with the cover plate removed.

Plate 616. The brass latch from the front door of a late 17th century spring clock case.

Plate 617. Spring clock case, veneered with ebony with repoussé metal dome, for a striking clock by Edward East. Circa 1680. Malcolm Gardner

Plate 618. Spring clock case, veneered with ebony with repoussé metal dome, for a striking clock by William Clement. Circa 1680.

Plate 619. Spring clock case, veneered with ebony with repoussé gilt metal dome and side panels, for a time-piece by Jacobus Markwick. Circa 1680.

Plate 620. Spring clock case, veneered with ebony with gilt metal dome, for a striking clock by Thomas Tompion. Circa 1680. The movement is inserted in the case through the bottom and is shown in Plates 495-496.

was in reality a metal dome. Normally it was made in repoussé, pierced and mounted on a moulded cast metal frame to which were brazed two or more metal screws with which the basket was fixed to the top of the case. It was lined with silk. These baskets were usually of gilt brass but examples exist that are made in silver (Plates 661 and 680). Apart from its obvious decorative purpose, the metal basket has the advantage of providing a good outlet for the sound of bells. The earliest baskets are usually small and shallow. The decorative motif is usually based on conventional acanthus scrollwork. Plate 617 shows a basket which is particularly small but it is by no means exceptionally so. It is of interest to compare the details of the design of the case of this clock with that in the illustration in Plate 618, for evidences can be seen that the same case maker has made both cases while the clocks are by different clockmakers.

A clockmaker whose cases do not appear to have been made by one of the specialist case makers, is James Clowes. One example of his work is seen in Plate 607. Often the proportions of his cases are not those of the general run and in this instance the handle is over large.

By 1680 the clockmakers had had twenty years of making the new pendulum clocks and were highly skilled and competent. The arts generally were flourishing in the country and there were available skilled craftsmen in all the trades. That the clockmakers availed themselves of some of these is demonstrated in the making of

Plate 621. Spring clock case of gilt metal with some wood in its foundation, the design reflecting that of the past decade. Made for a timepiece by Jonathan Loundes. Circa 1680-85.

Plate 622. The rear view of the case in Plate 621.

clock cases in metal. While there is some wood in the construction of the case illustrated in Plates 621-622, the exterior is nevertheless all of gilt brass. It is made in the style of cases that were in vogue before 1675, but since the maker was not free of the Clockmakers' Company before 1680, it cannot have been made before then but may have been one of his first productions.

When one thinks of metal cased clocks one naturally turns to those made by Thomas Tompion. Not because he made a great many, for he did not, but because of the unique quality and attractiveness of those which he did make. There are several which he made during this early period and two are illustrated in Plates 623-625 and 626. They are particularly small clocks and there is very little doubt that they were intended to be travelling clocks. Being so small and cased in blued steel, they would be less likely to be damaged by handling than a wood cased clock with its glued on mouldings. These clocks are particularly attractive with their gilded mouldings and mounts set against the blue of the steel background. In design they follow fairly closely Tompion's contemporary style and have elaborate frets in the back and sides. The movement entirely fills the case and Plate 624 shows how it has to be removed through the front after sliding off the front of the bottom moulding.

The case of the clock shown in Colour Plate 21, page 356, and Plates 627-628 is surely one of the most glamorous of Tompion's cases. It is constructed throughout

Plate 623. *Miniature spring clock case in blued steel with gilt metal mouldings and mounts for a timepiece by Thomas Tompion, No. 21. Circa 1680. (The movement is shown in Plate 497.)*

Fitzwilliam Museum, Cambridge

Plate 624. *The case in Plate 623 showing how, by removing the front of the lower moulding, the movement is withdrawn from the case.*

Plate 625. *The rear view of the case in Plate 623 showing the fine repoussé panels in the back and sides.*

Plate 626. Miniature spring clock case of blued steel with gilt metal mouldings and mounts for a timepiece by Thomas Tompion, No. 23. Circa 1680.

of brass, the surfaces are engraved and fire-gilt and there are fine chased silver mounts. The mounts are similar to those found on a few other clocks by Tompion including the tulip finials. Similar finials can be seen on the clock in Plate 634. The basic design and the size is almost identical with Tompion's wood cases of the period. The silver frets in the side windows and the back door are particularly delicately finished. Another small clock cased in a similar manner is shown in Colour Plate 22, page 437, and Plate 633 and is probably a further example of a clock made for travelling.

Two other clocks which, while they are not metal cased, would appear to come within the same design category, are illustrated in Plates 629 and 630-632. That the latter was indeed intended to be portable is demonstrated by the fact that it has been provided with its own carrying case. The cases of both of these clocks are veneered with ebony and the first is another very small clock with the movement so filling the case that it is necessary for it to be withdrawn through the bottom of the case. The mouldings and the mounts on both these cases are in silver. The second clock is somewhat larger and there is a wood fret in the back door. This is not the only clock to be supplied with a contemporary carrying case. There were probably many more originally than exist today. Most of these which do still exist are almost identical with this one and must have been made by the same joiner. All are constructed of wainscot oak and are made with opening front and top. The fittings are of wrought iron. Other examples are shown in Plates 703 and 704, while a somewhat different type with a glass front and with applied repoussé mounts is shown in Plate 677.

Plate 627. The back view of a gilt metal case for a grande sonnerie striking clock by Thomas Tompion shown in Colour Plate 21, page 356.

Plate 628. A view of the clock shown in Plate 627 showing the side panels.

433

Plate 629. Spring clock case veneered with ebony with silver mouldings and mounts. Circa 1700. (The hand is that of the late C.A. Ilbert who once owned it.) Victoria and Albert Museum

Another glamorous case very similar in design to that illustrated in Colour Plate 21 and Plates 627-628 is shown in Colour Plates 23-24 on pages 444-445. It has however a more conventional case veneered with ebony but mounted with fine silver mounts. This clock and that illustrated in Plate 634 are further examples of clocks, the movements of which have to be inserted through the base of the case. The bottom itself consists of a brass plate to which the movement is fixed and in the case of the first of these clocks the silver feet are also fixed to this plate while the gilt metal feet of the second are screwed to the wooden case.

Most of the wood cased clocks made after about 1680 have front doors with long fret apertures in the top rail. Only a few earlier cases had these and one of these is the clock by Joseph Knibb dated 1677 (Plate 599). At this period the frets are still being made of wood but are finer than the early frets and now have certainly been cut by a marquetry cutter. The design is fairly standard, very much as before, a reciprocal evolute scrolling stem with stylised flowers at the termination of each scroll. Most frets on ebony cases are cut in pearwood for ebony is too brittle for this purpose. Pearwood is also used in cases veneered with olivewood and sometimes on those with walnut. The side windows at this time were usually centrally placed and there is no doubt that more side apertures originally had wood frets than now have them. Examples of side frets are seen in Plates 651 and 659.

It is in the sixteen eighties that we see the individual styles of different makers

Plate 630. Spring clock case, veneered with ebony with silver mouldings and mounts, for a striking clock by Thomas Tompion, in its original carrying case. Circa 1700. (The movement is shown in Plate 545. The case is shown closed in Plate 704.)

Plate 631. The side view of the case in Plate 630 showing the side panel.

Plate 632. The rear view of the case in Plate 630 showing the wood fret panel in the back door.

435

Plate 633. *The rear view of the case in Colour Plate 22, opposite, showing the rear panel.*

Colour Plate 22. *A miniature spring clock case in gilt metal with silver mounts for a striking clock by Thomas Tompion. Circa 1680-85. (The rear panel is shown in Plate 633.)*
Science Museum, London. On loan from Mrs. M.L. Giffard

Plate 634. *Spring clock case, veneered with ebony with fine gilt metal mounts, for a grande sonnerie striking clock by Thomas Tompion known as the 'Tulip Tompion'. Circa 1680-85. (The movement is shown in Plates 503-508.)*

Plate 635. *Spring clock case, veneered with ebony with fine gilt metal mounts, for a grande sonnerie striking clock by Thomas Tompion. Circa 1680-85. (The movement is shown in Plates 509-511.)*

Plate 636. *Spring clock case, veneered with ebony with gilt repoussé metal mounts on the dome, for a striking clock by Peter Knibb. Circa 1680-85. (The movement is shown in Plate 530-531.)*

Plate 637 (above). Spring clock case, veneered with olivewood and with ebonised pearwood mouldings, for a striking clock by Joseph Knibb. Circa 1680.

Plate 638 (above right). Spring clock case, veneered with ebony with gilt metal mounts, for a striking clock by Robert Seignior. Circa 1680.

Plate 639 (right). Spring clock case, veneered with ebony with gilt metal mounts, for striking clock by Robert Seignior. Circa 1680. (The movement is shown in Plate 512.)

Plate 640. Spring clock case, veneered with ebony with gilt cast metal mounts, for a timepiece by John Knibb. Circa 1680-85.

Plate 641. The back of a spring clock case for a striking clock by Thomas Tompion shown in Colour Plate 26, page 469. (The dial is shown in Plate 518.)

440

Plate 642. Spring clock case, veneered with walnut with gilt cast metal mounts and small side fret apertures in the sides, for a timepiece by Thomas Tompion. Circa 1690.
Chas. Hobson

emerging. The cases which had been made for Joseph Knibb and his brother John, who evidently used the same case maker, continued to be made to approximately the same design as before. The cases are, however, somewhat smaller than they were and of more delicate proportions and the capping to the dome is thinner. They still have the top moulding providing a flat upper surface, retaining to some degree the effect of the former architectural cornice. The bottom member of the carcase extends to the limit of the bottom moulding to form the lower portion of that moulding and thus no joints are visible when the case is turned up. The dial size is now normally about 6ins. These makers retained this style of case almost to the end of the century, apart from the fact that a small fret aperture was cut above the side window later in the century. The handle on these cases is a slender bow with a straight top member with a knop of acanthus leaves in the centre. This is a handle which was popular with a number of makers and for a number of years. Indeed, it was used well into the following century. When the case has dome mounts they are now usually, but not always, of cast brass. One will frequently find that the ends of the dome have been cut away and are completely covered by a brass mount (Plate 640). The type of keyhole escutcheon favoured by the Knibbs consisted of a winged head suspended from the tip of the upper wing and covering the hole. That on the left hand side of the dial has to be swung to one side to expose the hole. In some instances these escutcheons have been pierced with a keyhole and fixed but usually this is a later modification. Many cases did not originally have one of these escutcheons on the right hand side

Plate 643. Spring clock case, veneered with ebony with gilt cast metal mounts, for striking clock No. 3 by Thomas Tompion. Circa 1685.

Plate 644. Detail of the mounts of the case in Plate 643.

Plate 645. Detail of the dome of the case in Plate 643 showing the apertures cut to make the bells more clearly heard.

Plate 646. Spring clock case, veneered with walnut inlaid with floral marquetry and with gilt repoussé metal dome, for a striking clock by Francis Stamper. Circa 1685-90.

Plate 647. Rear view of the case in Plate 646.

Plate 648. View of the decoration of the top of the case in Plate 646.

Colour Plate 23. Spring clock case veneered with ebony and with silver mounts for a semi-grande sonnerie clock by Thomas Tompion. Circa 1680. (The back is shown in Colour Plate 24 and the movement in Plates 498-502.) Courtesy Australian Consolidated Press Ltd.
(Photographs Camerer Cuss)

Colour Plate 24. The rear view of the case shown in Colour Plate 23.

although most have since had them added. The finials used by the Knibbs were quite small tulip vases.

In spite of the enormous output of the Knibbs, their case maker must have had spare capacity, for his cases were used by other clockmakers but, when they were, they were usually quite differently mounted. Examples can be seen in Plates 656, 664 and 667. There is no doubt that, whoever made the cases, it was the clockmakers who had the option of choosing the case mounts. The Knibbs' cases did not as a rule have feet at this period.

The fact that Knibb type cases are to be seen with other clockmakers' clocks may partly have been due to the fact that Tompion seems to have employed another case maker at about this time, for it is now that we find his clocks in cases of a very different style from those of the Knibbs. Whoever it was who actually designed the cases, there is not the slightest doubt that Tompion influenced the design for it is fully in keeping with that of his movements. The general impression which his cases give is of sturdiness and confidence, with bold convex features in evidence. Even the little convex moulding placed round the back door is bigger. The handle which he used was somewhat similar in shape to that used by the Knibbs but was considerably heavier, with the acanthus decoration much bolder. These handles are seldom seen on the clocks of other makers. On many of the cases holes have been cut in both the front, back and ends of the dome covered by mounts which are similar to those used by the Knibbs but slightly heavier in treatment (Plate 644) but, while the end mounts on Knibb clocks entirely cover the ends of the domes, Tompion's do not and are quite different in design. The escutcheons which Tompion used at this period consisted of a cartouche with a delicate string of acanthus husks above and below as seen in the clocks in Plate 643 and Colour Plate 26, page 469. The latter clock has repoussé mounts on the dome, of the pattern referred to earlier which is unusual on a Tompion, but this is an unusual clock, being one of only two made by him known to have been veneered in walnut. A number of Tompion clocks will be found with cast brass frets in the fret aperture in the front door of a design peculiar to him (Plate 643). These are usually on slightly later clocks but since wood frets are rather vulnerable and many have become broken, restorers have frequently replaced them with brass frets. A great many of the cases have the dial frame pierced with a similar aperture to the door and fitted with an identical fret. Sometimes it has been possible to replace a broken front fret with the contemporary one from the dial frame. It is interesting to see that the brass fret design is seen again, at a later date in an extended version, in the frieze of the clock in Plate 670, which suggests that both mounts were made by the same man. Towards the end of the century some Tompion clocks, as well as some signed Tompion & Banger, used a different type of escutcheon which can be seen in Plates 642 and 716. Henry Jones' escutcheons were rather similar to those on the early Tompions, but with the central cartouche being quite flat and the string of husks being replaced by open acanthus leaves (Plate 612). At the end of the century the same idea was used by him in a much larger form (Plate 668). If one closely studies the details of design of a large number of clocks, one can trace similarities in the design which may suggest that they are the work of the same case maker. Take for example the cases of the clocks in Plates 617 and 618.

Research has so far failed to provide us with very much information about the manufacture of many of the incidentals to the production of the seventeenth century clock. This is particularly true with regard to the decorative mounts. At a time when almost everything was individually made by hand, there is remarkably little variety in

Plate 649. *Spring clock case, veneered with ebony with gilt cast metal mounts, for a striking clock signed Fromanteel (probably Abraham). Circa 1690-95. (The back plate is shown in Plate 567.)*

Plate 650. *Side view of the case in Plate 649 showing the replacement fret with hole for the alarm winding square.*

Plate 651. Side view of an ebony veneered case for a clock by Thomas Tompion showing contemporary frets in the back door and the side window. Circa 1690.

Plate 652 (below left). Spring clock case, veneered with walnut, for a timepiece by John Knibb. Circa 1695.

Plate 653 (below). Spring clock case, veneered with walnut, for a timepiece by Joseph Knibb.

Plate 654. Spring clock case, veneered with walnut, for a timepiece by Joseph Knibb.

Plate 655. Spring clock case, veneered with walnut, for a timepiece by John Knibb.

Plate 656. Spring clock case, veneered with princes wood, with a striking movement by Daniel Quare. Circa 1695.

449

Plate 657. Spring clock case, veneered with ebony, for a timepiece by Mathias Unite. Circa 1695. (The movement is shown in Plate 494.)

the design of clock case mounts, at least until well into the seventeen eighties. While this might be understandable with regard to cast mounts, it is less so with regard to those made in repoussé. It is difficult to believe that the craftsmen who made the mounts were not artistic enough to vary the designs and yet we find very little variation. Take for instance the repoussé dome mount already referred to on the walnut Tompion in Colour Plate 26, page 469, and compare it with the various other similar mounts on other clocks in this book. They are not all exactly alike but are very similar indeed.

Repoussé work is done with very thin metal which is laid on pitch. The high relief of the decorative design is then produced by a selection of punches. The metal is then reversed for the addition of finer detail. Designs used during the 'seventies were often still being used at the end of the century. When one comes to the consideration of the clocks that were made in the last decade of the century, one does see some signs of something like quantity production.

It must be recognised that a great many of the metal mounts that are found on spring clocks today, have been added in quite recent times. A number of these are quite justifiable replacements of lost or broken ones but others, while being apparently suitable for the case to which they are applied and correct in design for the period, are nevertheless now on a case which was originally made without mounts. A very large number have, however, been quite indiscriminately applied, not only to the detriment of the aesthetic effect of the clock but perhaps more importantly, giving a totally incorrect appreciation of the taste of each period. These remarks apply particularly to mounts on the front doors which many people now regard as a period necessity, but it also applies to dome mounts, finials and brass feet. The vast majority of clocks made in the seventeenth century, except for those made at the very end, had very few mounts. Early mounts were restricted to keyhole escutcheons and then not always in pairs, to the occasional dome mount, the end mounts sometimes covering holes and a little later rail mounts. Cases made in decorative woods seldom had mounts, in particular the walnut clocks made by Joseph Knibb did not originally even have keyhole escutcheons.

Seventeenth century cast mounts were very rarely chased. That is, they were not tooled over after casting. They were always very fine castings which were merely well trimmed up. This even applies to the mounts on clocks by the famous makers such as Tompion and Knibb. For instance, if one examines the handle of a Tompion clock, one will find that where the joint in the mould has been, some of the detail of the acanthus decoration has been obscured. Where this is not the case, it usually means either that the handle has been improved in later years or indeed that it is not original. While this is true of the clocks in general, it does not apply to the many special productions which were made, particularly towards the end of the century, many of which were highly finished.

While makers like Tompion and Knibb retained their basically simple case designs for most of their work throughout the century, many other makers towards the end of the 'eighties added more detail to their mouldings and more variety in the way of

Plate 658. A spring clock case, veneered with ebony, for a timepiece by Thomas Tompion. Circa 1695. (The movement is shown in Plates 542-544.)

Plate 659. A side view of the case in Plate 658 showing the typical side fret of the period.

Colour Plate 25. Spring clock case veneered with ebony for a timepiece by Thomas Tompion. Circa 1685. (The side view is shown in Plate 660.)

Plate 660. Side view of the case in Colour Plate 25, opposite.

Plate 661. Spring clock case, veneered with ebony and with silver mounts of unconventional design, hallmarked for 1692, with a movement by Windmills.

Plate 662. Spring clock case, veneered with ebony, for a striking clock by Edward Burgis. Circa 1695. (The movement is in Plates 557-563.)

Plate 663. Spring clock case, veneered with ebony, for a striking clock by Richard Colston. Circa 1695.

Plate 664. Spring clock case, veneered with ebony with gilt repoussé mounts, for a timepiece by Jonathan Pullar. Circa 1695.

Sir Malcolm Stewart Bequest, Montacute House

Plate 666. Spring clock case, veneered with ebony, for an alarm timepiece by Henry Massey. Circa 1695. The finials are later additions.

Plate 667. Spring clock case, veneered with ebony with gilt repoussé mounts, the dome completely covered by the mount, for a striking clock by Cordery. Circa 1695.

Plate 668. *Spring clock case, veneered with ebony with gilt repoussé metal dome, for a striking clock by Henry Jones. Circa 1690. The finials are not contemporary.*

Plate 669. *Detail of the dome of the case in Plate 668.*

applied decoration. Although the process was very gradual it had the effect of drastically changing the overall appearance of many cases. Indeed by the end of the century some makers seem to have entirely thrown off the restraints which had controlled design for several decades, often to the detriment of the clock. Compare, for example, the little timepiece by Ebsworth in Plate 671 with the anonymous clock in Plate 673. The simplicity of the former is far preferable. In addition to more intricate moulding profiles, the domes were made larger and more convex and the mounts often added quite promiscuously. Handles lose their simple outlines and are more elaborately modelled, the designs including such features as dolphins (Plate 667), birds (Plate 674) and female caryatid-type figures (Plate 684). Tulip vase finials are also produced in more elaborate versions (Plates 696 and 699) and a variety of turned bun feet are used, some with relief decoration (Plate 707) and others with a claw (Plates 689 and 701).

A feature of a large number of cases at the end of the century is the profusion of repoussé mounts, or mounts which appear to be made in repoussé. Some of these clocks, whether they are to one's taste or not, have to be admired. That in Plate 673 is one of the best examples. Here the mounts are without doubt made in repoussé and yet there has been no initiative in the way of design. Escutcheons of the same

Plate 670. Spring clock case, veneered with ebony with a frieze and a dome of unusual shape entirely covered by its mounts, for a striking clock by John Garner. Circa 1690-95.

Plate 671. Spring clock case, veneered with ebony with a wood fret in the frieze, for a timepiece by John Ebsworth. Circa 1690.

Plate 672. Spring clock case, veneered with ebony with a gilt metal dome and repoussé mounts, for a striking clock by John Barnet. Circa 1690. The cast mount on the lower rail is a later addition.

Plate 673. Spring clock case, veneered with ebony with gilt metal dome and repoussé mounts on all sides, for an unsigned striking clock. Circa 1690-95.

Plate 674. The rear view of the case in Plate 673 showing the back plate with a space left in the engraving for a signature. There are mounts on the back door which cannot be seen.

design are commonly found as are the rail mounts, which, incidentally, are actually a series of swags suspended from ribbands but fitted upside-down which is not unusual. Many of these repoussé-type mounts have, however, been made by some reproductive method. They have frequently been produced in very thin metal which has disintegrated through the years. Examples of this type of mount are to be seen in Plates 698, 699 and 700. It would appear that escutcheon and rail mounts were made in a strip to be sheared off to the required length. It will be seen that there are parallel beaded edges to these mounts which are not continued round the ends.

The sides and backs of many of these clocks also came in for this type of decoration. Plate 673 is an example while Plate 678 shows a case for which a complete repoussé side covering has been made. The rail mounts on this clock are another example of a string of swags referred to with regard to Plate 673 but in this case the top mount is applied in the correct way. Several of these clocks (Plates 670, 671, 672 and 673-674) have friezes in which are frets of various kinds. While this is not very common at this period, it is nevertheless one of the signs of the changes that

Plate 675. *Spring clock case, veneered with ebony with gilt metal dome and repoussé mounts and side panels, for a striking clock by Nathaniel Hodges. Circa 1690-95.*

Plate 676. *The side view of the case in Plate 675.*

Plate 677. *Spring clock case, veneered with ebony and gilt metal dome in repoussé and incomplete repoussé mounts, for a striking clock by Nathaniel Hodges, in a glazed carrying case also with repoussé mounts. Circa 1690-95.*

Plate 678. *The rear view of the case in Plate 677 showing how the entire side is covered with a repoussé mount.*

460

Plate 679. Spring clock case, veneered with ebony with gilt metal dome in repoussé and repoussé mounts, for a striking clock by Jonathan Loundes. Circa 1690-95.

Plate 680. Spring clock case, veneered with ebony with pierced and engraved silver dome and mounts, for a three-train clock by Charles Gretton. Circa 1690-95. The hour hand is a replacement.

Victoria and Albert Museum, London

Plate 681. Spring clock case, veneered with princes wood with gilt metal repoussé dome and mounts, for a striking clock by Fromanteel. Circa 1690-95. The stand is part of an original bracket.

461

Plate 682. Spring clock case, veneered with princes wood with cast gilt metal mounts, for a timepiece by Jasper Taylor. Circa 1695.

were taking place at the end of the century. Occasionally one will find that a veneered dome has been entirely covered with repoussé, giving it the appearance of being a basket top. Two are shown in Plates 667 and 670.

The metal basket tops also developed considerably in the latter years of the century. The earlier ones were very restrained with the decoration usually in fairly low relief but as the century drew to a close they became bolder and the relief much higher. Compare, for instance, that on the Tompion case in Plate 620 with that shown in Plate 668. A number of the clocks illustrated also have repoussé panels in the side windows. These vary very much in quality and with a few exceptions they conform to just two or three basic designs almost proving that they are the work of the same man. Mostly they have an oval aperture in the centre through which the movement may be viewed while some of the later examples are designed for the aperture to represent a doorway or window (Plates 681 and 701).

While most of these mounts, whether made of brass or of silver, are made to standard patterns by men specialising in mounts for clock cases, there are at least two examples of clocks with the silver basket tops referred to earlier which are, however, quite different and individual. These would have been made by silversmiths who were not in the habit of making clock case mounts and were not, therefore, restricted by the habitual use of any design. The fact that one (Plate 661) is hallmarked for the year 1692 seems to confirm this for no other silver mounts are known to us that are hallmarked. The other clock referred to is that in Plate 680 where the mounts are not made in repoussé.

The end of the century also saw a much greater variety of veneers and finishes

Plate 683 (below). *The side view of a case veneered with tortoiseshell frets and with silver mounts for a clock by Jonathon Pullar shown in Colour Plate 28, page 481. (The back plate is shown in Plate 584.)*

Plate 684. The rear view of the case in Plate 683.

Plate 686. *Spring clock case, overlaid with relief-carved ebony, for a striking clock by John Barnett. Circa 1695-1700. The carving is believed to be Goanese.*

Plate 687. *The rear view of the case in Plate 686.*

Plate 688. Spring clock case, veneered with marquetry with straight grain mouldings and with a fretted frieze below the dome, for a timepiece signed Witherston, Hereford. Circa 1700-10. An identical case with counterpart marquetry with a movement by James Markwick, was exhibited at the Royal Academy of Arts.[1] (The movement is shown in Plate 587.)

Plate 689. Spring clock case, veneered with marquetry and with marquetry mouldings, for a striking clock by Francis Still. Circa 1700-1710.

being used. Marquetry had been used on longcases for some years but was rarely used on spring clock cases. However where it was used it was used to good effect. One of the earliest examples is probably that shown in Plates 646-648. It is the only spring clock known to the authors which is veneered with floral marquetry and has marquetry on the front, back and sides, with walnut background and cross-grain walnut mouldings. There are several examples of cases which were made at the turn of the century, which are decorated with marquetry in the arabesque style. Some of these are illustrated here in Plates 688, 689 and 690-691, while that in Plate 692 tends more to the seaweed style. Marquetry made from the reciprocal veneers to the clock in Plate 688 are to be found on a case of identical design with a movement by James Markwick.[1] Two cases are particularly interesting because the mouldings have also been made in marquetry (Plates 689 and 690-691); a very delicate operation requiring considerable skill. The Witherston clock is also slightly different from the normal run in that the dome is mounted on a frieze with a wood fret. Although not commonly found this is by no means unique.

---

1.   Royal Academy of Arts, ''The Age of Charles II'' Exhibition, 1960, exhibit no. 38.

Plate 690. *Spring clock case, veneered with marquetry and with marquetry mouldings, for a striking clock by John Martin. Circa 1700-10.*

Plate 691. *The rear view of the case in Plate 690.*

Another very popular material with which to veneer a better class clock at this time was tortoiseshell. When this was done the mouldings could also be made in shell. The shell was normally backed with vermilion colour which gives to the case a brilliant warm effect. Silver mounts in particular show well against this background and several cases so mounted are illustrated here. That by Jonathan Pullar in Colour Plate 28, page 481, and Plates 683-684 is an interesting example and has frets which are also cut in shell. When this is done, the shell is usually backed with a pearwood veneer to give added strength. The shaping of the dome is unusual but not unique. The vogue in France for veneering the cases with Boulle work was not much favoured here although a few examples do exist. The Tompion clock which is described in Chapter XI, page 528, is hardly relevant as the case is probably French. The case faced with mother-of-pearl shown in Plate 685 is, we believe, unique.

Princes wood was another wood which was used for a number of cases. This wood, popularly referred to as kingwood to which it is similar, is very attractive with its strongly marked straight grain and was normally used cross-grain for both the surface of the case and for the mouldings. However on the clock in Plate 681 the mouldings are not truly cross-grained. This illustration is of interest on account of the platform on which the clock stands. It is in fact all that remains of a contemporary bracket, the dovetails of the original back board still being in the shelf. There is no way now of telling what form the bracket took but it must have been one of the earliest clock brackets. Plates 655 and 682 are of cases with the more normal cross-grain mouldings.

A clock case with a quite unique finish is illustrated in Plates 686-687. It is covered with ebony of more than veneer thickness, which is shallow carved all over, including what, on a normal case, would be the mouldings. Since the carcase and overall design is quite conventional, it would be reasonable to assume that it was made in London. The carving has, however, been identified as Goanese work. It must, therefore, have been sent to Goa for this treatment to be added.

Several clocks were made about the turn of the century which were evidently intended for use in a coach or even perhaps at sea. Certainly they were intended to be hung by their handles, which were so constructed that the clock would, at least in theory, remain in a level position. Two such clocks are illustrated. One shown in Plate 693 in a tortoiseshell case is of quite normal design apart from the handle. Quite apart from the obvious doubt as to its performance if taken to sea, it is most unlikely that a tortoiseshell veneered case would survive sea conditions for very long. The other clock, like the last, by Quare, shown in Plate 694 is metal cased and would stand a better chance.

The new century saw many changes in the design of the spring clock case, but at first these were slow in emerging, just subtle changes of emphasis and small variations of outline. For instance the basket tops, when used, are given more prominence with much bolder outlines such as that on the Etherington clock in Plate 698. This was the beginning of a trend that evolved into the 'bell' basket, firstly as that in Plate 699 and then to the taller version shown in Plates 700 and 701. None of the baskets here illustrated are exactly alike but the treatment varies so little from one to the other that only a few men can have been involved in fashioning them. The final stage in the development of the basket top was the double basket where the bell basket is surmounted by a cast brass frame on which is a further small basket dome. This frame frequently has four small finials at each corner and the baskets often have a miniature cast medallion as a centrepiece. On the example shown in Plate 702

Plate 692. Spring clock case, veneered with marquetry with cross-grain princes wood mouldings, for a striking clock by Thomas Taylor. Circa 1700-10.

Plate 693. Spring clock case, veneered with tortoiseshell with trunnion suspension, for a timepiece by Daniel Quare. Circa 1700. The tortoiseshall is missing from the top moulding. Hessisches Landesmuseum, Kassel

468

Colour Plate 26. Spring clock case veneered with walnut with gilt repoussé mounts on the dome for a striking clock by Thomas Tompion. Circa 1680-85. (The back of the case is shown in Plate 641 and the movement in Plates 518-522.)

Plate 694. Spring clock case of unusual design in brass, for an alarm timepiece by Daniel Quare, with pierced dome and trunnion suspension.
Trustees of the British Museum

Plate 695. Spring clock case in gilt metal for a small timepiece by Richard Fennell. Circa 1700.

470

the centrepiece is worked in repoussé. This type of dome appears mainly in the second decade of the eighteenth century.

The new century also saw the beginnings of change to the standard square dial. Taller dials than square had been made in the early days of the pendulum clock and just a few later in the seventeenth century but at the beginning of the eighteenth they were made in larger numbers again. The earliest were probably those with just a narrow band of engraving or the maker's name at the top (Plates 709 and 710). The fully developed rectangular dial however usually had subsidiary dials above the chapter ring which emphasised the extra height. Clocks with square dials continued to be made however until they were superseded by the break-arch dial.

The wooden dome also came in for attention early in the century, a small concave addition being made to produce what has become known as the inverted bell top. The concave section was not very tall in the early period but later was made taller. This change is in keeping with developments which we have considered in regard to longcases where concave features gradually became more in evidence. This, together with the taller dial, made for greater elegance in design. Plates 706 and 715 are of cases which have the front door glass framed in a wide bolection moulding. While this is by no means a common feature, a number of other examples are known.

The Garrard clock (Plate 715) also is an example of the early use of a wall bracket for a spring clock. These are very rarely found dating from this period and whether many more were made at the time is not known. One other is illustrated here in Plate 716 made for a clock by Tompion and Banger. These are both examples of the earliest type of bracket made for clocks and consist of a shelf secured to a back board which is fixed to the wall. The corbel moulded part slides on to this on runners and has inside a small box which will hold the winding key, which is probably the reason why the type is known as a box bracket. The carving on the Tompion and Banger bracket is certainly unusual and may be unique.

The feet on the cases made at this time are usually rectangular and often of brass, several are shown here, some have mouldings mitred round and some plain. The eighteenth century also saw a greater variety in the shapes of the side fret or glass apertures. The small upper fret aperture is now sometimes rectangular. It is more often discarded until later in the century when a circular aperture is made. The break-arch panel is more usual in the 1720s and '30s. Into these panels were inserted some of the most delicate frets that are found in clocks (Plate 720). The cases at this time usually have mouldings which are decidedly concave, and the earlier traditional moulding is less often used.

It was probably in the second decade of the eighteenth century that the break-arch dial began to be popular and this opened up entirely new design possibilities, but these lie outside the period covered by this book.

Colour Plate 27. *An oil painting, signed ''Arnold 1682'', which includes a representation of a clock similar to that in Plate 634.*

Plate 696. Spring clock case, veneered with tortoiseshell with silver mounts and doors at the sides, for a three-train clock by Peter Garon. Circa 1700.

Plate 697. Spring clock case, veneered with tortoiseshell with silver mounts, for a striking clock by George Etherington. Circa 1700. (The back plate is shown in Plate 579.)

Plate 698. Spring clock case, veneered with ebony and with gilt metal dome and mounts, for an alarm timepiece by George Etherington. Circa 1705. The finials are of later date.

Plate 699. Spring clock case, veneered with ebony with gilt bell basket dome and pressed mounts, for a striking clock by Markwick. Circa 1705-10.

Plate 700. Spring clock case, veneered with ebony with gilt tall bell basket top and pressed mounts, for a striking clock by John Shaw. Circa 1705-10.

Plate 701. Spring clock case, veneered with tortoiseshell with tall bell basket dome and repoussé mounts, for a grande sonnerie-clock by Fromanteel and Clarke. Circa 1710.

Plate 702. *Spring clock case, veneered with ebony with gilt double-basket dome and repoussé mounts, for a striking clock by Windmills, in contemporary carrying case. Circa 1710.*

Plate 703. *The oak carrying case of the clock in Plate 702.*

Plate 704. The oak carrying case of the clock in Plate 630.

Plate 705. Spring clock case, veneered with ebony with gilt cast metal mounts, and the handle of the design particularly associated with the maker of the movement, Daniel Quare. Circa 1710.

Plate 706. Spring clock case, veneered with ebony with bolection moulding to the front door, for a striking clock by William Walfall. Circa 1710.

Plate 707. *Spring clock case, veneered with ebony with repoussé silver mounts, for a striking clock by Windmills. Circa 1710. The finials are a later addition.*

Plate 708. *Small spring clock case, veneered with burr walnut with silver mounts, for a striking clock by Windmills. Circa 1710. The extra base is modern.*

Plate 709. *Spring clock case, veneered with ebony, with an elongated dial and the handle in the style of Daniel Quare, for a striking clock by Francis Robinson. Circa 1710.*

Plate 710. *Spring clock case, veneered with ebony and with elongated dial, for a striking clock by Daniel Quare. Circa 1710. The movement is shown in Plates 532-536.*

Plate 711. *Miniature spring clock case, veneered with ebony, with elongated dial for a striking clock by Thomas Tompion. Circa 1690-95. The fret in the door rail is a replacement.*

Plate 712. *Miniature spring clock case, veneered with ebony, with elongated dial for striking clock No. 227 by Thomas Tompion. Circa 1690-95.*

Colour Plate 28. *A spring clock case for a striking clock by Jonathan Pullar. It is veneered with tortoiseshell, with tortoiseshell frets and silver mounts. Circa 1700. (Other views of the case are shown in Plates 683-684 and the backplate is shown in Plate 584.)*

Plate 713. Spring clock case, veneered with ebony, with elongated dial and gilt cast metal mounts, for a striking clock by Thomas Tompion. Circa 1700. (The movement is shown in Plates 548-549.)

Plate 714. Spring clock case, veneered with ebony with gilt cast metal mounts, the rectangular feet with gadrooned moulding, for a striking clock by Thomas Tompion. Circa 1710.

Plate 715. *Spring clock case, veneered with ebony, with elongated dial, bolection moulding to the front door and contemporary box bracket, for a striking clock by John Garrard. Circa 1710-15.* R.A. Lee

Plate 716. *Spring clock case, veneered with ebony, with elongated dial and inverted bell top, on contemporary box bracket with carving, for a striking clock by Tompion and Banger. Circa 1705-10.*

Colour Plate 29. *Spring clock case veneered with burr walnut with an inverted bell top for a striking clock by Windmills. Circa 1710.*

Plate 717. *Spring clock case, veneered with ebony, with elongated dial, inverted bell top with additional moulding and pedestals to the finials, for a three-train clock by Charles Goode. Circa 1710.*

Plate 718. *Spring clock case, veneered with ebony, with elongated dial, for a three-train clock by George Graham. Circa 1715.*

Plate 719. *Spring clock case, veneered with ebony, with elongated dial, inverted bell top and silver mounts, for a three-train clock by Daniel Delander. Circa 1715-20. (The movement is shown in Plates 585-586.)*

Plate 720. *Spring clock case, veneered with burr walnut, with inverted bell top, break-arch top to the side windows and fine frets, for a three-train grande sonnerie clock by George Graham. Circa 1720.*

R.A. Lee

Plate 721. *The rear view of a spring clock case, veneered with ebony, for a clock by George Graham, showing the fine fret in the back door. Circa 1720.*

Plate 722. *Spring clock case, veneered with ebony, with elongated dial, for a timepiece by Daniel Delander. Circa 1720.*

Chapter X

Cases for Weight-driven Clocks of Short Duration

Although in the period following the introduction of the pendulum, eight-day clocks were produced in considerable numbers, many clocks were still being made which had a duration of only about thirty hours. These movements were in posted frames either as lantern clocks or open movements or they were between plates. They would have been made for humbler situations in a house, probably below stairs and the cases which were made for them were usually, but not always (e.g. Plate 402), far below the standard of the eight-day clock case.

The lantern clock, which remained popular for many years, was housed in a wooden case far more often than is realised. It is probably because most of these cases were so unpretentious and indeed frequently quite crude, that the vast majority have since been destroyed. In many cases the lantern clock, which is itself attractive, may have been preferred uncased. It is quite understandable that the lantern cases which do remain are those which are attractive, but like the movements which they contain they are usually simple, low cost productions.

Lantern clock cases may be divided into two main types; the hooded wall bracket and the long case. While the latter were probably the more numerous originally, it is the former that is more readily found today. Both types are also found with the open posted frame movements and plated movements to which square dials have been fitted. Most of the hooded lantern clock cases which are to be found are for quite small lantern clocks and are of good quality, obviously made by one of the specialist clock case makers, and the lantern clocks in them have frets with flat tops in line with the glazed apertures of the cases. A number of cases of this type were made for clocks by Joseph Knibb, one of which is illustrated in Plate 723. The arched top moulding is necessary in order to provide space for the bell. Where there is no arched moulding a shallow dome is usually provided to accommodate the bell and this is frequently hidden behind a carved cresting as in Plates 725 and 726. The later marquetry example by Gould in Plate 728 has a fully developed dome in keeping with its period. The majority of the extant earlier cases of this type were made for clocks by Joseph Knibb and two of these shown here have movements made in Oxford, so, presumably, they were made before he came to London in 1670 (Plates 724 and 725) although this may be doubted. The maker most associated with the later period is Christopher Gould.

Some of these little hoods have had trunks added in contemporary or near con-

Plate 723. A thirty-hour lantern timepiece alarm by Joseph Knibb on a hooded wall bracket veneered with walnut and with fret front.

Plate 724. Thirty-hour ting-tang repeating clock with 5½ ins. square dial by Joseph Knibb, Oxon, on a hooded wall bracket veneered with walnut and with carved brackets.

Plate 725. Thirty-hour
timepiece alarm with
carved pediment by
Joseph Knibb, Oxon,
on a hooded wall
bracket.

Plate 726. Thirty-hour timepiece by Christopher Gould with 4½ ins. square dial on a hooded wall bracket. Veneered with olivewood and with floral marquetry and carved brackets and pediment.

Plate 727. The side view of the case in Plate 726.

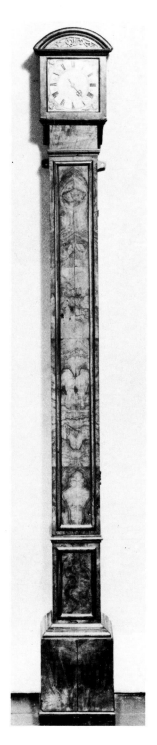

Plate 728. *Thirty-hour clock by Christopher Gould, on a hooded wall bracket. With a dome, veneered with walnut and with seaweed marquetry. The carved brackets are a replacement.*

Plate 729. *Thirty-hour timepiece by Joseph Knibb, on a hooded bracket converted into a longcase with walnut veneer in contemporary times.*
Country Life

temporary times and some, indeed, have had them added in this century. An example of one of the former is seen in Plate 729, where the original brackets are clearly visible. A case of somewhat similar proportions was made for a lantern clock almost identical with that in Plate 723, but in unveneered pine. This case is shown in Plates 730-732. It is by no means a fine case but is typical of many made in the seventeenth century which have in later years been discarded. Not only were they made for

Plate 730. *Thirty-hour lantern timepiece alarm by Joseph Knibb in a pine longcase. The columns are replacements.*

Plate 731. *The upper part of the long-case in Plate 730.*

Plate 732. *The timepiece alarm in Plate 730 with the hood removed.*

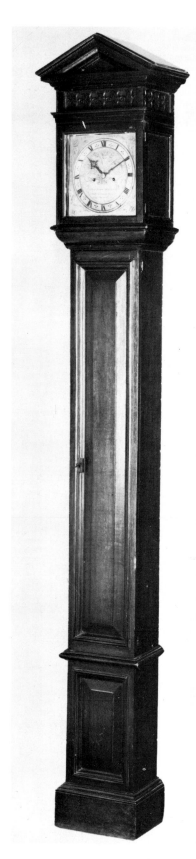

Plate 733. Oak longcase for a posted frame movement by John Wise of 1672. With original dial but modern movement.

Plate 734. Painted longcase for posted frame movement by Edward Clement. (The movement is shown in Plates 302-304.)

Plate 735. Painted longcase for posted frame thirty-hour movement by Thomas Tompion. The carved pediment is an addition.

Worshipful Company of Clockmakers

Plate 736. The short duration time-piece made for St. Andrew's University by Joseph Knibb in 1672, in a hooded bracket converted into a longcase.

small lantern clocks but also for larger ones. Usually, however, they were not made by the specialist case makers and were often of crude design and workmanship with no decorative merit and consequently no longer exist.

The case illustrated in Plate 733 was made for a posted short duration clock by John Wise for presentation in 1672. Unfortunately, although the original dial has been retained a new movement has been fitted to it. The case is, however, one of the better examples of a case *not* made by a clock case maker. One of the more normal thirty-hour clock cases is seen in Plate 734 but there were many cases made by clock case makers in pine for these movements which in design and construction were up to the best standards but finished with japanning. Most of these good pine cases were during the early years of this century either veneered with walnut, lacquered or were refinished as stripped pine cases. One is however preserved in the Clockmakers' Company Museum and is illustrated in Plate 735.

The trunk which has been added to the hood of the timepiece in Plate 736 does not conform to the high quality of the rest and must have been added at a later date.

Chapter XI
Some Special Clocks

The preceding chapters of this book have attempted to describe the history of the domestic clock in such a way that the reader can see how one mechanical development led to another and how the style of cases reflected both the prevailing tastes of the day and were adapted to the demands of the clockwork. Inevitably there are some clocks of such exceptional design that they refuse to fit neatly into prescribed categories, or which are of such interest that they justify individual and lengthy descriptions. Such clocks have been brought together in this concluding chapter. It will not surprise the reader that among them are two clocks by Ahasuerus Fromanteel and three by Thomas Tompion.

An Early Long Duration Timepiece by Fromanteel

Ahasuerus Fromanteel, in his advertisements in the *Commonwealth Mercury and Mercurius Politicus* in 1658, claimed that a way had been found for making "clocks that go exact and keep equaller time than any now made . . . and may be made to go a week, a month, or a year with once winding up." The wording should be noted, they "may be made to go . . . a year". In fact, no clock made by Ahasuerus Fromanteel is known that goes for a year and indeed few were made until later in the century by any maker. Was Fromanteel indulging in wishful thinking in this advertisement? Had he conceived a train of wheels without taking into consideration the problems of friction involved? Had he rushed into print before putting the project to the test? The clock here described may provide us with an answer (Plates 737-743).

The clock was discovered in a Suffolk farmhouse in about 1935 by an East Anglian antique dealer. When found it had no back and was standing against a wall. Since it had to be wound from the back, this had to be done through the wall from an adjoining room. It had at that time already been converted from verge to anchor escapement and had a one seconds pendulum.

It would appear that the dealer who had acquired it, in order to make the clock more readily saleable, reversed the winding arbor so that it could be wound from the front, and evidence that this change has been made in recent years is found in a newly made depression in the front of the trunk cover to take the protruding winding square. A heavy oak back board was also added at the same time to cover the otherwise open back. To gain access to the winding square it is now necessary to remove the trunk cover. This consists of the entire front of the trunk to which are fixed the sides and it would appear that this has always been detachable.

During 1935 the clock came into the possession of Mr. Ernest Watkins and for

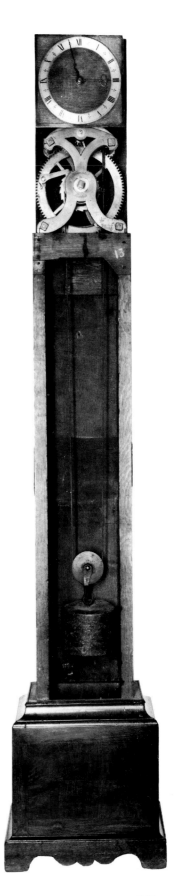

Plate 737. Three-month timepiece by Ahasuerus Fromanteel in an unusual princes wood longcase.

Plate 738. The hood of the clock shown in Plate 737 with a broken pediment from which the central feature is missing.

Plate 739. The case and movement of the clock shown in Plate 737 with the hood and trunk cover removed.

some time was in his shop in Carey Street. While there he had the verge escapement replaced, the work being done by Mr. J.W. Parkes. Apart from some superficial repairs to the case, nothing further was done to the clock at that time. It then went into the collection of Mr. Montague Meyer at Avon Castle where it remained until his death, when it again came on the market and was lot No. 99 at Sotheby's sale on April 18th, 1958. It was then bought by Mr. James Oakes who later sold it to its present owner.

Apart from the alterations mentioned, the movement appears to be in its original state (Plate 740). It has two main parts. The top part is similar to a normal timepiece movement of about 1665, but where the main wheel would have been in such a time-piece, there is an intermediate wheel and pinion. This part is screwed to the lower part using specially made brackets which are screwed to the plates of the top part and to the two top pillars of the lower part. This lower part is of quite massive construction, consisting of a cross-frame with the barrel arbor at the centre. It is made of brass with four pillars and contains the main wheel and barrel, the main wheel running into an intermediate pinion on the arbor of which is mounted another intermediate wheel which runs into the pinion running in the upper part.

There are twelve turns on the barrel and the wheel and pinion numbers appear to be as follows:

Main wheel	98	1st intermediate pinion	14
1st intermediate wheel	60	2nd intermediate pinion	12
2nd intermediate wheel	48	Centre pinion	8

One turn on the main wheel will therefore produce $^{98}/14 \times {}^{60}/12 \times {}^{48}/8 = 210 \div 24 = 8.75$ days running $\times$ 12 for the 12 turns of the barrel = 105 days or three months with some days to spare.

The wheels and pinions of the lower part are of conventional material and construction except the main wheel which is of steel. Its running into a steel pinion appears to have worked well, there being no deep cuttings, pittings or wear marks in either.

The first intermediate pinion runs in bushes but is positioned above the centre of the bushes. The question follows, did Fromanteel originally set the train out with the first pinion in the centre of the bushes? With different numbers in wheel and pinion the train could in theory, have been given a duration of six months. He could have intended the barrel to have been larger, which, again, with altered numbers could have given more power and a duration of twelve months, but a greater fall. This seems to be quite likely. He may have attempted to achieve the twelve-month duration that he evidently thought he could achieve by the addition of massive train wheels at the driving end, but he failed. It would appear that for almost another twenty years no clockmaker did succeed and when they did, it was by modifications at the other end of the train.

This timepiece has attracted little notice since it came to light more than forty years ago and it is difficult to understand why. It is true that it is unconventional in almost every respect. Even the signature has been the subject of doubt. It is to be found on the lower frame surrounding the barrel arbor and its form, "Fromanteel London", is unique for the period, although it is similar to that on the dated example in Plate 89 which has the addition of the initial "A" and also to that in the Fogg Museum in Plate 96, which is almost contemporary, which is signed on one of the square pillars. However, it appears to be contemporary and authentic. The main wheel click and spring are of the shape, fixing and method of operation which one

Plate 740. The movement of the clock shown in Plate 737 showing how the two separate parts are fitted together.

Plate 741. A view of the dial and the lower part of the movement of the clock shown in Plate 737 showing the signature and the eccentric pivot of the intermediate wheel just below the dial.

Plate 742. The trunk cover of the clock shown in Plate 737 with the hood in position.

Plate 743. The inside of the hood and trunk cover of the clock shown in Plate 737 showing the evidence of former latches and hinges.

finds on Fromanteel clocks of the early period, with the spring working under the tail of the click.

The dial plate is of brass, 8⅝ ins. square, with a chapter ring and is mounted on the upper part of the movement. The part of the dial plate not covered by the chapter ring is worked over methodically up and down and across by wriggling a narrow chisel, with the edging left plain. The hands are well made and appear to be original. The weight is of lead and cylindrical, 5 ins. in diameter by 4 ins. deep with part of it flattened, presumably because it was slightly large. It weighs about 30 lbs.

The movement rests on a heavily constructed stand which is almost identical in dimensions with the main trunk carcase of a longcase of the period. The hood, also, is very similar superficially, with the contemporary longcase hoods. The most obvious differences are the broken pediment from which a central feature is missing (Plate 738), and the flat pilasters. Both the capitals and bases of the pilasters and the top section of the cornice moulding are all of well finished fire-gilt brass. It may well be that Fromanteel anticipated when he set out to make the clock, that it would fit into a reasonably conventional case but that it proved impossible as the work progressed. There is no doubt that it was intended to be an important clock and is veneered with princes wood. The opening front to the hood is not normal on early longcases.

The trunk cover is a most unusual feature and may have been necessitated by the size of the weight which would have made a door inset in the trunk impossible. If the depth of the case was increased to accommodate the weight, a similar amount would need to be added to the width to maintain the proportions with the hood. The trunk cover must be placed in position before the hood as the hood rests directly upon it, is positioned by two pegs and held down by two hooks on the inside of the trunk cover.

From the nature of the veneer on the base and the mouldings associated with it, it would appear that this part of the case is not in its original state.

It is the construction of the case at the back which produces most surprises for it shows that both the hood and the trunk were originally fitted with back doors. In fact, part of a wrought iron "H" hinge remains as proof, let into the princes wood with which the back of the hood is veneered. It would suggest that the hood door had also been veneered. There is however no sign of veneer ever having been on the back edge of the trunk cover. As will be seen from the illustrations, the cut-outs for wrought-iron hinges of the type used on longcase doors are clearly visible while on the left hand side there is a shallow rebate to receive the door and there is a cut-out to receive the bolt of the lock.

A further interesting feature is the remains of a latching arrangement which can be seen in Plate 743. The hood door at the moment has no lock or other latching device and the internal dial frame is a later feature. A possible reconstruction of this latch could be made from the evidence available including the latches for holding down the hood, parts of which have survived on the trunk cover. Since the hood is veneered at the back and the trunk is not, the question arises as to where the clock was intended to stand. It could not, in any case have stood against a solid wall because the doors had to be opened for winding. The answer to this and other questions posed by this very interesting timepiece will, I fear, remain with us for a very long time.

An Early Spring-driven Musical Clock by Fromanteel

While this clock may be thought to lack some of the refinement and elegance of

Plate 744. The musical thirty-hour spring clock by Ahasuerus Fromanteel.

some clocks of the period (Plate 744), it has so many features of outstanding importance, that questions of elegance and superficial attractiveness are secondary matters. Indeed, its rather simple design, so unusual at this period, is one of the clock's interesting features.

There can be no doubt that the clock is one of very early workmanship. It must have been designed well before 1670 and probably as early as 1665. It must be emphasised that this was when the clock was probably designed and started but owing to the nature of the task that Fromanteel had set himself and because of unforeseen difficulties which occurred as the work progressed, it was not completed until some years later. It could well be that the new style of casemaking was by that time coming into vogue, and a decision was taken to modify the design to harmonise more with contemporary practice.

Probably the most interesting feature is that it is a full musical clock, playing a

Plate 745. The left hand side of the clock shown in Plate 744.

selection of tunes three times in each twelve hours. The music is released by one of three pins in the striking count wheel. There is, however, evidence of other pins having been in the plate, and it is more than likely that it was originally intended that the tunes should be played four times in each twelve hours — which was normal practice in later days — probably at three, six, nine and twelve o'clock. The tunes are played on ten bells by the use of twenty hammers.

This is the earliest known example of an English spring-driven musical clock; and as the maker was engaged in an operational experiment, it is not surprising that the movement is unconventional in many respects.

The case of this clock is virtually the hood of a longcase clock of the period, except that it does not quite conform to the architectural design. Like the longcase hood, it slides upwards off the back board (see Plates 748 and 749) which has the advantage of exposing the whole of the movement.

Unlike contemporary longcases, it is not necessary in the case of this clock to lift off the hood for winding because the front opens to expose the dial. The door is pivoted on the capital and base of the left hand column (Plate 746). The capitals are of the Doric and not the Corinthian order, which was the more usual at the period.

As to the latching of the door, the hasp is seen on the lower part of the inside on the door in Plate 746. The reconstructed locking device which can be operated by the

Plate 746. *The right hand side of the clock shown in Plate 744 with the door open and the top removed.*

504

Plate 747. *The front view with the hood removed of the clock shown in Plate 744.*

Plate 748. *The music side of the movement of the clock shown in Plate 744.*

Plate 749. The striking side of the movement of the clock shown in Plate 744.

Plate 750. The back of the movement of the clock shown in Plate 744 showing the roller cage.

Plate 751. *The pendulum suspension and roller cage of the clock shown in Plate 744.*

Plate 752. *The top of the movement of the clock shown in Plate 744 with the bells removed.*

Plate 753. *The front view of the movement of the clock shown in Plate 744.*

507

winding key, can be seen in Plate 749, while the hole through which the key goes is visible in the side of the hood in Plate 746.

The shutters of the bolt and shutter maintaining power are sometimes used merely for the purpose of tidying up the dial by obscuring the winding holes. (The authors know of at least one year clock and several month clocks which have for them the unnecessary refinement of bolt and shutter maintaining power.) In this clock, Fromanteel seems to have gone a stage further and avoided winding holes altogether. To do this, it has been necessary to introduce a most elaborate and ingenious system of cranked connections between the separate winding arbors and the fusee arbors (Plate 750). The result is that it has been possible to position the winding squares on the outside edge of the dial.

It is unlikely that Fromanteel intended that the clock should be wound in this way when he started making it, for had he done so he would have made the plates wide enough to take the arbors instead of having them in cocks as he did. This is one of the pieces of evidence which shows that the maker had to modify his plans as the work progressed.

The general view of the dial, seen in Plate 747, shows how the winding squares are positioned round its edge. The dial is 8⅛ ins. high and 7¾ ins. wide. It may be that the dial was made higher than it was wide merely to accommodate the signature and the squared regulation arbor at the top. Square dials were not necessarily the rule however at this time, for a number of early spring clocks by such makers as Edward East and John Hilderson are known with tall dials; so this feature on this clock may be further evidence that it was at least started at an early date. While this dial is on the one hand very typical of Fromanteel's early work, it has on the other hand a number of quite unusual features. The engraving of the initial 'A' above the rest of the signature is exceptional. The central zone is finely matted and the whole mercury gilt. The chapter ring is engraved in silver superimposed upon brass in Fromanteel's customary manner.

One of the features on the dial is the mock-pendulum aperture. This is the curved opening just below the figure XII in which a small engraved mock pendulum swings in time with the actual pendulum. It is difficult to understand why this should be thought necessary since it only appears with a verge escapement, which is a noisy escapement, and one can always hear whether the clock is going. Fromanteel must have thought it important, for in this case it was only achieved with some difficulty. Perhaps it was something that his customer particularly wanted. It is a feature not normally associated with the early period and must be another indication that the clock was some years being made.

The escapement is particularly low in the movement. It is, in fact, below the centre of the dial. Accordingly, it was necessary to have the mock pendulum independently pivoted above the verge, and for it to be oscillated with the pendulum by levers on the arbors linked with a connecting wire. These levers and the rod have had to be counterpoised and the little spherical counter-weight can be seen beside the large bell in the top centre of Plate 755.

Above the mock pendulum aperture is another aperture through which can be seen a segment of the rise and fall disc. The provision of means of regulating a clock from its dial was not in general use for some decades after the date when this clock was made. In fact it is the earliest example with this feature known to the authors. The mechanism is very ingenious and as it requires some height above the point of suspension of the pendulum, its inclusion may have influenced Fromanteel in

Plate 754. *The movement of the clock shown in Plate 744, partly dismantled.*

Plate 755. *The top of the movement of the clock shown in Plate 744, with the bells in position.*

Plate 756. *The pin barrel for the music of the clock shown in Plate 744.*

Plate 757. *The hammer assembly of the clock shown in Plate 744.*

placing the escapement. The pendulum rod is not fixed to the verge as was the practice at the time, but is independently suspended with a suspension spring and motivated by a crutch attached to the verge (Plates 748 and 749). There is, still in position, a roller cage for the back end of the verge which was certainly completed, with its rollers and then discarded. A further sign of modification as the work progressed.

Instead of the suspension spring being retained at the top by a brass block riveted to it, there is a long square steel rod passing through a helical spring upon the top of which it is supported (Plate 751). The suspension spring is held loosely below in a fixed brass nib. The helical spring causes the squared rod to press upwards on the under edge of a brass 'snail' which is riveted to the back end of the rise and fall arbor (Plate 750). The front end of this arbor is squared and passes through the dial above the figure XII. By turning this arbor with the winding key in an anticlockwise direction one will depress the helical spring, increase the effective length of the pendulum and cause the clock to go slower. Conversely, turning the arbor in a clockwise direction will allow the pendulum to rise and the clock to go faster. The regulation disc, visible through the dial, turns with the arbor and enables one to make exact adjustments. It is engraved with one hundred divisions, each fifth one being numbered.

A general front view of the movement with the dial removed is illustrated in Plate 753. On the left are the main parts of the musical movement. The spring barrel is at the bottom, the fusee and main wheel in the centre and the pin barrel above, all of which are considerably deeper than the rest of the movement (also seen in Plate 753). The right hand front plate is divided into two parts to enable the going train (top) or the hour and quarter striking trains (bottom) to be assembled separately. All the bells and hammers are mounted on a plate which is latched to four posts on the top of the movement. This top plate is rather reminiscent of the top plate of a lantern clock.

510

Having regard to the early date of this clock and the heavy demand made upon both the musical and the striking trains, it is not surprising that it only has a duration of thirty hours when fully wound. The striking train for instance actuates the hammers for both the hours and the ting-tang quarters and to do this it has to strike 375 blows in thirty hours. The going train is remarkable for the ingenuity with which it is stowed into such a small compass. The layout is quite unconventional, and the plane of the very low crown wheel is at an angle of 50° from the vertical (Plate 754).

Three views of the musical movement are given in Plates 748, 753 and 756. It has already been mentioned that the spring barrel, fusee and pin barrel occupy all the space provided between the plates. Plate 750 shows how the rest of the train is placed outside the back plate with the back pivots of the arbors in gracefully shaped cocks. The pin barrel, which can be seen removed from the plates in Plate 756, has been pinned for two tunes, the names of which are engraved on the end of the barrel.

There is no doubt whatever that this clock was constructed with the intention that it should be able to play a greater variety of tunes, for the barrel is retained on the barrel arbor by a spring-loaded catch, upon the release of which it may be withdrawn out of the side of the movement without any further dismantling of the clock. It is a matter for speculation whether in fact any further barrels were ever provided, but the fact that the titles of the tunes are engraved on the end of the barrel where they cannot be seen at all when it is in place in the clock, is fair proof that they were in-

Plate 758. The back of the dial of the clock shown in Plate 744.

tended to be readable when stowed — with other barrels — in some container out of the clock (Plate 756).

The titles of these tunes are interesting. Nothing is known today of the "Western March" but the "Granadeers March" is to be found in Playford's Dancing Master of 1686, twenty years after the suggested date of this clock. It is known that the Granadeers were a Royalist infantry regiment which served with the exiled Charles II and came to England at the restoration in 1660.

In addition to the automatic playing of a tune at five, nine and twelve o'clock, the musical train may be set in motion by pressure on the scroll-ended lever on the top of the movement (see Plates 748 and 749). The alternative tunes on the barrel can be brought into use by the movement of a lever on the top plate which can be operated with the hood in place. The lever pushes the entire barrel forwards or backwards, thus bringing different rows of pins in line with the hammers.

The hammers for the musical train are all mounted in one frame which can be detached complete from the top plate (Plate 757). Ten of the hammers strike from one side of the frame and ten from the other. The division is achieved by having the hammer tails independently pivoted at the base of the frame, with connecting wires to operate the hammers themselves going alternatively to the left hand side and the right hand side of the frame.

There are no fretted apertures to this case to allow for the full sound of the bells to be heard, but the top panel, which is removable — presumably to give access to the tune set-off lever — could always be removed to increase the volume of the music.

It would prove of great interest if some documentary evidence were to be discovered which would date this clock more exactly, but it certainly belongs to the period prior to any kind of standardisation of either the layout of the movements or the design of the clock case.

The Night Clock

The night clock was introduced in this country in the middle 1660s and, while few examples now remain, it is quite possible that they were more numerous in their day. In spite of the excellence of the craftsmanship involved, the method of illuminiating the dials of many of these clocks was very primitive and it is not difficult to imagine that many may have been damaged or even destroyed by fire. They were produced in the main, over a very short period, for they were rendered redundant by the introduction of repeating mechanisms; for these made the clock not only a much more convenient one for use during the hours of darkness, but also one which was a good deal safer.

Night clocks are known to have been made by a number of the well known makers, including Fromanteel, Edward East, Joseph Knibb, Henry Jones, Robert Seignior and James East. R.W. Symonds records a bill for a night clock by the latter, dated 23rd June, 1664, "a pendilum clocke to goe 8 days with a lamp to show the houre of the night, £45".[1] While a few longcase night clocks are known, the majority of those extant are spring-driven.

One example made by John Hilderson is illustrated here in Plates 759-763. It has

---

1. R.W. Symonds, "The night clock from Mediaeval times", Parts 1 and 2, *Country Life,* 24th September and 15th October, 1948.

Plate 759. *Night clock with alarm by John Hilderson. The feet are a later addition.* Gerald Marsh

Plate 760. *The movement of the Hilderson clock.*

an exquisitely engraved dial with a floral design and leaves at the base forming a grotesque mask. It has a chapter ring which seems small for the plate but it allows space above it for the aperture through which the illuminated hour disc is seen. Above this aperture and pierced in the dial plate is a pointer to indicate the time. The large disc in which the hours and quarters are pierced, is fixed to the hour socket, close to the dial plate, leaving no room for cross pinning pegs in the chapter ring. Consequently this has had to be screwed on from the front. Also it has been necessary to cross out the disc to enable the winding key to reach the squares.

No provision appears to have been made in the case for the incorporation of a lamp; instead there is a large glazed panel in the back door and presumably a lamp had to stand behind the clock for its light to illuminate the dial. This is also the case with some other night clocks. The movement appears to be an adaptation of an eight-day clock of the traditional school associated with Edward East. In order to allow the light from the lamp to illuminate the dial all the work had to be below the

Plate 761. *The dial of the Hilderson night clock showing the fine engraving.*

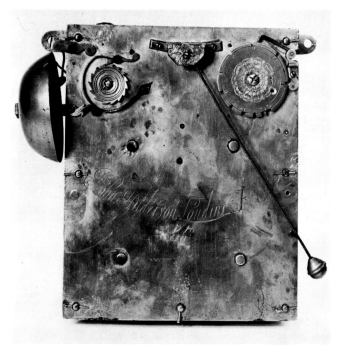

Plate 762. *The back plate of the Hilderson clock showing the position of the alarm bell.*

Plate 763. *The front plate of the Hilderson clock showing the position of the hour bell.*

514

disc aperture. The bell is mounted on the front plate and the hammer positioned downwards. Also in order to accommodate the large pierced disc, lugs have had to be pinned on the front plate to take the dial feet.

There is an alarm mechanism which will go for eight days without re-winding and the alarm hammer hangs downwards from its horizontal verge at the side of the movement and a separate bell is mounted there.

There are more spring-driven night clocks to be found by Joseph Knibb than any other maker and four almost identical examples are known to the authors. The dials, in particular are very similar except for the variety in the painted zone. One of these four is not now in its original case and another has had its superstructure replaced without an air vent. The other two are illustrated here in Colour Plate 30 and Plates 764-767, and Colour Plate 31 and Plates 768-769.

The method of illumination used in these clocks was an oil lamp inside the case, undoubtedly both smelly and smoky. The lamp consisted of a rectangular metal cistern, with one, two or three wick-holders and a lid. This was inserted through a hole in the side of the case. The principle commonly used for indicating the time was for the hour numerals to traverse a semi-circular aperture in the dial plate above which the minutes were indicated by small scallops around the edge and the quarters by large pierced Roman figures I, II and III through the dial plate backed with silk. There are also small holes to mark each five minutes. The hours are pierced in Arabic numerals in two secondary discs mounted on the rear of the main hour disc on diametrically opposite sides, the even hours on one disc and the odd on the other. These are visible from the front through circular holes in the hour disc. Beneath each hour numeral a pin protrudes from the disc and when the rotating hour disc carries the numeral for the past hour to the bottom of its circuit, the pin makes contact with a brass cock on the front plate of the movement, holding the pin while the hour disc rotates and thus turns the subsidiary disc until the next hour is opposite the hole, when the pin is released. The hour disc, by revolving once in two hours will show the hours in correct order. The dial plates are engraved, fire gilded and have painted decoration.

The cases of both the clocks illustrated are very interesting, for both show signs that the clockmaker was not sure of his ultimate requirements when he obtained the case. That of the first clock is shown in Colour Plate 30 and Plates 764-765 and is probably the earlier of the two. It was evidently constructed without knowledge of how the mechanism was being arranged. Indeed, it may well have been that it was a case made for quite a conventional movement which had to be adapted as a night clock. This could be possible for these night clocks have dials which are square and are the same size as many of the ordinary clocks of the period. The main difference is that the centre of the dial is not the centre of the movement but above it, making it necessary in this case to cut away the bottom of the case and add a false bottom. A superstructure is added to the gable to provide more space above the flame of the lamp. To ensure a sufficient flow of air a large square hole has been cut in the bottom of the case and ventilation at the top is provided by slits under the top moulding of the superstructure.

The second clock illustrated (Colour Plate 31 and Plates 768-769) is one in which the case maker had been aware that it was necessary to allow extra space below the dial which he provided by increasing the height of the dado. However, even in this case he failed to provide a door aperture at the back sufficiently low for the convenient assembly of the movement and dial. A glance at Plate 768 will show that

Plate 764. A night timepiece by Joseph Knibb. The dial is shown in Colour Plate 30, opposite.

Colour Plate 30. The dial of the Knibb night time-piece shown in Plates 764-767.

Colour Plate 31. Archbishop Sharp's night clock by Joseph Knibb. (Other views of the clock are shown in Plates 768-769.)

National Museum of Antiquities of Scotland

Plate 765. The rear of the clock shown in Plate 764 showing the lamp above the movement.

Plate 766. The movement and lamp of the clock shown in Plate 764.

Plate 767. The movement of the clock shown in Plate 764 showing the hour disc with one numeral subsidiary disc removed.

Plate 768. *The rear of the timepiece in Colour Plate 31, page 517, showing the three wick holders, the altered door, the ventilation holes and the chimney.*

Plate 769. *The bottom of the case and the lamp of the timepiece in Plate 768.*

it has been necessary to cut away the bottom rail of the case and to add an equivalent amount to the door. The problems of air-flow were also aggravated by the attempt to improve the illumination of the dial by providing the lamp with three wick holders, presumably, one for each quarter hour mark. This greatly increased the consumption of oxygen and generated more heat. As will be seen in Plate 768, a series of holes have been drilled in the door and back of the case just above the level of the flames, and there is also a considerable hole in the bottom of the case. Even these evidently did not prove sufficient, for a large aperture was cut in the door into which a fret was inserted. That this aperture was not planned for when the case was being made, is obvious from the fact that this door is not framed up but made as was that in the other clock, with the grain running vertically.

The superstructure of this clock has a properly constructed chimney which is metal lined with the opening at the back of the central block (Plate 768). This is a much more confident production than the other Knibb clock and the movement is better finished. The back plate is also well engraved. It was bequeathed to the Society of Antiquaries of Scotland and is now in the National Museum of Antiquities of Scotland in Edinburgh. Miss Elizabeth MacLaurin, whose property it was, has written about it as follows: "This timepiece was brought down from London by Archbishop

Colour Plate 32. *The small Boulle case made for a spring-driven clock by Thomas Tompion. (Other views of the clock are shown in Plates 784-790.)*

Plate 770. The dial of a striking night clock by Henry Jones.

Sharp along with another timepiece of ordinary construction & appearance. The latter he presented to the College of St. Andrews, with which he had been so long connected, and the former he retained for his own use. It remained in the possession of his family until upwards of seventy years ago. At the death of Major Johnson, one of the Archbishop's descendants, it and other family relics were dispersed and the valuable timepiece came into the possession of my father, who prized it very highly as an antique. Sir John Leslie and the old Earl of Buchan (founder of the Society of Antiquaries of Scotland) both came to see it and, being old St. Andrews students, distinctly remembered to have seen the other timepiece there, which Archbishop Sharp had given to the College; and also to have heard of another and rarer one which he had purchased at the same time for himself, and which, at the time when they were students, was still in the possession of his family."[2]

Night clocks were by their nature most often made for use in bedrooms and consequently were not always made to strike the hours. Some were however made which did strike and the dial of one of these made by Henry Jones is shown in Plate 770. There is also a very unusual three-train night clock with a beautifully engraved back plate extant which was made by Robert Seignior.[3]

The Tompion Astrolabe Longcase Clock

This clock with an astrolabe dial was presented to the Fitzwilliam Museum, Cambridge, by the late Mr. Ernest Prestige. It is the only known example of such a clock to be made by Thomas Tompion (Plates 771-780).

Reference has already been made to this clock in an earlier chapter (page 133) and to the transitional nature of its recoil escapement. This, and other features of the movement suggest that the main body of it is quite early and indeed may have been constructed very shortly after Tompion came to London, which is presumed to be just before he was admitted as a brother of the Clockmakers' Company on September 4th, 1671. (He became a freeman on April 6th, 1674.) The movement is of one month's duration and at least two other Tompion movements are known which have the same basic layout, one of which is in the British Museum. This latter however has a normal Tompion anchor escapement so may be a slightly later example. These clocks do not conform to the standard layout of the period. There is no true centre pinion. The going train consists of main wheel, first, second and escape wheels and their pinions. Part of the motionwork is mounted between the plates, a wheel of 60 being carried by spring friction on the first wheel arbor engaging a pinion of 20 on an arbor which, passing through the front plate, carries the minute hand. The front end of the first pinion also passes through the front plate and is pivoted on a cock and it carries a pinion which turns the hour wheel.

Thus far, the movement shows every evidence of being of quite early construction, but to drive the motions on the astrolabe dial, additions to this basic movement were necessary. In the first place the main arbors, although squared, could not be used for winding owing to the revolving heavens disc on the dial; consequently extension plates were screwed to the base of the movement to take separate winding arbors which are geared to the main arbors by a pair of winding wheels. Also additional gearing was needed to drive the moon and heavens disc which rotate about the dial centre and this is taken from the pinion driving the hour wheel. None of this extra work appears to be quite contemporary with the rest of the movement; the heavens wheel in particular is of a distinctly different metal.

Some confirmation that the clock had alterations made to it quite early in its existence is to be found in the case. When Mr. Prestige acquired the clock it needed some restoration and the marquetry panel in the long door of the case was rising and in order to effectually re-lay it, it was completely lifted out. Beneath, in the foundation wood were found unmistakable signs of earlier chopped-in inlaid decoration. This meant that at some time after the case was first made, new marquetry had been applied and since all the present marquetry is evidently by the same

2. *Proceedings of the Society of Antiquaries of Scotland,* March, 1901.

3. *Antiquarian Horology,* Vol. 1, p. 39.

Plate 771. The Tompion Astrolabe Clock. The case is constructed of oak and veneered with olivewood and with olivewood mouldings. The front is decorated with crossbanding and unusual marquetry inlays against a background of olive oyster pieces. (Another view of the clock is shown in Plate 523.)

Fitzwilliam Museum, Cambridge

Plate 772. The hood of the clock shown in Plate 771 showing the olivewood oyster pieces and the gilt metal mounts. The carved cresting is a later addition.

Plate 773. The upper part of the case of the clock shown in Plate 771 with the long door open showing that the thickness of the trunk sides alone provides the framework for the door.

Plate 775. The left hand side of the movement of the clock shown in Plate 771 showing the going train, the extension plates and the gearing for the motions on the dial.

Plate 774. The movement of the clock shown in Plate 771 with the front plate and extension plates removed.

Plate 776. The right hand side of the movement of the clock shown in Plate 771 showing the striking train and the gearing for the motions on the dial.

Plate 777. The dial with the twenty-four hour silver-faced chapter ring and astrolabe disc of the clock shown in Plate 771.

Plate 778. The lower portion of the dial plate of the clock shown in Plate 771, with the blue paint removed exposing what remains of an engraved cartouche and the word "Crepusculum".

Plate 779. The back of the chapter ring and the astrolabe disc of the clock shown in Plate 771, showing the manner in which the silver face is fixed to the brass ring.

hand and undoubtedly seventeenth century, it suggests that somewhere about 1680 the case was upgraded and that this was probably when the clock was completed as an astrolabe clock.

The case has some unconventional constructional features such as the back board fitting between the trunk sides instead of behind them, as was the normal practice, and the clamps on the long door are grooved on, which is unusual.

The dial has a twenty-four hour chapter ring showing meantime in hours and minutes. In addition the declination of the sun and its position in the zodiac is shown

Plate 780. The cleaning mark of Henry Taylor with the date 1779 scratched on the dial plate beneath the chapter ring of the clock shown in Plate 771.

as also is that of the moon and its age. The altitude and azimuth of the sun, moon and certain stars can also be read.

The central zone of the dial is engraved in the upper part to show the arc of the horizon with a scale of azimuth lines. An area below this, which is matted, is coloured blue and shaded from light to a darker blue at the bottom, on the crepuscular or twilight line. Below this, the area has been coloured dark blue for many years to indicate night. A close examination of this, however, showed vague signs that beneath there might be some engraving. We were therefore allowed to remove the blue paint and below was found the remains of a very attractively engraved cartouch and the word "Crepusculum". The whole area had however been scraped over in an attempt to obliterate it before painting. This can be seen in Plate 778.

The central zone is covered by a circular disc which is water gilt, and fretted and mounted with two silver circles, one of which is eccentric. The decorative fretwork around these has been ingeniously designed to bear at the leaf points selected stars in their correct positions. Around the circumference of this fretted disc are engraved the ecliptic circle, the names and signs of the zodiac and the months and days. The eccentric silver ring also gives the ecliptic circle and the names of the zodiac, the smaller circle the age of the moon and the time of high water at London Bridge. The minute hand makes one revolution each hour, the sun hand one revolution a day to show mean sun time and the moon hand indicates lunar time. As the sun and moon hands cross the edge of the eccentric circle, their positions in the heavens may be read.[4] The chapter ring is of silver attached to a brass ring in the manner of the Fromanteels. The silver facing overlaps the heavens disc and thus the chapter ring has to be mounted last.

---

4.   The authors acknowledge the help of Dr. F.A.B. Ward with regard to the indications on the astrolabe dial.

A Wall Timepiece Alarm by Joseph Knibb

This is an unusual, if not a unique, wall timepiece alarm made by Joseph Knibb (Plates 781-783), housed in a case which has the appearance of a picture frame hung on the wall from its corner. The movement, which is long and narrow, is constructed as a plated, rope-driven thirty-hour timepiece with a verge escapement but since it has an intermediate wheel and pinion it has a longer duration. The alarm mechanism is attached to the side of the movement which is suspended from the dial in the manner of the early spring-driven clocks, and the dial is retained in the case by turn buttons. The case consists of an ebonised bolection moulding on an oak frame fixed to an oak box. The back board is removable and is held in place by pegs with latches which are replicas of those on the movement. The clock hangs diagonally on the wall, a hinged loop being provided for the purpose. The dial plate is engraved with traditional flowers and is signed in the lower spandrel corner, Joseph Knibb, London.

A Small Boulle Clock by Tompion

The little tortoiseshell spring clock decorated with Boulle-work, which is shown in Colour Plate 32, page 520, and Plates 784-790, is a unique example amongst the special productions made by Thomas Tompion at about the turn of the century. The fact that it is so constructed that it appears to have a circular dial is but one of its unique features. This clock was at one time in the Wetherfield Collection and is quite small, being only 10½ ins. high to the top of the finial. It is very probable that this clock was a special order for an important French client or for one who had a taste for things French. Apart from its general design, its construction suggests that the case was made in France. If, however, this was not the case and it was made in England, then it must have been made by a Frenchman working here.

There has been some speculation that the case may have been designed by Daniel Marot, who came to England after the Revocation of the Edict of Nantes and who was employed by King William III. Certainly Marot did design many ormolu mounted cases, engravings of some of which still exist but most of these cases are considerably larger than this case. Tardy, in *La Pendule Français,*[5] illustrates a clock which is almost identical with this Tompion clock, which was made by Passerat at the end of the nineteenth century and was claimed to be a reproduction of a clock case by Marot. Whoever made the case cannot have been in very close touch with Tompion while it was being made, for he made it with an inset back door, the rebate for which may be seen in Plate 786. When the movement was being fitted, this had to be removed as there was insufficient room for the pendulum and the present engraved and gilt brass door fitted on the back. The cut-out for the hinge of the first door can be seen if the present door is removed. This must not be taken to suggest that the case was made without any reference to the requirements of the movement, for both case and movement must have been made for each other.

The movement is typical of Tompion's work and is special only in that it had to be adapted to a special shape. It is one of the few spring clocks which Tompion made which do not have pull-quarter repeating mechanism. Owing to the shape of the case it has been necessary to site the bell at the top centre of the movement, and the

---

5.   Tardy, *La Pendule Francaise,* Paris, Part 2, p. 94.

Colour Plate 33. *William III's year spring clock by Tompion. (Other views of the clock are shown in Colour Plates 34-35, pages 532-533, and Plates 791-800.)*

Christie, Manson and Woods Ltd.

Plate 781. Wall timepiece by Joseph Knibb.

Plate 782. The rope-driven movement and dial of the timepiece shown in Plate 781.

Plate 783. The back view showing the latched back board of the timepiece shown in Plate 781.

Plate 784. The dial of the Tompion Boulle clock with the front door open and showing the lever for opening the back door, in the lock plate. This clock is also shown in Colour Plate 32, page 520.

Plate 785. The back of the case of the clock in Plate 784 with the overlaid back door and showing the movement fixing screws.

Colour Plate 34. The finely engraved front plate of the lower part of the movement of the clock shown in Colour Plate 33, page 529.

Colour Plate 35. The clock in Colour Plate 33, page 529, shown without its case.

Plate 786. The clock in Plate 784 with the back door open showing the engraving on the inside.

Plate 787. The top of the clock in Plate 784 with the dome removed.

hammer also placed where there is sufficient room for draw. Its operation is by a linking mechanism from the hammer's customary position. A rise and fall dial is situated above the chapter ring in such a position that it is obscured when the front door is closed. The pointer operates a single lead worm which is capable of making a very fine adjustment to the pendulum. There is a pull-string attached to the striking side lifting-piece by an extra lever for that purpose, by which the last hour may be struck.

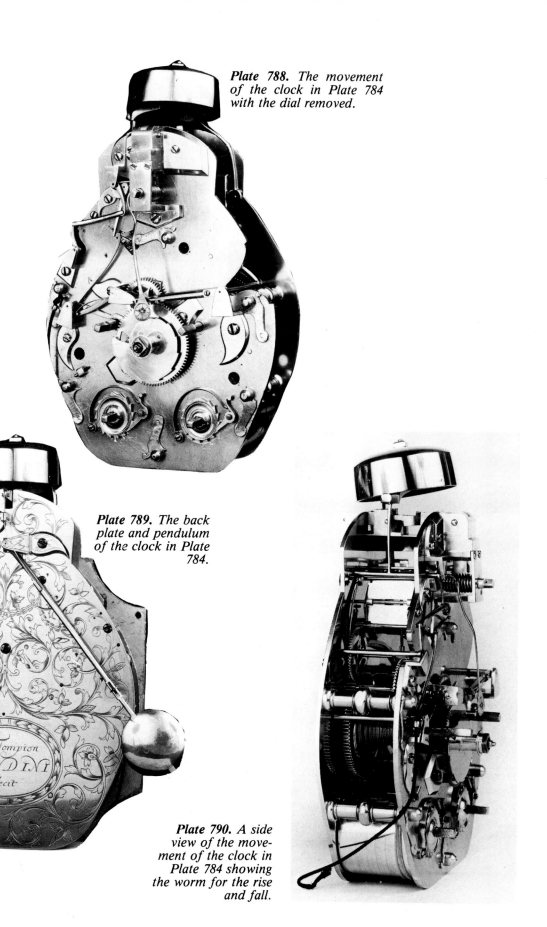

Plate 788. *The movement of the clock in Plate 784 with the dial removed.*

Plate 789. *The back plate and pendulum of the clock in Plate 784.*

Tho.Tompion
LONDINI
Fecit

Plate 790. *A side view of the movement of the clock in Plate 784 showing the worm for the rise and fall.*

To insert the movement into the case it is necessary to remove the dome. This is done by unscrewing the central finial, when it may be lifted off (Plate 787). The movement is held in the case by four long screws through the depth of the case into the dial (Plates 784 and 785). The back door is held closed by a latch which is operated by depressing the small lever which can be seen in the lower part of the front lock plate in Plate 785. The latch for the front door is key-operated through the side of the case.

William III's Year Spring Clock by Tompion

This clock, which has been known in recent years as the "Mostyn Tompion", is not only one of the finest clocks ever made but it also has a most impeccable pedigree. It was made for King William III by Thomas Tompion and passed on his death amongst the contents of his bed chamber, to Henry Sydney, Earl of Romney, a Gentleman of the Bed Chamber and Groom of the Stole, from whom it has passed by descent to Lord Mostyn. In 1982 it was purchased for the nation by the British Museum.

Plate 791. The whole movement of the Mostyn Tompion from the striking side. Three views of the clock are shown in Colour Plates 33-35, pages 529 and 532-533.

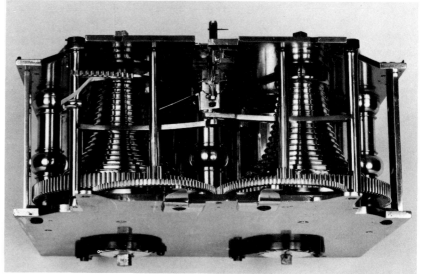

Plate 793. *The top of the power part of the movement showing the back plate and the delicate escapement.*

Plate 792. *Another view of the striking side of the Mostyn Tompion with parts removed including the back stay and the second intermediate wheels and pinions.*

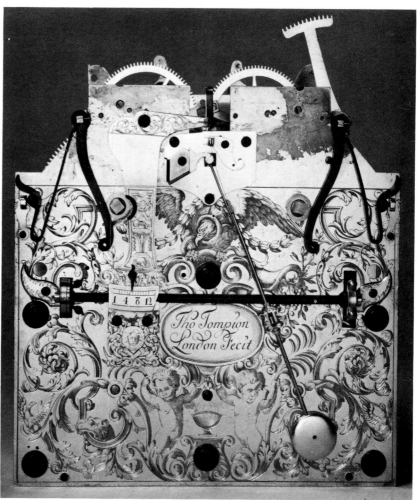

Plate 794. *The front plate of the lower part of the movement showing the rise and fall mechanism and the pendulum.*

It is a truly magnificent clock (Colour Plates 33-35, pages 529 and 532-533, and Plates 791-800) which, when seen only in book illustrations, can give one the impression that it is of monumental proportions when in fact it is a little gem. It stands only 28 ins. high overall and the dial is but 5 ins. square. It is the first spring clock to be made in England that will go for a year with one winding. In this clock we see a supremely satisfactory example of collaboration between a highly gifted and imaginative horological craftsman and equally talented case designers and makers. No standard basis of case design would have been appropriate to accommodate the exceptional requirements of a movement capable of functioning for a year and the movement itself would have needed to have been designed with due regard to the constraints of a suitable case design. The clock strikes the hours and has pull quarter-repeat. It was made between 1695 and 1700.

It will be seen from the illustrations in Plates 791 and 792 that the movement is constructed in two parts. The lower part is heavily made and contains the power source while the upper is more delicately made. The plates of the lower part are held together by six stout pillars which are riveted into the back plate while the front plate is attached by large blued steel screws. In addition to the pillars, where there is insufficient room for pillars beside the main wheels, there are two flat brackets screwed to the back plate and latched through the front. Between these plates are two enormous barrels, fusees and main wheels together with the first intermediate wheels and pinions of each train. The tops of the plates are shaped with slight projections to take the repeat arm arbors. In Plate 791 it will be seen that the clock has fusee chains which are of the two and three plate type. These wind anticlockwise. The barrel ratchets have been turned in a similar fashion to those on Fromanteel's early clocks. One of the clicks has had its tail broken off.

A view of this part of the movement taken from above (Plate 793) shows the linking pin and slot levers of the pull arm arbors of the repeat mechanism and also the quadrant on the right hand side arbor which engages the first pinion of the repeat train. The very delicate verge escapement can also be seen mounted on cocks on the front plate. Contrary to normal practice, the crown wheel pinion rises from the wheel making it necessary for the verge arbor to be cranked in order to avoid it.

Colour Plate 34, page 532, and Plate 794 show views of the front plate of this part of the movement and show the superb engraving, the blued steel repeat arms and their springs, the pendulum and its rise and fall mechanism. This latter is quite precise. There are two visual aids to precision. The shaft pivoted across the plate will be seen. It has at its right hand end a wheel with knobs round its circumference to facilitate turning. At the other end is another wheel with engraved divisions and a fixed pointer. A single lead worm on the shaft, hidden by the plate with twelve divisions, engages the teeth on the lower edge of the angled arm, to the upper end of which is fixed the nib for the pendulum suspension. Thus, by turning the shaft by the wheel at its right hand end, the pendulum is raised or lowered and this action precisely indicated by the pointer on the angled arm against the engraved scale. The pendulum rod is of steel and there is an engraved silver masking over the impulse slot which appears to be merely for decoration.

The upper part of the movement is mounted on the front plate of the lower by a cranked bottom extension of its front plate. Thus it is carried backwards and the dial can be in the same plane as the engraved lower plate. There is an additional support at the back for extra stability. The front plate is narrower than the dial with the pillars riveted to it. These are latched on the back plate, the latches being retained by

Plate 795. The front of the upper part of the movement showing the under dial work.

Plate 796. The upper part of the movement seen from below.

Plate 797. The complete movement seen from the front.

screws. The second intermediate wheels and pinions are pivoted into the lower part of the front plate but are cocked on to the back plate of the lower part of the movement.

Plate 796 shows that the repeat train is pivoted at the back into a small plate screwed to the back plate, and the first pinion which engages the quadrant from the repeat pull-arms, may be seen engaging the quadrant from the repeat arm arbor. Thus the two quadrants engage into the same pinion head. These upper plates contain what is virtually a normal eight-day movement but the going train is far from being a straightforward one. The large wheel, which can be seen in this illustration, is the centre wheel, the arbor of which carries the minute hand. It is driven by a wheel of one third of its count. Since the drive from the second intermediate wheel comes into the pinion upon which this last wheel is mounted and goes out through the large wheel on the same pinion, the centre wheel is an idler. For this reason it has been necessary for the minute hand to be counter-balanced to prevent it dropping backwards on its upward travel and forwards on the other. The fusee has 16½ turns, which gives a running of 396 days including 31 days of grace if not wound on time.

The train numbers are $^{120}/_{10} \times {}^{96}/_8 \times {}^{84}/_7 = 1728 \div 3$ because the solid wheel turns three times an hour, therefore 576 hours for one turn of the main wheel, or 24 days × 16.5 turns for 396 days. As the pinion which carries the solid wheel turns three times an hour, the 72 tooth wheel taking the motion on through the train must be multiplied by three. Thus the remainder of the train is this wheel, the contrate wheel and pinion and crown wheel and pinion, expressed as (72 × 3 = 216) thus $^{216}/_8 \times {}^{56}/_7 \times {}^{21}/_{30} = 151.2$ vibrations of the pendulum per minute, giving a theoretical pendulum length of six inches.

Not much of the striking train can be seen in the illustration, but it has the same count as the going train up to the pin pinion with 30 pins in the pin wheel and sixteen turns on the fusee. Therefore $^{120}/_{10} \times {}^{96}/_8 \times {}^{30}/_1 \times {}^{16}/_1 = 69,120$ blows when fully wound. With 156 blows needed each day and 365 days for a year, only 56,940 blows are actually required. The 12,180 additional blows have been provided to allow for the pull-string to be used when necessary. The remainder of the train has the usual parts performing their normal functions with an inside rack and rack hook. The big cock seen at bottom right in Plate 796 takes the back pivot of the lifting piece arbor, the front pivot being in the cock seen bottom left in Plate 795. The lower of the two levers on this arbor is lifted by the cannon wheel pin and the top one prevents the repeat arm being pulled during the warning period. In Plate 796 a long lever may be seen rising from the back of the same arbor. It is for the warning pin and that which rises from the centre of the arbor is the strike/silent lever (Plate 792), the lower part of which can just be seen in Plate 791. This lifts a lever on the rack hook arbor, the highest part of which extends upwards and rides in the fork end of the bell crank lever that is pivoted in a cock at the top of the movement. The upper end of this latter lever protrudes through an aperture in the dial plate above the chapter ring.

The repeat arm has all the usual working parts (Plate 795). Normally the motive power spring works upon the repeat arm arbor driving the train. In this clock, however, the drive comes from the springs working on the pull-string arms through their quadrant and from the same pinion head on to the repeat arm quadrant, the arm of which is shaped to avoid several arbors. The bridge across the hour socket is also

Plate 798. The day of the week disc.

Plate 799. A view of the rear and side of the clock in its case.

Plate 800. The right hand side of the complete clock.

seen in Plate 795 and it is upon this that the day-of-the-week disc turns, which is driven by a six leaf pinion carried by the four-armed twenty-four hour wheel. The crossings on this wheel are not quite square at the corners, which may suggest that it is a replacement.

The movement stands upon a solid cast brass plate which also forms the platform for the case and as the edges of this plate are visible they have been gilded. This is raised up on four gilded metal feet, each consisting of two voluted scrolls with leaf decoration and silver floral pendants. The centrepiece is a gilded mask with silver floral swags on each side. There are also silver swags between the feet on the sides of the case. This type of finish to the base of a clock is not unique and we have already seen it on some fine longcase clocks of the same period (Plates 412 and 415). The case is not fixed to this platform in any way but may be lifted off complete and is positioned by four pegs in the plate.

It will be seen that the case, like the movement, appears to be in two parts, the larger pedestal base and the smaller upper part surrounding the dial, more like a normal bracket clock case. They do not separate and the only way in which to gain access to the movement is by lifting off the entire case. There is, however, a door in the base part to give access to the mechanism for regulating the clock. This is the only door in the case. It is constructed of wainscot oak and veneered with ebony and, although the general effect of the design is architectural, the mouldings are in the main the conventional mouldings of the period and not strictly classical. Tompion made a number of clocks about the time that this clock was made, usually with grande sonnerie movements, which can be compared with this clock in respect of its case except, of course, that they do not have the pedestal base. Symonds illustrates three in his book.[6] The possibility that Daniel Marot may have had some hand in the design of the little tortoiseshell clock described in the previous section has been mentioned. That his influence is to be found in these and in particular this year clock is fairly obvious. Here, however, there is no sign of a breakdown of contact between the clockmaker and the case maker, as in the tortoiseshell clock, for everything fits exactly.

The aperture in the base door with the break-arch ends is glazed and the silver repoussé fret over the glass depicts a pair of cherubs holding up a floral wreath through which Tompion's signature and the pendulum may be seen. The design of the mounts on the frame of this door are almost the only ones on this clock which can be found on other clocks for all the other mounts appear to have been made especially for it. The finish of all is the highest possible and the condition excellent. In the centre of the inverted bell top there are the arms of King William III in silver and there are four finials set on pedestals at the corners in the form of a lion, a unicorn, a rose and a thistle. An impressive figure of Britannia surmounts the whole. The four columns are free-standing and are of gilt brass with silver capitals and bases of the Tuscan order.

The back of the case is very much like the front and all the horizontal mouldings are continued round it but in place of the glazed aperture in the base there is a sunken panel while above there is a fine rectangular gilt metal fret. Otherwise the back is quite plain. The sides are fully mounted, the base having large ormolu handles with foliated back plates set in rectangular sunken panels and there are silver mounts on the rails above and below which match those on the front. The frets in the side apertures are of silver.

The dial is gilt, the central zone being finely matted with sector shaped apertures in the upper part revealing the day of the week and its planet, engraved on a silvered revolving disc and in the lower part a silver cartouche with Tompion's signature. The spandrel corners have elaborate silver mounts.

It seems particularly fitting that the last clock described in this book should be by that supreme master of the seventeenth century clock, Thomas Tompion. In these days of the microchip, and the quartz watch, we have lost any sense of wonder that a clock should be of a year's duration. To Tompion's contemporaries this clock must have represented the epitome of the clockmaker's skill.

---

6.   R.W. Symonds, *Thomas Tompion, his Life and Work,* London, 1951, pp. 162, 163 and 170.

Bibliography

This list does not include all the works which have been consulted by the authors in writing the present book, but they are all recommended for further reading. All are available in Guildhall Library, London (except where indicated by an asterisk).

Antiquarian Horology. The Journal of The Antiquarian Horological Society. December 1953 — the present.

C.E. Atkins, *Register of Apprentices of the Clockmakers' Company from its Incorporation in 1631 to 1931,* London.

S.E. Atkins and W.H. Overall. *Some Account of the Worshipful Company of Clockmakers of the City of London,* London, 1881.

G.H. Baillie, *Watchmakers and Clockmakers of the World,* London, 1929, 1947, 1951. (*See also* B. Loomes.)

* F.J. Britten, *Old English Clocks. The Wetherfield Collection,* London, 1907, reprinted by the Antique Collectors' Club, 1980.

* F.J. Britten, *Old Clocks and Watches and their Makers.* Antique Collectors' Club edition, Woodbridge, 1977. Reprint of the 1911 3rd edition with additional material.

Britten's Old Clocks and Watches and their Makers. 7th edition by G.H. Baillie, C. Clutton and C.A. Ilbert, London, 1956.

H. Cescinsky, *The Old English Master Clockmakers, 1670-1820,* London, 1938.

H. Cescinsky and M.R. Webster, *English Domestic Clocks,* London, 1913, reprinted Woodbridge, 1976.

P.G. Dawson, *The Design of English Domestic Clocks, 1660-1700,* London, 1956.

W. Derham, *The Artificial Clockmaker, A Treatise of Clock and Watch Work,* London, 1696, 1700, 1714, 1734, 1759, 1962.

R.K. Foulkes, *Thirty Hour Tompion Clocks,* London, 1951. An illustrated extract from *Apollo,* Vol. 54, pp. 99-102, 106.

W.J. Gazeley, *Clock and Watch Escapements,* London, 1956, 1973.

N.P. Goodison, "Clocks in the Collection of Lord Harris at Belmont Park, Kent" (two parts), *The Connoisseur,* Vol. 168, London, 1968.

* W.F.J. Hana, *English Lantern Clocks,* prepared by E.J. Tyler from the Dutch original of 1977, 1979.

R.A. Lee, *The First Twelve Years of the English Pendulum Clock; or the Fromanteel family and their contemporaries, 1655-1670,* London, 1969.

R.A. Lee, *The Knibb Family,* Byfleet, 1964.

H.A. Lloyd, *The Collector's Dictionary of Clocks,* London, 1964.

H.A. Lloyd and C.B. Drover, "Nicholas Vallin (circa 1565-1603)", *The Connoisseur Year Book, 1955,* London, pp. 110-116.

B. Loomes, *Watchmakers and Clockmakers of the World,* Vol. 2, London, 1976. Intended as a companion volume to G.H. Baillie (q.v.).

* B. Loomes, *The Early Clockmakers of Great Britain,* London, 1982.

T. Robinson, *The Longcase Clock,* Woodbridge, 1981.

J. Smith, *Horological Dialogues,* London, 1675, 1962. The earliest book dealing with clocks and watches to be published in England.

J. Smith, *Horological Disquisitions concerning the Nature of Time,* London, 1694, 1962.

R.W. Symonds, *A Book of English Clocks,* London, 1947, 1950.

R.W. Symonds, *Masterpieces of English Furniture and Clocks...of the 17th and 18th Centuries,* London, 1940.

R.W. Symonds, *Thomas Tompion, his Life and Work,* London, 1951, 1969.

H. von Bertele, *The Book of Old Clocks and Watches,* London, 1964 (translated from the German by H.A. Lloyd).

Makers' Index

Illustrations are listed after text references and are identified by plate number

Subject Index

This is a selective index. An exhaustive one would have produced a daunting document with a book of this size. Main entries are in bold type, and other entries have been restricted to those which make a useful contribution.

Illustrations are listed after text references and are identified by Plate number.

continued